Springer Texts in Business and Economics

Springer Texts in Business and Economics (STBE) delivers high-quality instructional content for undergraduates and graduates in all areas of Business/Management Science and Economics. The series is comprised of self-contained books with a broad and comprehensive coverage that are suitable for class as well as for individual self-study. All texts are authored by established experts in their fields and offer a solid methodological background, often accompanied by problems and exercises.

Kuo-Ping Chang

Corporate Finance: A Systematic Approach

Springer

Kuo-Ping Chang
Xi'an Jiaotong University
Xi'an, China

ISSN 2192-4333 ISSN 2192-4341 (electronic)
Springer Texts in Business and Economics
ISBN 978-981-19-9118-9 ISBN 978-981-19-9119-6 (eBook)
https://doi.org/10.1007/978-981-19-9119-6

This Springer imprint is published by the registered company Springer Nature Singapore Pte Ltd.
The registered company address is: 152 Beach Road, #21-01/04 Gateway East, Singapore 189721, Singapore

To my parents, my grandparents, and m., a., l., d., j., for their endless love

Preface

This textbook takes on a systematic approach to elaborate on the different subjects within corporate finance. The chapters bring together existing concepts with examples and stories that allow students to easily understand and apply financial tools. In doing so, this book strives to clarify misconceptions in the literature on topics related to firms' ownership and control, problems of the Modigliani-Miller first and second propositions and firms' payout policy, relationship between options and corporate finance, behavioral finance versus corporate finance, etc. The book takes the growing importance of the Asian economy and financial markets in recent years into consideration, as well as constructs the p-index to measure and compare the risk structures of US and China's stocks and stock indexes. Risk here is defined as the likelihood that you can deliver your promise. The p-index, constructed from the European put option, measures the insurance fees for each insured dollar if the asset delivers at least δ rate of return.

This book is a primary text written for the introductory courses in corporate finance at the MBA level and for the intermediate courses in undergraduate programs. However, it can also be of great use to Ph.D. students as well as professionals. The content of this book has evolved from a series of courses I have taught and learned since the early 1980s. While it has been a long and lonely journey, I did benefit greatly from interacting with my former students at Tsing Hua University (Hsinchu) and Xi'an Jiaotong University (Xi'an). I am grateful to all those who have aided in the development of this book. Much appreciation also goes out to reviewers for taking their time and providing valuable feedback and comments. Finally, I would like to express my sincere thanks to Vidyaa Shri Krishna Kumar, Anushangi Weerakoon, Shinko Mimura, Lavanya Devgun and William Achauer of Springer for their kind help and patience in coping with the inevitable delay in finishing this book.

Xi'an, China Kuo-Ping Chang

Contents

Introduction 1

Every person on every day needs to make decisions (choices) on many things: to do or not to do. Decision-making is based on cost and benefit analysis. If benefit is greater than cost, then it is worthwhile to do it. Benefit and cost can be money or utility. However, cost must be opportunity cost which means you still have an opportunity (choice) to spend or not to spend. That is, opportunity cost is ex-ante and related to decision-making. After a choice (decision) is made, the rest are: making a budget and recording accounting numbers. Budgeting is making a plan of predicted future revenues and expenses for the choice which has been made. Accounting numbers are the results or outcomes of the decision (choice). Hence, budget and accounting numbers are ex-post, which are not opportunity costs and have nothing to do with decision-making (choice). Another important point in decision-making (choice) is the marginal analysis. As long as the marginal benefit (the revenue of producing one more unit) is greater than the marginal cost (the cost of producing one more unit), carry out the decision that has been made can increase wealth.

In any organization (corporation), every resource provider contributes something, i.e., investment, and hence, is entitled to get something back, i.e., payments for consumption. Every resource provider is free to do her own cost–benefit analysis and to decide to join or not to join the company. Therefore, it is difficult to determine the objective of a group of people (e.g., a corporation) and not meaningful to talk about 'balance of power' in a corporation. This book systematically discusses the subjects of corporate finance, i.e., ownership and objectives of the firm (Chap. 2), basic concepts of valuation (Chap. 3), financial statements and financial analysis (Chap. 4), cash flows and investment appraisal (Chaps. 5 and 6), estimating the discount rate under uncertainty (Chap. 7), capital structure puzzle (Chap. 8), how options and corporate finance are related (Chaps. 9 and 10), behavioral issues in economics and finance (Chap. 11), capital structure in imperfect market (Chap. 12), payout policy (Chap. 13), mergers and acquisitions, and corporate governance (Chap. 14), and multinational corporations (Chap. 15).

K.-P. Chang, *Corporate Finance: A Systematic Approach*, Springer Texts in Business and Economics, https://doi.org/10.1007/978-981-19-9119-6_1

1.1 Decision Making and Cost–Benefit Analysis

Without the transaction costs of discovering, informing, bargaining, contracting and monitoring, the maximum value of production by the firm or by markets is the same. Chap. 2 uses a robber's story to illustrate that there is no such thing as the owner of the gang (firm) nor the residual claimant of the gang (firm). In the firm, each resource provider (e.g., labor, material provider, debtholder, and equityholder) has property rights only on the resource she provides, and only the entrepreneurs who can innovate to create excess profits can have the power to control the firm and determine the firm's objectives. Also, when people cooperate, types of contracts are determined by the transaction costs of contracting. The transaction costs of contracting are dependent on the contracting parties' risk attitudes which are dependent on the sizes of their choice sets. Under certainty, the Modigliani–Miller First Proposition holds (i.e., the market value of the firm is independent of the firm's capital structure), but the Modigliani–Miller Second Proposition does not hold (i.e., changing the debt-equity ratio does not affect the rate of return on equity).

When the objective of the firm is determined by the entrepreneurs, the cost and benefit analysis of an investment will be made. Since costs usually happen at the current time and benefits happen in the future, a discount rate (i.e., opportunity cost of capital) needed to discount future cash flows back to the current time. Forecasted income statement of the investment project and the discounted rate are used to estimate the current values of capital providers' cash outflows and inflows for evaluating the investment project, i.e., the net present value (NPV) analysis.

1.2 Risks and Returns

Under uncertainty, when a person takes high 'risk', there is no guarantee that she will earn high return. But if a person suddenly becomes very rich not because of winning a lottery or inheriting a big fortune, she must have taken a great risk before. Risk in finance is usually defined as variance or beta (as in the capital asset pricing model: CAPM). In the CAPM, the discount rate (the opportunity cost of capital) contains two parts: risk-free interest rate and risk premium. Higher beta means higher discount rate for the project's future cash flows. These are all assuming the mean–variance analysis, i.e., assuming that people prefer high expected rate of return and lower variance of rate of return. However, diversification in investment, such as organizing a portfolio, cannot increase or decrease value, i.e., an example of financial diversification irrelevancy.

1.3 Derivatives and Corporate Finance

In the put-call parity, the European call option can be interpreted as the equity of the firm. The Modigliani–Miller first proposition is a corollary of the put-call parity and an example of financial diversification irrelevancy. In the binomial option pricing case, (i) under riskless debt, increasing the debt-equity ratio increases the variance of the rate of return on equity and has no effect on the rate of return on debt; and (ii) under risky debt, increasing the debt-equity ratio increases the variance of the rate of return on debt but does not affect the probability density function of the rate of return on equity. These findings refute the Modigliani–Miller second proposition that the expected rate of return on the equity of the levered firm increases in proportion to the debt-equity ratio. Also, in a complete market with no transaction costs, i.e., a perfect market, the market value of the firm is independent of the firm's payout policy, i.e., an example of financial diversification irrelevancy. However, cash dividends or share purchase can increase equityholders' wealth at the expense of debtholders.

The p-index introduced in Chap. 9 defines the risk of an asset (a firm) as the likelihood that the asset (the firm) can deliver at least a specific rate of return. European put option is used to construct the p-index to measure risk levels (likelihoods) of asset's providing various rates of return, i.e., risk structure of asset. In the binomial case with up move and down move, (i) assets having lower down move have higher p-index, i.e., higher risk; (ii) all call options (firms' equities) have the same p-index, i.e., the same risk level, and all put options have the same p-index; and (iii) underlying asset (the firm) may be riskier than its put option and may have the same risk level as its call option (equity).

1.4 Behavioral Finance and Corporate Finance

Behavioral economics and Behavioral finance, incorporating the concepts and methods in psychology science into traditional economics, have found pervasive anomalies in common people's behaviors. However, by using the concepts in traditional economics (e.g., choice, relative price, and opportunity cost) to analyze these anomalies, it is found that quite a few anomalies do not exist. Especially, relative price ratio (or rate of return) can explain why people decides to invest or not to invest, equity premium puzzle, and the disposition effect (i.e., why investors have a tendency to sell winners too early and keep losers too long).

The Ownership and Objectives of the Firm

2

The essence of economics and management is choice (i.e., decision-making). Choice is about cost and benefit analysis. For an individual, examine her past behaviors probably can tell what her future strategies and objectives are. But for a group of people, e.g., a firm, it won't be easy to understand what the objectives of the firm are, who can determine what, and who should contribute and get what. Section 2.1 of this chapter uses a robber's story to illustrate that there is no such thing as the owner of the gang (firm) nor the residual claimant of the gang (firm). In the firm, each resource provider (e.g., labor, material provider, debtholder, and equityholder) has property rights only on the resource she provides, and only the entrepreneurs who can innovate to create excess profits can have the power to control the firm and determine the firm's objectives. Section 2.2 explains that when people cooperate, types of contracts are determined by the transaction costs of contracting. The transaction costs of contracting are dependent on the contracting parties' risk attitudes. Section 2.3 shows that the contracting parties' risk attitudes are dependent on the sizes of their choice sets.

2.1 The Ownership of the Firm—A Story of Robin Hood

Imagine Robin Hood plans to organize a group of gangsters to rob banks. Here the resource providers are: a planner (the boss: Robin Hood), an archer, a lookout, and an old lady who cooks for the gang. According to the ex-ante contracts among these resource providers, after each robbery, the cook will be the first to get $2,000, and the rest of the money will be split among the archer (50%), lookout (30%), and boss (20%). If the cook obtains only $1,600 this time, she may get compensations ($400 plus some interests) next time. In any case, it is an ex-ante contract between the cook and other members of the gang.

After each robbery, the gangsters will hide out for two to three months, and redo it again.

K.-P. Chang, *Corporate Finance: A Systematic Approach*, Springer Texts in Business and Economics, https://doi.org/10.1007/978-981-19-9119-6_2

Several interesting conclusions can be drawn from this example:

(1) *There is no such thing as "the owner of the gang (firm)".* People organize through voluntary contracts. Each resource provider has property rights only on the resource she provides, i.e., she has an ex-ante choice to join or not to join the firm (gang), and after she invests her resource in the firm (gang), she obtains a right to ex-post share the big pie generated by the firm (gang). If it is wrong to say that Robin Hood is the owner of the gang, it is also wrong to say that shareholders (or stockholders) are the owners of the firm. Suppose that these gangsters are captured by the authority, all members (including the cook) will be prosecuted since they all are responsible for the "product" they have produced. Thus, if a firm's product causes harm to its customers, it will be unfair to hold only the equityholders (the so-called 'owners') responsible and ask them to compensate. For example, it could be the case that a new stockholder who just bought some shares yesterday.

(2) *This gang acts like a firm.* The cook is like a debtholder of the gang (the firm): she obtains fixed income, and the archer, lookout and boss are like equityholders: they obtain non-fixed income. Usually, after splitting the big pie generated, the resources providers of a firm will put back some resources to continue production. The only difference between a gang and a firm is that the latter does not need to liquidate and hide out for a period of time.

    The gangsters need to hide out because they are unlawful. They are unlawful because they don't pay taxes. Can these gangsters pay taxes so that they can be lawful? The answer is no, because they don't have the property rights to rob (milk) those banks. An example is Sir Francis Drake, who was considered a hero in England and a pirate in Spain for his raids. On September 26, 1580, *Golden Hind* sailed into Plymouth with Drake and 59 remaining crew aboard, along with a rich cargo of spices and captured Spanish treasures. Queen Elizabeth appropriated the lion's share of the proceeds. On April 4, 1581, Drake was awarded a knighthood.

(3) *First claim or seniority between stockholders and debtholders is not meaningful.* Although the cook has first claim on the firm's assets and operating income, her first claim does not affect the ex-post distributions among the resource providers. No matter who has first claim (or everyone has the same first claim), the big pie generated ex-post will be split exactly according to the resource providers' ex-ante contracts (i.e., the cook's first claim is meaningless). Also, only in the cases where there are no clear definitions for property rights (such as public goods: fish in a lake owned by no one) can we say that first claim has some advantage. But firms (or gangs) always have clear definitions for the resource providers' property rights, and there is no such thing as: "stockholders do receive more earnings per dollar invested, but they also bear more risk,

because they have given lenders first claim on the firm's assets and operating income" (Myers, 1984, p. 94).[1]

2.2 Power (Authority), Entrepreneur, and Objectives and Boundary of the Firm

The above discussions seem in line with the contractual theory of the firm, i.e., view the firm as "a nexus of contracts" among participants in the organization. The strongest (and most quoted) statement of the contractarian viewpoint may be found in Alchian and Demsetz (1972, p. 777): "It is common to see the firm characterized by the power to settle issues by fiat, by authority, or by disciplinary action superior to that available in the conventional market. This is delusion. The firm does not own all its inputs. It has no power of fiat, no authority, no disciplinary action any different in the slightest degree from ordinary market contracting between any two people". Jensen and Meckling (1976, pp. 310–311) also argue that "the private corporation or firm is simply one form of legal fiction which serves as a nexus for a set of contracting relationships among individuals. ... Viewing the firm as the nexus of a set of contracting relationships among individuals also serves to make it clear that the personalization of the firm implied by asking questions such as 'what should be the objective function of the firm,' or 'does the firm have a social responsibility' is seriously misleading". But this kind of legal fiction (or contractual relations) view of the firm has one problem: Who in the firm has the power (authority) to make decisions to direct the resources?

The firm should be more than a nexus of contracts. Otherwise, because we all have contracts with government, each country will become a big "super-firm". Coase (1937, 1960) have pointed out that there are five kinds of transaction costs involved when people interact: the costs of discovering, informing, bargaining, contracting, and monitoring. In the absence of transaction costs, the maximum value of production by the firm or by markets is the same, i.e., the Coase theorem. The Coase theorem emphasizes that "in the absence of transaction costs, there is no economic basis for the existence of the firm ... it does not matter what the law is, since people can always negotiate without cost to acquire, subdivide, and combine rights whenever this would increase the value of production. In such a world the institutions which make up the economic system have neither substance nor purpose" (Coase, 1988, p. 14).

Coase argues that the size of the firm is determined by two different sets of transaction costs in directing resource allocation: (1) the cost of using the price mechanism (i.e., costs of discovering, informing, bargaining and contracting), and (2) the cost of using authority or power (i.e., monitoring cost). An activity will be included within the firm if its costs of using markets are greater than its costs

[1] This important point will be elaborated more in later chapters.

of using direct authority. However, an activity will not be counted as a part of the firm just because it has a contract with the firm (e.g., firm's outsourcing). It is only when a resource is under the direction of the firm can we say it is included as a part of the firm. Coase emphasizes the entrepreneur of the firm has the power and authority to direct resources. But Coase has never clearly pointed out where this power or authority comes from. He argues that since the purchaser will not know which of several courses he will want the supplier to take, "the details of what the supplier is expected to do are not stated in the contract but are decided later by the purchaser ... A firm is likely, therefore, to emerge in those cases where a very short-term contract will be unsatisfactory" (Coase, 1937, p. 40). That is, in Coase's view, long-term contract gives purchaser the power to direct resources. However, since every resource provider has free choice to join or leave the firm, Coase's long-term contract is, in fact, a short-term contract, and it cannot give the firm (the purchaser) any power.[2]

I argue that power or authority comes from choices: If you have more choices (i.e., have a larger choice set), you will have more power than the persons you cooperate with. For example, assume that Michael Jordan is the only person having special talent in playing basketball, and his five-member basketball team can earn $70 a year. Other basketball teams, because of having no special talent, can only earn $50 a year, i.e., each player obtains $10 opportunity cost. It is clear that the $20 excess profit (70 – 50 = 20) generated in Michael Jordan's team belongs to Michael Jordan only (because Michael Jordan can cooperate with other players, and other players can earn only $10 a year). Suppose Michael Jordan takes $4 from the $20 excess profit and split it equally among his four other team members (i.e., now each of them can have $11 a year). Then we can imagine that because Michael Jordan owns the excess profit and can use it to "bribe or buy" people, he will have the power (authority) in his team, and more importantly, his objectives will be the objectives of his team. In the firm, according to Schumpeter's idea, only those entrepreneurs who can innovate and create excess profits (and hence, have more choices and can bribe or buy people) can have power or authority. Other resource providers of the firm can only obtain the opportunity costs of their resources.[3] Once Robin Hood loses his ability to innovate and create excess profits,[4] but his

---

[2] Alchian and Demsetz (1972) also argue that "it is not true that employees are generally employed on the basis of long-term contractual arrangements any more than on a series of short-term or indefinite length contracts" (p. 784).

[3] Schumpeter (1934) argues that entrepreneurs are those who can innovate to devise new product, new producing method and new organization structure, and find new markets and new resources. He terms capitalists as the persons who do not innovate but only provide capitals and take risks, and entrepreneurs as the persons who innovate and do not take any risk. Coase, on the other hand, follows Adam Smith and Alfred Marshall's idea that capitalists and entrepreneurs are the same, and entrepreneurs do not have the feature to innovate, i.e., "... I shall use the same term 'entrepreneur' to refer to the person or persons who, in a competitive system, take the place of the price mechanism in the direction of resources" (Coase, 1937, footnote 10, p. 36).

[4] Sociologists may call it: lose charisma, and management (organizational) scholars may call it: lose leadership.

subordinate Little John can, then Little John will replace Robin Hood as the leader of the gang and have the power to direct. An employee currently may be willing to accept a lower pay (in comparison with the opportunity cost he can earn from other employers) if he believes in the future his firm will have a great chance to successfully innovate, and he can have a piece of the possible excess profits.

In sum, the boundary (the size) of the firm is determined by two sets of transaction costs: If monitoring cost is greater than the costs of searching, approaching, bargaining and contracting, the employee (or the whole division) will be fired, and the firm's size decreases; if monitoring cost is less than the sum of other four transaction costs, the firm will hire (integrate) people, and the firm's size increases. People may have contracts with the firm but only those who also follow the firm's flexible directions are included as a part of the firm. Within the firm, the person(s) who is capable of innovating and creating excess profits has the power to direct resource allocation, and her objectives will be the firm's objectives. (Appendix of this chapter shows that under certainty maximizing the firm's excess profits or maximizing different resource providers' wealth are equivalent.)

There are several different thoughts of the existence of the firm in the literature.

Alchian and Demsetz (1972) use three factors to explain the existence of the firm. First, because of shirking in the team production of the firm, a monitor is needed to detect and determine each individual's contribution to the output of the cooperating inputs. The monitor, as a residual claimant, earns the net earnings of the team (i.e., net of payments to other inputs) through the reduction of shirking. Second, "to discipline team members and reduce shirking, the residual claimant must have power to revise the contract terms and incentives of *individual* members without having to terminate or alter every other input's contract" (p. 782).[5] Third, "how can residual-claimant, central-employer-owner, demonstrate ability to pay the other hired inputs the promised amount in the event of loss? He can pay in advance or he can commit wealth sufficient to cover negative residuals. The latter can take the form of machines, land, buildings, or raw materials committed to the firm" (p. 791). I will argue that, first, just like other input providers, Alchian et al.'s monitor is also an input (resource) provider of the firm. Unlike Marxist's capitalist, Alchian et al.'s monitor does not have any power to pressure labors (and other resource providers) to work harder and exploit them to receive the residual since each resource provider (including the monitor) can freely choose to leave or stay in the firm. Second, whether the firm will make contracts with new or additional suppliers is not the resource providers' concern because they have free choice to leave or stay and only care whether they can earn the opportunity costs of the resources they have provided. The monitor will not have any power just

[5] This view point is similar to Coase's (1937) argument: "It is true that contracts are not eliminated when there is a firm, but they are greatly reduced. A factor of production (or the owner thereof) does not have to make a series of contracts with the factors with whom he is co-operating within the firm, as would be necessary, of course, if this co-operation were a direct result of the working of the price mechanism" (p. 39).

because he can make new contracts or revise or terminate old contracts.[6] Third, the monitor will not have the power because "he can pay in advance or he can commit wealth sufficient to cover negative residuals". The monitor will have the power or authority to direct only when he is a Schumpeterian entrepreneur who can innovate and create excess profits to buy or bribe people.

Hart (1995) argues that "the concept of nonhuman assets is also helpful in clarifying the notion of authority … Coase … argued that the distinguishing feature of the employer-employee relationship is that an employer can tell an employee what to do … When nonhuman assets are present, it is not difficult to understand the difference between the employer-employee situation and the independent contractor situation. In the former case, if the relationship breaks down, the employer walks away with all the nonhuman assets, whereas in the latter case each independent contractor walks away with some nonhuman assets. This difference gives the employer leverage" (pp. 57–58).[7] But again, as long as the so-called 'employee' can innovate to create excess profits, she will have the power and can "fire the employer" and cooperate with others (e.g., headhunters will contact the employee). Nonhuman assets (such as machines, land or money) do not provide authority or leverage.

Alchian and Woodward (1987, 1988) propose that within the firm, team members have some specific knowledge, and departure of part of the team can threaten the team's value. Members will want assurance of performance and compensation before they will be willing to make any self-financed investments in the team's efforts (hence, long-term contracts and teamwork co-exist). Alchian and Woodward also argue that team members who own resources (human as well) whose values depend most heavily on the performance of the team (i.e., are the most team-specific) will be willing to pay the most for the right to control the team and own the residual value.[8] The team members, whose resource values most dependent on the performance of the team, are "the directors, administrators and managers (or their principals) of the team's activities, and by convention, are called the 'owners of the firm'".[9] Williamson (1988) emphasizes credible commitments (not credible threats) as a protection from post-contractual opportunism (shirking). He concludes that whether labor serves on the board of directors depends

[6] Contrary to Coase's argument, producing by markets might also not need to make a series of contracts. For example, a merchant makes contracts with different firms (labors) to manufacture different parts of a machine, and then organizes these parts to make the machine (i.e., it is a kind of outsourcing). These firms (labors) will only care about the opportunity costs they can earn, and do not need to make contracts with each other. In this case, the merchant (the 'organizer') will not have any power since everything will be done according to well-specified ex-ante contracts.

[7] Rajan and Zingales (1998) also argue that the person who has the ability to grant, deny, or terminate access to the firm's productive assets has power.

[8] Klein, Crawford and Alchian (1978) suggest that the "monitoring the monitors" problem may be solved by making the owners of the most firm-specific assets the residual claimants.

[9] Some law professionals (e.g., O'Kelley, 2012) argue that the corporation is a by-product of contractual bargaining between a subset of the firm's constituents who voluntarily choose to organize their business relationship by forming a corporation and agreeing to act as the corporation's

on whether employees have made firm-specific investments (e.g., develop skills or knowledge with firm-specific value). It is interesting to note, however, that even in human's smallest organization—marriage, "long-term contract" and "credible commitments" don't seem plausible.

Berle and Means (1932) argue that dispersed owners of the modem corporation do not have the incentive to effectively control corporate management—directors and officers—and that managers often act in their own interests rather than in the stockholders' interests (hence, a rise in the power of managers). Williamson (1975) suggests hierarchy in organizations may mitigate the problem of controlling opportunism. Holmstrom (1979) and Grossman and Hart (1983) argue that the least easily monitored agent (i.e., the manager) whose effort makes the most difference to output should be the residual claimant. Fama and Jensen (1983) claim that in large open corporations, agency problems arise when the decision managers who initiate and implement important decisions are not the major residual claimants and therefore do not bear a major share of the wealth effects of their decisions. Fama and Jensen propose to control the agency problems by separating the management (initiation and implementation) and control (ratification and monitoring) of decisions. In sum, hierarchy or the separation of management and control decisions in large organizations can be used to mitigate agency problems in ex-post operations. But the powers to determine the firm's (ex-ante) objectives are still in the hands of innovative entrepreneurs.

2.3 Choice Set, Risk Attitude, and Types of Contract

In the modern economy, under private ownership of resources, the contracting parties can freely choose among different contracts: a wage contract, a fixed-rent contract, a share contract, or a combination of each. Cheung (1969) suggests that the choice of contracts is determined by weighing the gains from risk dispersions and the costs of contracting associated with different contracts. He argues that "given the transaction cost, risk aversion implies that asset values and the variances of income are negatively related. While in itself the dispersion of risk under a share contract will lead to higher values for the contracted resources, the higher associated transaction cost will lead to lower asset values" (p. 27).

I argue that the transaction costs of contracting are dependent on the contracting parties' risk attitudes, and the contracting parties' risk attitudes are dependent on the sizes of their choice sets. For example, if a person doesn't have much saving and her spouse is not working, then we say this person has a smaller choice set and is risk averse in the sense that she needs to choose a wage (fixed payment) contract and cannot choose a share (uncertain payment) contract. If on the other hand, a person who has some wealth and, hence, can choose a wage, a fixed-rent,

officers, directors and shareholders. Corporation law assigns to the corporation the role of sole-proprietor-surrogate. The sole proprietor possesses a position within the firm and a bundle of property rights which are generally described as the powers and position of an owner.

or a share contract, then she is termed as having a larger choice set and is less risk averse. The transaction costs of contracting will be prohibitively high if all contracting parties want a wage contract (i.e., all have smaller choice sets). The costs of contracting will be lower if one of contracting parties has a larger choice set (i.e., less risk averse), and can take an uncertain payment contract.[10]

Cheung (1969) reports that in China, share tenancy appears more frequent in the wheat region than in the rice region, and higher proportional variances for wheat than for rice. He suggests that share rent is generally slightly higher than fixed (crop) rent, and this premium may be regarded as a return for risk bearing to the landowner. I argue that higher share rent may be due to the fact that tenants in the wheat regions have less choices: In China's north (wheat) region, tenants are much poorer because except farming they cannot find much work to do (and landowners can charge "monopolistic rents"); whereas in the south (rice) region with a more prosperous economy, tenants can also work in other jobs (e.g., owning small workshops) and hence, can choose the fixed-rent contract. Atack and Passell (1996) also find that after the American Civil War, former slaves in the south still worked for their previous masters with "dependent" share contracts. This is because the newly liberated slaves didn't have other job opportunities—labor markets were closed to them then, and they still needed protections from their previous masters.[11] In the tenant-landowner case, if the tenant chooses fix-rent contract, an interesting question arises: *Who is the owner of this 'firm'?*

In the modern public firm, the relationship between equityholder and debtholder is like a wage or a fixed-rent contract, i.e., the equityholder is like a landowner, and the debtholder is like a tenant. On the other hand, manager and equityholder seem to have a share contract. In a society with a big middle class, capital markets can gather large capital from people who have small amount of wealth. Limited liability means that the most you may lose is the resource you invested. Limited liability helps lower the transaction costs of investing: If shareholders were liable for debts of the firm, both creditors and shareholders would need to investigate the wealth of each shareholder. But limited liability is not only limited to stock. All the resource providers in the firm (shareholders, bondholders, material providers and workers) have limited liability. Also, whether a resource provider's rights can be transferred or sold to other investors depends on whether the service provided by the resource is homogeneous. For example, in the previous Robin Hood's story, all the gangsters (including the cook) have limited liability, but they cannot sell their rights to outsiders unless other members of the gang agree. However, if there is a capitalist who provides the gang weapons (i.e., capitals), then this capitalist's

---

[10] Still, it is the entrepreneur who innovates to earn excess profits can have the power to direct even if she has no wealth and needs a wage (or a mixed) contract: "One entrepreneur may sell his service to another for a certain sum of money, while the payment to his employees may be mainly or wholly a share in profits" (Coase, 1937, p. 41).

[11] In a complete market with no transaction costs and no arbitrage, all types of labor contract have the same value. See Chang's (2015) Chap. 5.

rights can be transferred to another capitalist without the agreement from other members.

2.4 Legal Forms of Firms, and the Market Value and Capital Structure of the Firm

Basically, there are three different legal forms of organizing firms: sole proprietorships, partnerships and corporations.

(a) Sole Proprietorship. A sole proprietorship is a business owned and run by one person. The firm may have a few employees, but the owner has unlimited personal liability for the firm's debt and pays only individual income taxes. The life of a sole proprietorship is limited to the life of the owner.
(b) Partnership. Partnership has more than one owner. Income from a partnership is taxed as personal income to the partners. There are two kinds of partnership: general partnership and limited partnership. In general partnership, all owners contribute some capital and labor to the firm and have unlimited liability. Limited partnership has at least one general partner and other limited partners do not manage the business of the firm. Limited partners have limited liability and may transfer their ownership.
(c) Corporation. Corporation is a legal entity. Like a natural person, corporation can enter into contracts, buy (acquire) assets, lend or borrow (incur obligations). Hence, it needs to pay corporate income tax. According to the corporate law, the owners of corporation are shareholders (or stockholders or equityholders) who are the residual claimants after labor, material providers and debtholders. All the stakeholders of corporation have limited liability.

The market value of the firm does not mean the total value of physical assets such as land, buildings, machines, etc. We have two ways to define the market value of the firm:

(1) When the firm liquidates (e.g., being acquired, 'bought' by another firm), after giving money to non-capital providers (such as labor and material providers), the share that belongs to capital providers (e.g., debtholders and equityholders) is the market value of the firm.
(2) When the firm continues operation, in year t, after giving money to labor and material providers, the money distributed to capital providers is termed as cash flow (CF_t) where the discount rate is r, the market value (MV) of the firm is:

$$MV = \frac{CF_1}{1+r} + \frac{CF_2}{(1+r)^2} + \frac{CF_3}{(1+r)^3} + \dots \tag{2.1}$$

These two methods should give the same the market value of the firm since every asset's present value (market value) is determined by its future cash flows. Under uncertainty, asset's market value is determined by its future possible cash flows and their probabilities.

The way to divide cash flows to pay debtholders and equityholders will determine the market/present value of debt and of equity. For example, suppose that under uncertainty, the risk-free annual interest rate of banks is 10%. You have a patent (a particular technology) so that if you invest \$8, 000 now, you will receive certain \$1, 200 annually. Note that the rate of return on this totally equity-finance firm (investment) is not 15%(= 1, 200/8, 000), but 10%(= 1, 200/12, 000). This is because the market value of this firm (investment) is not \$8, 000, but \$12, 000(= \$8, 000 + \$4, 000) where \$8, 000 is the cash investment and \$4, 000 is the market value of the patent for the production. The market value of the patent \$4, 000 is calculated as follows: Suppose that the firm borrows \$8, 000 from a bank (i.e., it is a totally debt-financed firm) and pays the bank interests \$800 annually. Then you will receive \$400(= 1, 200 − 800) annually by investing no money but a patent, and hence, the market value of the patent is: \$4, 000 = 400/10%. This shows that the capital structure (e.g., totally equity-finance or totally debt-financed) of the firm does not affect the market value of the firm. This is **the Modigliani–Miller First Proposition**: capital structure irrelevancy proposition.

The above example can be generalized as follows. The annual cash flow of the levered firm X (i.e., \$1, 200) belongs to and is distributed to the debtholders and equityholders:

$$X \equiv X_B + X_S \tag{2.2}$$

where X_B is the cash flow for debtholders, and X_S, the cash flow for equityholders. Equation (2.2) is equality by definition. Define $V_L \equiv S_L + B$, $X \equiv (r_{WACC})(S_L + B)$, $X_B \equiv r_B B$, and $X_S \equiv r_S S_L$, where V_L (i.e., \$12, 000 = \$8, 000 + \$4, 000) is the market value of the firm; S_L is the market value of equity; B is the market value of debt; r_{WACC} is the weighted average cost of capital (WACC) on the levered firm's assets; r_B is the rate of return on debt; and r_S is the rate of return on equity. Equation (2.2) can be rewritten as:

$$(r_{WACC})(S_L + B) \equiv r_B B + r_S S_L, \tag{2.3}$$

or

$$r_S = r_{WACC} + (B/S_L)(r_{WACC} - r_B). \tag{2.4}$$

The cash flow of the firm, X, is independent of the debt-equity ratio (B/S_L). The firm's market value $V_L \equiv S_L + B$ is also independent of the debt-equity ratio. Hence, r_{WACC} must be independent of the debt-equity ratio. Suppose that the firm borrows \$4, 000 from a bank and the equityholder invests \$4, 000. Then, annually after paying the bank interests \$400, the equityholder will receive \$800, and hence, the market value of the equity is: \$8, 000 = 800/10%, and the rate of return on equity is still 10% = 800/8, 000. This result shows that Eq. (2.4) is meaningless since $r_S = r_B = r_{WACC} = 10\%$. This result also refutes the Modigliani–Miller Second Proposition which claims that increasing debt-equity ratio increases the rate of return on equity. In Chaps. 8 and 9, we will see the same result when the firm has uncertain cash flows.

Summary and Conclusions

This chapter uses a robber's story to illustrate that there is no such thing as the owner of the gang (firm) nor the residual claimant of the gang (firm). Each resource provider has property rights only on the resource she provides, and only those entrepreneurs who can innovate to create excess profits can have the power to control the firm and determine the firm's objectives. When people cooperate, types of contracts are determined by the transaction costs of contracting. The transaction costs of contracting are dependent on the contracting parties' risk attitudes. The contracting parties' risk attitudes are dependent on the sizes of their choice sets.

- There are three different legal forms of organizing firms: sole proprietorships, partnerships and corporations.
- The market value of the firm is defined as the share that belongs to capital providers (such as equityholders and debtholders) when the firm liquidates or is acquired by another firm.
- Under certainty, the Modigliani–Miller First Proposition holds (i.e., the market value of the firm is independent of the firm's capital structure), but the Modigliani–Miller Second Proposition does not hold (i.e., changing the debt-equity ratio does not affect the rate of return on equity).

Appendix: Equivalency between Maximizing Profits and Maximizing Resource Providers' Wealth

Assume a one-period model: In the beginning of the period, the firm employs labor (L) and capital (K) to produce output ($q = q(L, K)$). At the end of the period, the capital has no scrap value, and the firm sells outputs and liquidates. The firm's profit-maximizing problem is:

$$\underset{L,K}{Max} \quad \pi = p(q(L, K)) \cdot q(L, K) - wL - (1 + r)K, \tag{2.5}$$

where w is the wage rate, $1+r$ is the rental price of capital. In Eq. (2.5), a Schumpeterian entrepreneur owns and tries to maximize excess profits, π, by choosing optimal labor and capital inputs. The resource providers (labor and capitalist) can only earn opportunity costs: w and $1 + r$, respectively.

The first-order conditions for Eq. (2.5) are:

$$\frac{\partial \pi}{\partial K} = \frac{\partial}{\partial K}[p(q(L, K)) \cdot q(L, K)] - (1 + r) \equiv 0 \tag{2.6}$$

$$\frac{\partial \pi}{\partial L} = \frac{\partial}{\partial L}[p(q(L, K)) \cdot q(L, K)] - w \equiv 0. \tag{2.7}$$

From Eq. (2.6) we get $K = K(L, r)$, and from Eq. (2.7), $L = L(K, w)$. The optimal inputs: $L^* = L(r, w)$ and $K^* = K(r, w)$ can be obtained by jointly solving Eqs. (2.6) and (2.7).

We can also use a two-step approach to solve the profit-maximization problem. First, solve Eq. (2.7) for $L = L(K)$, and substitute it into Eq. (2.5):

$$\underset{K}{Max} \quad \pi(K) = p(q(L(K), K)) \cdot q((L(K), K) - w \cdot L(K) - (1+r) \cdot K, \quad (2.8)$$

where "$p(q(L(K), K)) \cdot q(L(K), K) - w \cdot L(K)$" is the capitalist's quasi-rent. Note that deriving $L = L(K)$ from Eq. (2.7) implies that for any given capital K, the capital provider can choose an optimal L to maximize excess profitsπ. Thus, Eq. (2.8) is the capital provider's wealth-maximizing problem, i.e., it assumes that the capital provider owns the property rights of the production (i.e., in addition to the opportunity costs of capital input, the capital provider also owns the excess profits). The capitalist chooses optimal capital input K^* to maximize profits by equalizing the marginal revenue (i.e., marginal quasi-rent) with the marginal cost (i.e., the cost of capital):

$$\left.\frac{\partial \pi(K)}{\partial K}\right|_{K=K^*} = \left.\frac{\partial [p(q(L(K), K)) \cdot q(L(K), K) - w \cdot L(K)]}{\partial K}\right|_{K=K^*} - (1+r) \equiv 0. \quad (2.9)$$

After deriving the optimal capital input $K^* = K(r, w)$, the optimal labor input $L^* = L(r, w)$ can be calculated from $L = L(K)$. Comparing Eq. (2.5) with Eq. (2.8), we can conclude that in the absence of transaction costs, no matter who (either the capitalist or the entrepreneur) owns the property rights of production, the market value of production remains the same.

If on the other hand, we solve Eq. (2.6) first for $K = K(L)$, then substitute it into Eq. (2.5):

$$\underset{L}{Max} \quad \pi(L) = p(q(L, K(L)) \cdot q((L, K(L)) - (1+r) \cdot K(L) - w \cdot L, \quad (2.10)$$

where "$p(q(L, K(L))) \cdot q(L, K(L)) - (1+r) \cdot K(L)$" is the labor's quasi-rent. Deriving $K = K(L)$ from Eq. (2.6) implies that for any given L the labor can choose an optimal K to maximize excess profits π. Equation (2.6) is the labor's wealth-maximizing problem, i.e., it assumes that the labor owns the property rights of the production (i.e., in addition to the opportunity costs of the labor input, the labor also owns the excess profits). The labor chooses optimal labor input L^* to maximize profits by equalizing the marginal revenue (marginal quasi-rent) with the marginal cost (the wage rate):

$$\left.\frac{\partial \pi(L)}{\partial L}\right|_{L=L^*} = \left.\frac{\partial [p(q(L, K(L)) \cdot q(L, K(L)) - (1+r) \cdot K(L)]}{\partial L}\right|_{L=L^*} - w \equiv 0. \quad (2.11)$$

After deriving the optimal labor input $L^* = L(r, w)$, the optimal capital input $K^* = K(r, w)$ can be calculated from $K = K(L)$. Comparing Eq. (2.5) with Eq. (2.10), we conclude that in the absence of transaction costs, no matter who (either the labor or the entrepreneur) owns the property rights of production, the market value of production is the same.

In sum, in the absence of transaction costs, maximizing Schumpeterian entrepreneur's excess profits and maximizing any resource provider's wealth are equivalent. For example, assuming in equation (2.5), $q(L, K) = L^{1/2}K^{1/2}$, $w = 1$, $r = 56.25\%$, and $p(q) = 10 - q$. Solve any of Eqs. (2.5), (2.8) or (2.10), we get the same $\pi^* = \$14.0625$, $L^* = 4.6875$, and $K^* = \$3$. These are the results of the Coase theorem: in the absence of transaction costs, who (or even no one) owns the property rights of production (excess profits) is irrelevant to the market value of production.

In the above example, suppose that the capital provider owns the property rights of the production (as in Eq. (2.8)) and invests three units of K (\$3) of her own money in the production, i.e., no debt. Then the market value of equity is: $\$12 = (14.0625 + 3 \times 1.5625)/1.5625$, which implies: If the capital provider sells her capital \$3 plus the present/market value of the property rights of the excess profits to the market, she will get \$12. The rate of return on equity is: $56.25\% = [(14.0625 + 3 \times 1.5625)/12] - 1$. If the capital provider invests only \$1 and borrows \$2 from a bank, then the market value of equity is: $\$10 = (14.0625 + 1 \times 1.5625)/1.5625$, and the rate of return on equity is still the same: $56.25\% = [(14.0625 + 1 \times 1.5625)/10] - 1$. This result refutes the Modigliani–Miller Second Proposition increasing debt-equity ratio increases the rate of return on equity.

Similarly, suppose that the labor provider owns the property rights of the production (i.e., Eq. (2.10)) and invests 4.6875 units of L in the production. Then the market value of her labor input is: $\$18.75 = 14.0625 + 1 \times 4.6875$, which implies: If the labor provider sells her 4.6875 units of L plus the present/market value of the property rights of the excess profits to the market, she will get \$18.75. The return per unit of labor provider's input is: $\$1 = (14.0625 + 1 \times 4.6875)/18.75$. If the labor provider invests only one unit of L and hires 3.6875 units of L from the labor market, then the market value of labor provider's input is: $\$15.0625 = 14.0625 + 1 \times 1$, and the return per unit of labor provider's input is still the same: $\$1 = (14.0625 + 1 \times 1)/15.0625$.

Problems

1. What kind of assumptions do we need if the firm is a nexus of contracts? Can a family be regarded as a nexus of contracts?
2. Use the concept of choice set to explain the existence of interest rate. Explain the meaning of the negative interest rate.
3. "With no transaction costs, maximizing profits is equivalent to maximizing resource providers' wealth." Comment on this statement. Who owns the property rights of excess profits?

4. Some scholars argue that ‘check and balance’ is needed in corporation. Is this argument correct?
5. Suppose that under uncertainty, the risk-free annual interest rate of banks is 10%. You have a patent (a particular technology) so that if you invest \$10, 000 now, you will receive certain \$2, 000 annually. Suppose that the firm borrows \$8, 000 from a bank and pays the bank interests \$800 annually. What is the rate of return on equity?

References

Alchian, A., & Woodward, S. (1988). The firm is dead; long live the firm: A review of Oliver E. Williamson's The Economic Institutions of Capitalism. *Journal of Economic Literature, 26*, 65–79.

Alchian, A., & Woodward, S. (1987). Reflections on the theory of the firm. *Journal of Institutional and Theoretical Economics, 143*, 110–136.

Alchian, A., & Demsetz, H. (1972). Production, information costs, and economic organization. *American Economic Review, 62*, 777–795.

Atack, J., & Passell, P. (1996). *A new economic view of American history*. W.W. Norton Company, Chapters 12 and 14.

Berle, A., & Means, G. (1932). *The modern corporation and private property*. Harcourt, Brace & World, Inc.

Chang, K.-P. (2015). *The ownership of the firm, corporate finance, and derivatives: Some critical thinking*. Springer Nature.

Cheung, S. (1968). Private property rights and sharecropping. *Journal of Political Economy, 76*, 1107–1122.

Cheung, S. (1969). *The theory of share tenancy*. The University of Chicago Press.

Coase, R. (1988). *The firm, the market and the law*. The University of Chicago Press.

Coase, R. (1960) The problem of social cost.*Journal of Law and Economics 3*, 1–44; also in Coase, R. (Ed.). (1988). *The firm, the market and the law* (pp. 95–156). The University of Chicago Press.

Coase, R. (1937). The nature of the firm. *Economica 4*, 386–405; also in Coase, R. (Ed.). (1988). *The firm, the market and the law* (pp. 33–55). The University of Chicago Press

Demsetz, H., & Lehn, K. (1985). The structure of corporate ownership: Causes and consequences. *Journal of Political Economy, 93*, 1155–1177.

Fama, E., & Jensen, M. (1983). Agency problems and residual claims. *Journal of Law and Economics, 26*, 327–349.

Fama, E. (1978). The effect of a firm's investment and financing decisions on the welfare of its security holders. *American Economic Review, 68*, 272–284.

Grossman, S., & Hart, O. (1986). The costs and benefits of ownership: A theory of vertical and lateral Integration. *Journal of Political Economy, 94*, 691–719.

Grossman, S., & Hart, O. (1983). Unemployment with observable aggregate shocks. *Journal of Political Economy, 91*, 907–928.

Hart, O. (1995). *Firms, contracts and financial structure*. The Oxford University Press.

Holmström, B. (1979). Moral hazard and observability. *Bell Journal of Economics, 10*, 74–91.

Jensen, M., & Meckling, W. (1976). Theory of the firm: Managerial behavior, agency costs and ownership structure. *Journal of Financial Economics, 3*, 305–360.

Klein, B., Crawford, R. G., & Alchian, A. (1978). Vertical integration, appropriable rents, and the competitive contracting process. *Journal of Law and Economics, 21*, 297–326.

Myers, S. (1984). The search for optimal capital structure. *Midland Corporate Finance Journal 1*, 6–16; also in Stern, J. M., & Chew, D. H. Jr. (Eds.). (1986). *The revolution in corporate finance* (pp. 91–99). Basil Blackwell.

O'Kelley, C. (2012). Coase, Knight, and the nexus-of-contracts theory of the firm: A reflection on reification, reality, and the corporation as entrepreneur surrogate. *Seattle University Law Review, 35*, 1247–1269.

Rajan, R., & Zingales, L. (1998). Power in a theory of the firm. *Quarterly Journal of Economics, 113*, 387–432.

Schumpeter, J. (1934). *The theory of economic development: An inquiry into profits, capital, credit, interest, and the business cycle.* Harvard University Press.

Williamson, O. E. (1975). *Markets and hierarchies: Analysis and antitrust implication: A study in the economics of internal organization.* Free Press.

Williamson, O. E. (1988). The logic of economic organization. *Journal of Law, Economics, and Organization, 4*, 65–93.

Basic Concepts of Valuation

3

In a one-period model, deposit money in a bank, and on the maturity date, in addition to the principal, the depositor usually can get interest payment. But why is the bank willing to provide interest? In Sect. 3.1 of this chapter, we explain that time value of money is not the main reason of the existence of interest. Section 3.2 introduces how to calculate the present value and the future value of an asset. In the multi-period case, the discounted cash flow (DCF) method or the net present value (NPV) method assumes that the predicted reinvestment rate is the discount rate for future cash flows. Section 3.3 discusses annuity and perpetuities. Annual interest rate and effective annual rate are in Sect. 3.4. Section 3.5 explains bond price volatility and term structure of interest rates.

3.1 The Time Value of Money Versus Choice Set

When we use cost–benefit analysis to make decision, we usually need consider its time line: cost happens at the current time and benefit, in the future. To have a meaningful comparison between benefit and cost we need to use the discount rate to discount those future benefits back to the current time. The difference between the present value of benefit and that of cost is called the net present value (NPV). This kind of method is termed as the discounted cash flow (DCF) method.

When a person borrows money (principal) from a bank, on the maturity date of the debt the borrower must pay to the bank both principal and interest. The interest rate (the discount rate) of debt is calculated by dividing interest by principal. It makes sense to pay back principal, but why pay interest? Traditionally, in finance and economics, there are five reasons for paying interest: (1) time preference (**the time value of money**)—even with the same quality and quantity, people prefer current goods to future goods; (2) default risk—borrower may fail to pay back the principal; (3) inflation risk—because prices may go up, the same amount of money may buy less amount of goods in the future; (4) opportunity costwhen people lend

K.-P. Chang, *Corporate Finance: A Systematic Approach*, Springer Texts in Business and Economics, https://doi.org/10.1007/978-981-19-9119-6_3

money, they can no longer use this money to fund their investment; and (5) cost of liquidity (inconvenience)—for example, fiat money doesn't provide interest but government bond does. This is because the latter is less convenient to use to buy goods.

The following example shows, however, that even if the above five reasons do not exist, people will still pay interest. Imagine Robinson Crusoe and Friday live all alone in a remote and uninhabited island. Friday wants to borrow a salted fish from Robinson Crusoe, and promises to give back on the next full moon another salted fish with the same size and quality. Robinson Crusoe replies that in addition to a salted fish, Friday should also give him a coconut as an interest payment. Friday is illiterate and couldn't understand what interest payment means. Robinson Crusoe therefore lectures him about the five reasons for paying interest (i.e., Econ 101 and Finance 101). After the lecture, Friday refutes his professor: Your five reasons do not make sense; (1) no time preference—you have in your warehouse so many salted fish which are more than you can eat for the rest of your life, (2) no default risk—I am quite healthy and cannot leave this island, (3) no inflation risk—there is no money in this island, (4) opportunity cost – there is no other place you can invest, (5) cost of liquidity (inconvenience)—there is no liquidity or inconvenience problem.

My answer for paying interest is: When Robinson Crusoe lends a salted fish to Friday, his **choice set** becomes smaller and Friday's **choice set** becomes larger. In order to have a voluntary agreement between these two people, even with no default, Friday must pay an extra coconut to compensate Robinson Crusoe. When fewer people want to borrow money from banks, the interest rate will go down. In the case of economic recession, people may deposit money in banks to earn no interest (zero interest rate), i.e., the time value of money is zero. This is because even if the depositors' choice sets become smaller, the banks' choice sets do not become larger (because no one borrows for consumption or investment), and hence, interest rate is zero. The so-called negative interest rate is just the fee for renting a bank's safety deposit box. In this Robinson Crusoe-Friday example, if Friday has a salted fish and wants to lend it to Robinson Crusoe, Robinson Crusoe will not accept it unless Friday is willing to earn a negative interest rate for renting Crusoe's warehouse.

3.2 Present Value, Future Value and Compounding

The following example explains how reinvestment affects the discounted cash flow method (i.e., the Net Present Value Method and Internal Rate of Return Method).

Example 3.1 Suppose on January 1, a 5-year government bond has par value \$100 and coupon rate 10% (i.e., at the end of each year the coupon payment or the interest payment is \$10). The cash flows of this bond in the next five years can be represented as:

$t = 0$	$t = 1$	$t = 2$	$t = 3$	$t = 4$	$t = 5$
0	10	10	10	10	10 + 100

The question is: How much are you willing to pay to own these cash flows?

The answer depends on the annual interest rate these coupon payments can use to reinvest during the five years. For example, if people predict (expect) the reinvestment rate is 8%, the future values of the five coupon payments and the principal will be:

$t = 0$	$t = 1$	$t = 2$	$t = 3$	$t = 4$	$t = 5$	
0	10	10(1+8%)	$10(1+8\%)^2$	$10(1+8\%)^3$	$10(1+8\%)^4$	Reinvest the first year interest for 4 years
		10	10(1+8%)	$10(1+8\%)^2$	$10(1+8\%)^3$	Reinvest the second year interest for 3 year
			10	10(1+8%)	$10(1+8\%)^2$	Reinvest the third year interest for 2 year
				10	10(1+8%)	Reinvest the fourth year interest for 1 year
					10+100	The fifth year interest plus the principal

Add them up, the future/final value (FV) of the investment at the end of the fifth year is:

$$\begin{aligned} FV &= 10(1+8\%)^4 + 10(1+8\%)^3 + 10(1+8\%)^2 + 10(1+8\%) + (10+100) \\ &= \left(10/1.08 + 10/1.08^2 + 10/1.08^3 + 10/1.08^4 + 110/1.08^5\right)(1+8\%)^5 \\ &= (107.9854)(1+8\%)^5. \end{aligned} \tag{3.1}$$

Divide both sides of Eq. (3.1) by $(1+8\%)^5$, we can estimate the present value (PV) of this investment:

$$\begin{aligned} PV &= \frac{FV}{(1+8\%)^5} \\ &= \frac{10}{(1+8\%)} + \frac{10}{(1+8\%)^2} + \frac{10}{(1+8\%)^3} + \frac{10}{(1+8\%)^4} + \frac{110}{(1+8\%)^5} \\ &= 107.9854. \end{aligned} \tag{3.2}$$

The future value of this government bond: $\$158.6660 = (107.9854)(1+8\%)^5$ is equal to the future value of investing \$107.9854 in a bank with annual risk-free interest rate 8% for five years. Equation (3.2) can also be stated as:

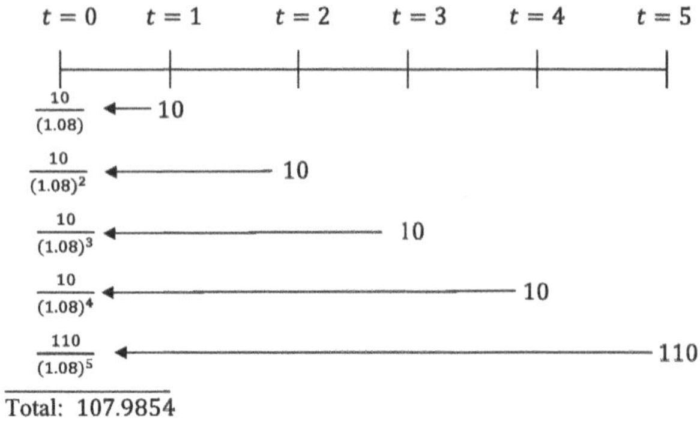

That is, at $t = 0$, this coupon bond can be 'stripped' to and sold as five different zero-coupon bonds, i.e., as Treasury STRIPS (Treasury Separate Trading of Registered Interest and Principal of Securities):

(1) The first year cash flow \$10 can be sold as a one-year zero-coupon bond with present value $\$9.2593(= 10/1.08)$;
(2) The second year cash flow \$10 can be sold as a two-year zero-coupon bond with present value $\$8.5734(= 10/(1.08)^2)$;
(3) The third year cash flow \$10 can be sold as a three-year zero-coupon bond with present value $\$7.9383(= 10/\left(1.08\right)^3)$;
(4) The fourth year cash flow \$10 can be sold as a four-year zero-coupon bond with present value $\$7.3503(= 10/\left(1.08\right)^4)$;
(5) The fifth year cash flow \$10 and par value \$100 can be sold as a five-year zero-coupon bond with present value $\$74.8642(= 110/\left(1.08\right)^5)$.

Equation (3.2) can be rewritten as a net present value (NPV), where predicted (expected) 8% reinvestment rate (discount rate) makes the NPV equal to zero:

$$NPV = 0 = -107.9854 + \frac{10}{(1+8\%)} + \frac{10}{(1+8\%)^2} + \frac{10}{(1+8\%)^3} + \frac{10}{(1+8\%)^4} + \frac{110}{(1+8\%)^5}. \tag{3.3}$$

Similarly, with predicted 10% reinvestment rate (discount rate),

$$NPV = 0 = -100 + \frac{10}{(1+10\%)} + \frac{10}{(1+10\%)^2} + \frac{10}{(1+10\%)^3} + \frac{10}{(1+8\%)^4} + \frac{110}{(1+8\%)^5}; \tag{3.4}$$

with predicted 12% reinvestment rate (discount rate),

$$NPV = 0 = -92.7904 + \frac{10}{(1+12\%)} + \frac{10}{(1+12\%)^2} + \frac{10}{(1+12\%)^3} + \frac{10}{(1+12\%)^4} + \frac{110}{(1+12\%)^5}. \tag{3.5}$$

In Eq.'s (3.3), (3.4) and (3.5), the discount rate (the reinvestment rate) that makes the net present value equal to zero is called internal rate of return (IRR) in corporate finance or yield to maturity (YTM) in bond management.

In sum, we conclude:

1. *Our expectations for the future will determine our current behavior (valuation).* In the muti-period case, the discounted cash flow (DCF) method or the net present value (NPV) method, e.g., Eq. (3.2), assumes that the predicted reinvestment rate is the discount rate for future cash flows. This is a very strong assumption.
2. Any coupon bond can be transformed into a summation of several zero-coupon bonds.
3. Higher yield to maturity (or higher yield) of government bond indicates higher inflation risk and/or default risk. For example, comparing Eq. (3.4) with Eq. (3.5), when the YTM of the government bond increases from 10 to 12%, it implies the bond is less valuable, i.e., its market price drops from \$100 to \$92.7904. Decreasing government bond price indicates that this country may have higher inflation risk (if it is a developed country) or higher default risk (if it is a less developed country).

3.3 Annuity and Perpetuities

The following example explains how to calculate the market price (present value) of a stock.

Example 3.2 Suppose a company's stock provides Ccash dividends each year for an infinite amount of time. With reinvestment rate (i.e., opportunity cost of capital) r, the present value of this stock is calculated as[1]

$$\begin{aligned} PV &= \frac{C}{1+r} + \frac{C}{(1+r)^2} + \cdots + \frac{C}{(1+r)^n} + \cdots \\ &= \frac{C}{1+r}\left[1 + \frac{1}{1+r} + \frac{1}{(1+r)^2} + \cdots\right] \\ &= \frac{C}{1+r} \cdot \frac{1}{1-\frac{1}{1+r}} = \frac{C}{r} \end{aligned} \tag{3.6}$$

[1] Because $(1-R)(1+R+R^2+R^3+\ldots+R^n) = 1-R^{n+1}$, $1+R+R^2+R^3+\ldots+R^n = (1-R^{n+1})/(1-R)$. Let $r > 0$ and $0 < R = 1/(1+r) < 1$. We have: $1+R+R^2+R^3+\ldots+R^n = 1/(1-R)$ if $n \to \infty$.

where C/r is the present value of a perpetuity, which assumes the asset (stock) can perpetually generate cash flow C with reinvestment rate r. Suppose the annual rent of a piece of land is \$1,000 and the predicted reinvestment rate is 5%. Then the present value of the land is: $C/r = 1,000/0.05 = \$20,000$.

Some assets may produce cash flow only for a certain period of time. This is the annuity.

Example 3.2 Suppose on January 1, the government plans to give you \$2,000 for the next thirty years, starting from January 1 next year. Assume the reinvestment rate is 5%. The present value of this annuity is calculated as follows.

From Eq. (3.6) we can calculate the present values of the two cash flows:

(1)

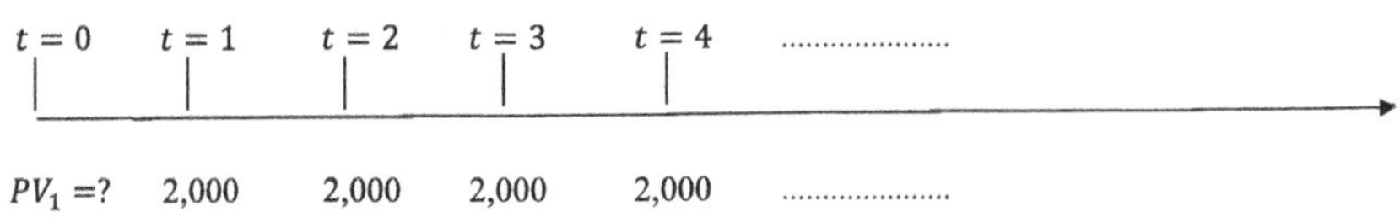

at $t = 0$, $PV_1 = C/r = 2,000/0.05 = \$40,000$;

(2)

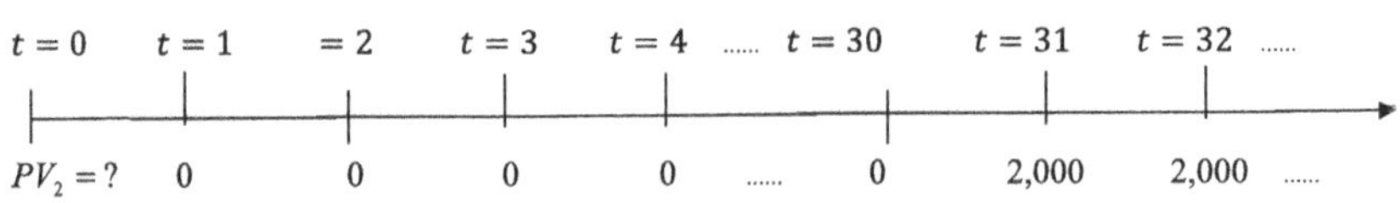

at $t = 30, PV' = C/r = 2,000/0.05 = \$40,000$
and hence, at $t = 0$,

$$PV_2 = PV'/(1+r)^{30} = 40,000/(1+0.05)^{30} = \$9255.0979$$

The present value of an annuity (PVA) is calculated by subtracting PV_2 from PV_1:

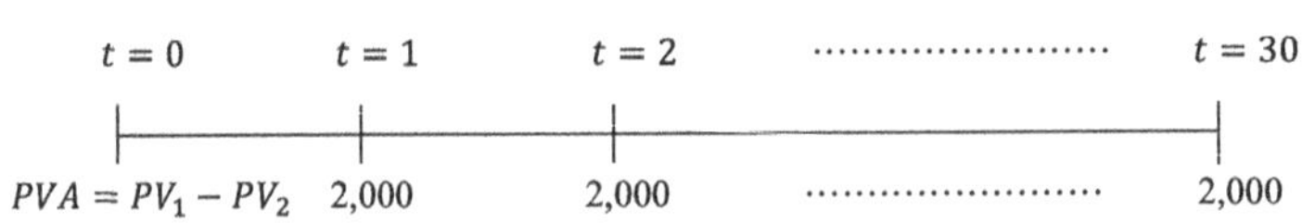

$$PVA = PV_1 - PV_2 = \frac{C}{r} - \frac{C}{r}\frac{1}{(1+r)^{30}} = \frac{C}{r}\left[\frac{(1+r)^{30}-1}{(1+r)^{30}}\right] = \$30744.9021.$$

Thus, the formula for present value of an annuity (PVA) is:

$$PVA = \frac{C}{r}\left[\frac{(1+r)^n - 1}{(1+r)^n}\right] \tag{3.7}$$

where n the number of years, C the yearly payment, and r is the reinvestment rate (the discount rate or the opportunity cost of capital).

The future value of an annuity (FVA) is:

$$FVA = PVA \cdot (1+r)^n = \frac{C}{r}\left[\frac{(1+r)^n - 1}{(1+r)^n}\right] \cdot (1+r)^n = \frac{C}{r}\left[(1+r)^n - 1\right]. \tag{3.8}$$

Suppose that the yearly payment starts from $t = 0$ for thirty years. Then the present value of annuity due (PVAD) is calculated as:

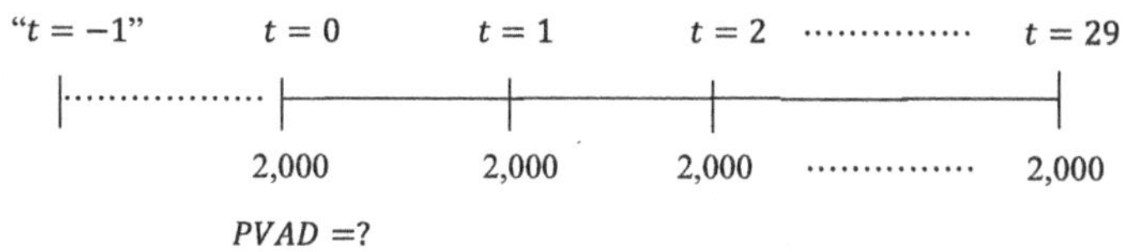

$$PVAD = (PVA) \cdot (1+r) = \frac{C}{r}\left[\frac{(1+r)^n - 1}{(1+r)^n}\right](1+r) \tag{3.9}$$

and the future value of an annuity due (FVAD) is:

$$FVAD = (PVAD) \cdot (1+r)^n = \frac{C}{r}\left[(1+r)^n - 1\right](1+r) \tag{3.10}$$

3.4 Annual Interest Rate and Effective Annual Rate

Example 3.3 Suppose that on January 1, the market price of a one-year government bond is \$100. The bond has par value \$100 and coupon rate 10%, but will provide interest payment \$5 every six months.

If the reinvestment rate of six months is 5%(= 0.10/2), the future values of the interest payments and the principal will be:

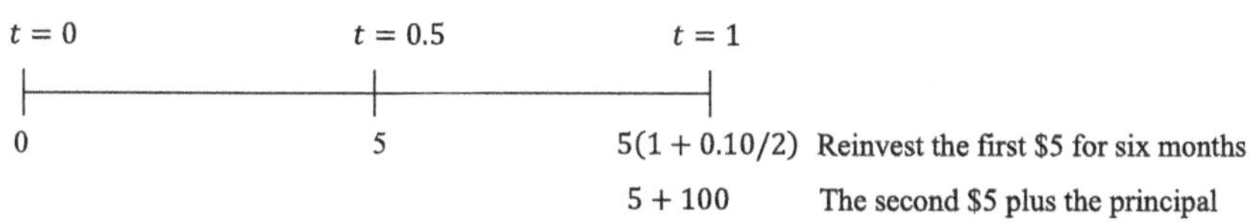

That is, at the end of this year, the owner of the bond will receive: \$110.25 = 5(1 + 5%) + (5 + 100). The annual interest rate that the owner actually earns is: (110.25 − 100)/100 = 10.25%, where 10.25% is called the effective annual rate (EAR).

We can rewrite the calculation as:

$$5\left(1+\frac{10\%}{2}\right)+5+100=100\left(1+\frac{10\%}{2}\right)^2=100(1+EAR)$$

or

$$\left(1+\frac{10\%}{2}\right)^2=1+EAR.$$

If the bond provides interest payment every quarter, then we will have (where r is the annual reinvestment rate):

$$100\left(1+\frac{10\%}{4}\right)^4=100(1+EAR)\text{ or }\left(1+\frac{r}{4}\right)^4=1+EAR \qquad (3.11)$$

If in a year the bond provides interest payment m times, the EAR is calculated as:

$$\left(1+\frac{r}{m}\right)^m=1+EAR$$

or

$$EAR=\left(1+\frac{r}{m}\right)^m-1 \qquad (3.12)$$

When m approaches infinite, $EAR = e^r - 1$.

The following table shows that because interest payment can be reinvested, increasing the frequency of paying interests will increase the EAR:

From Table 3.1 we can conclude three principles about money.

1. Receive money as early as possible (so that you have more choices to use it even if the reinvestment/interest rate is zero).
2. Pay as late as possible (so that you have more choices to use it even if the reinvestment/interest rate is zero).
3. If money is not in your pocket, it may disappear (i.e., agency cost: someone may steal it).

Table 3.1 Effective annual rates when annual reinvestment rate is 10%

Time period	Number of times (m)	Interest of the period (r/m)	$(1+\frac{r}{m})^m$	EAR
Yearly	1	10%	1.10^1	10%
Semiannually	2	5%	$(1.05)^2$	10.25%
Quarterly	4	2.5%	1.025^4	10.3813%
Monthly	12	0.8333%	1.008333^{12}	10.4713%
Weekly	52	0.1923076%	1.001923076^{52}	10.5065%
Daily	365	0.027397%	1.00027397^{365}	10.5156%
Continuously	$+\infty$	–	$2.71828^{0.10}$	10.5171%

3.5 Bond Price Volatility and Term Structure of Interest Rates

Bond Price Volatility

As shown in Eq. (3.2), suppose that a coupon bond provides yearly interest payment C for n years with par value M and annual reinvestment rate (or opportunity cost of capital) y. The present value of the coupon bond is calculated as:

$$P = \frac{C}{1+y} + \frac{C}{(1+y)^2} + \cdots + \frac{C}{(1+y)^n} + \frac{M}{(1+y)^n}. \tag{3.13}$$

Obviously, when the required rate of return y increases, the present value of the bond P will decrease, i.e.,

$$\frac{dP}{dy} = \frac{-1}{1+y}\left(\frac{C}{1+y} + \frac{2C}{(1+y)^2} + \cdots + \frac{nC}{(1+y)^n} + \frac{nM}{(1+y)^n}\right) < 0. \tag{3.14}$$

Divide both sides of Eq. (3.14) by P:

$$\frac{dP}{dy}\cdot\frac{1}{P} = \frac{-1}{1+y}\cdot\frac{1}{P}\cdot\left[\sum\nolimits_{t=1}^{n}\frac{tC}{(1+y)^t} + \frac{nM}{(1+y)^n}\right]. \tag{3.15}$$

Let $\Delta y = 1\%$. Then $(\Delta P/P)/\Delta y$ measures the percentage change of the present value of the bond. In Eq. (3.15), "$\frac{1}{P}\cdot\left[\sum\limits_{t=1}^{n}\frac{tC}{(1+y)^t} + \frac{nM}{(1+y)^n}\right]$" is termed as Macaulay duration, and "$\frac{1}{P(1+y)}\cdot\left[\sum\limits_{t=1}^{n}\frac{tC}{(1+y)^t} + \frac{nM}{(1+y)^n}\right]$" is the Modified duration. Thus, higher Macaulay duration of a bond means higher modified duration and higher volatility to interest rate (y) changes. Equation (3.15) also shows that duration can be expressed in terms of years. For example, if it is a zero-coupon bond (i.e., C is zero) with market price P and required rate of return y, the bond's remaining time to its maturity date is equal to its Macaulay duration (n years). On the other hand, if it is a coupon bond (i.e., $C > 0$) with the same market price P

Table 3.2 Lower coupon rate means greater price volatility

y (%)	(Coupon rate 10%)		(Coupon rate) 12%	
	p	Effects on bond price when required rate of return changes from 10%	p	Effects on bond price when required rate of return changes from 12%
8	$1,135.90	+13.59%	$1,271.81	+13.09%
10	$1,000	–	$1,124.62	–
12	$885.30	- 11.47%	$1,000	- 11.08%

and required rate of return y, the bond's duration number will always be less than the maturity date.

The following table shows that when required rate of return y changes, the changes of bond's price are not symmetric. Suppose two coupon bonds have the same par value: $1,000 and the same maturity date: 10 years, and pay interest semiannually. One has annual coupon rate 12%, and another, 10% (Table 3.2).

For the bond with 10% coupon rate, when it's required rate of return increases from 10 to 12%, its bond price decreases 11.47%; and when it's required rate of return decreases from 10 to 8%, its bond price increases 13.59%. For the bond with 12% coupon rate, when it's required rate of return increases from 10 to 12%, its bond price decreases 11.08%; and when it's required rate of return decreases from 10 to 8%, its bond price increases 13.08%. This shows that with the same amount of change in the required rate of return (i.e., $\Delta y = 2\%$), the bond with a lower coupon rate has greater price volatility.

Term Structure of Interest Rates

The term structure of interest rates is the relationship between interest rates or bond yields and different terms or maturities. According to Eq. (3.15), bonds with longer maturities will have higher interest rate risk (i.e., duration) than similar bonds with shorter maturities. It is believed that because long-term bonds have higher duration and are exposed to a greater probability that interest rates will change, long-term bonds should have higher interest rates than short-term bonds. However, there may be another reason: the buyer (loaner) of a long-term bond for a longer time cannot sell back the bond to the seller (borrower) to obtain the par value. In the case of renting an apartment, we find the opposite: short-term lease has higher rent than long-term lease because it is not easy for the landlord (loaner) to frequently find another tenant (borrower).

The following example shows how to use a six-month zero-coupon bond, a 1-year coupon bond, and a 1.5 year-coupon bond (where the two coupon bonds pay $5.25 semiannually) to construct the term structure of interest rates.

Maturity	Present value of the bond	Semiannual interest payment	Par value
0.5 year	101.69	0	105.25
1 year	102.36	5.25	100

Maturity	Present value of the bond	Semiannual interest payment	Par value
1.5 years	102.06	5.25	100

The yields (internal rates of return) for the three bonds are:

0.5 years: $101.69 = \frac{105.25}{1+r_1}$, and $r_1 = 3.50\%$;
1 year: $102.36 = \frac{5.25}{1+r_2} + \frac{105.25}{(1+r_2)^2}$, and $r_2 = 4.00\%$;
1.5 years: $102.06 = \frac{5.25}{1+r_3} + \frac{5.25}{(1+r_3)^2} + \frac{105.25}{(1+r_3)^3}$, and $r_3 = 4.50\%$.

The yield assumes that for each bond, the semiannual reinvestment rate is the same for every six-months.

The theoretical spot rates for the three bonds are:

0.5 years: $101.69 = \frac{105.25}{1+z_1}$, and $z_1 = 3.50\%$;
1 years: $102.36 = \frac{5.25}{1+z_1} + \frac{105.25}{(1+z_2)^2}$, and $z_2 = 4.01\%$;
1.5 years: $102.06 = \frac{5.25}{1+z_1} + \frac{5.25}{(1+z_2)^2} + \frac{105.25}{(1+z_3)^3}$, and $z_3 = 4.536\%$.

The theoretical spot rate assumes that all bonds have the same semiannual reinvestment rate for the next six-months.

For the first six-months, $r_1 = z_1 = 3.50\%$. From the one-year coupon bond, we can calculate the forward rate $f_1$for the second six-months:

$$\begin{aligned} 102.36 &= \frac{5.25}{1+z_1} + \frac{105.25}{(1+z_1)(1+f_1)} \\ &= \frac{5.25}{1+3.5\%} + \frac{105.25}{(1+3.5\%)(1+f_1)}, \text{ and } f_1 = 4.523\%. \end{aligned} \tag{3.16}$$

Equation (3.16) shows that the one-year coupon bond (with present value: \$102.36) is equivalent to a combination of a six-months zero coupon bond (with present value: \$5.07 = 5.25/1.035) and a one-year zero coupon bond (with present value: \$97.29 = 105.25/(1.035 × 1.04523)). The one-year zero coupon bond is equivalent to such a contract: at $t = 0$, the loaner loans \$97.29 to the borrower for six months with semiannual interest rate 3.5%, and in the meantime, signs a forward contract with the borrower to promise that at $t = 0.5$, she will lend out \$100.70 (= 97.29 × 1.035) to the borrower for another six months with semiannual interest rate 4.523%. Thus, the forward rate $f_1 = 4.523\%$is the second six-months interest rate both parties (i.e., the loaner and the borrower) agree at $t = 0$.

From the 1.5 years coupon bond, we can calculate the forward rate $f_2$for the third six-months:

$$102.06 = \frac{5.25}{1+z_1} + \frac{5.25}{(1+z_1)(1+f_1)} + \frac{105.25}{(1+z_1)(1+f_1)(1+f_2)}, \text{ and } \tag{3.17}$$

$f_2 = 5.594\%$.

The third term of the right-hand side of Eq. (3.17) represents: at $t = 0$, the loaner lends \$92.136 to the borrower for six months with semiannual interest rate 3.5%, and in the meantime, signs two forward contracts with the borrower to promise that (1) at $t = 0.5$, she will lend out \$95.36 (= 92.136 × 1.035) to the borrower for the second six months with semiannual interest rate 4.523%; and (2) at $t = 1.0$, she will lend out \$99.67 (= 95.36 × 1.04523) to the borrower for the third six months with semiannual interest rate 5.594%. Thus, the forward rate $f_1 = 4.523\%$is the second six-months interest rate and the forward rate $f_2 = 5.594\%$is the third six-months interest rate that both parties (i.e., the loaner and the borrower) agree at $t = 0$.

There are several theories of term structure of interest rates.

1. Unbiased expectations theory. The unbiased expectations theory emphasizes that current long-term interest rates contain an implicit prediction of future short-term interest rates. Hence, investors earn the same amount of interest from an investment in a single two-year bond today as that person would with two consecutive investments in one-year bonds.
2. Liquidity premium theory. The liquidity premium theory argues that investors prefer short-term bonds that can be sold quickly over long-term ones. Hence, yields on long-term bonds should be higher than short-term bonds.
3. Market segmentation theory. The market segmentation theory states that long- and short-term interest rates are not related to each other because they have different investors. It suggests that investors only care about yield and will buy bonds of any maturity.

   In practice, when the gap between short-term and long-term government bond yields shrinks, it usually means that short-term bond price decreases and long-term bond price increases, i.e., people feel less confident about the near-term economic situation. If yields on short-term bond rise above those on long term bond (i.e., the so-called yield curve inversion), it may signal an economic recession ahead.

Summary and Conclusions

This chapter explains the reasons why interest exists. In the multi-period environment, the reinvestment rate is assumed to calculate the present value and future value of an asset. The reinvestment rate also explains the three principles of money: receive money as early as possible; pay as late as possible; and keep money in your pocket (to avoid agency cost). Duration measures how sensitive a bond's price to the changes of yields.

- The main reason why interest payment exists is that the borrower's choice set becomes larger and the loaner's choice set becomes smaller.
- In the multi-period case, the discounted cash flow (DCF) method or the net present value (NPV) method, e.g., Eq. (3.2), assumes that the predicted reinvestment rate is the discount rate for future cash flows. This is a very strong assumption.

- Let r be the annual interest rate, C the interest payment, n the number of years before maturity, m the frequency of paying interest within a year.

Present value	$PV = \sum_{i=1}^{n} \frac{C}{(1+r)^i}$
Future value	$FV = \sum_{i=1}^{n} C(1+r)^{n-i}$
Present value of annuity	$PVA = \frac{C}{r}\left[\frac{(1+r)^n-1}{(1+r)^n}\right]$
Future value of annuity	$FVA = \frac{C}{r}\left[(1+r)^n - 1\right]$
Present value of annuity due	$PVAD = \frac{C}{r}\left[\frac{(1+r)^n-1}{(1+r)^n}\right](1+r)$
Future value of an annuity due	$FVAD = \frac{C}{r}\left[(1+r)^n - 1\right](1+r)$
Effective annual rate	$EAR = (1+\frac{r}{m})^m - 1$

- The Macaulay duration: $\frac{1}{P} \cdot \left[\sum_{t=1}^{n} \frac{tC}{(1+y)^t} + \frac{nM}{(1+y)^n}\right]$. The Modified duration: $\frac{1}{P(1+y)} \cdot \left[\sum_{t=1}^{n} \frac{tC}{(1+y)^t} + \frac{nM}{(1+y)^n}\right]$.

Problems

1. Explain that in the multi-period case, why the discount rate is also the reinvestment rate.
2. Suppose that a five-year investment project needs \$1,200 initial investment and at the end of each year will give \$50 payoff and \$1,200 at the end of the fifth year. The annual interest rate is 4%. Is this investment worthwhile?
3. In the previous question, if the annual interest rate is 8%, will you invest in this project?
4. Suppose that today is September 1 and you need to pay tuition \$10,000 in the next four years starting from next year's September 1. With annual interest rate 4%, how much money do you need now?
5. A young worker is twenty years old and plans to work until sixty years old. She hopes that after she retires, she can receive \$60,000 annuity until she is eighty years old. With 4% annual interest rate, how much does she need to save in each year between twenty- and sixty-year-old?

4 Financial Statements and Financial Ratios

As the report of physical examination for a person, financial statements provide information about financial conditions of a firm. Financial statements can help the management team to discover potential problems of the firm and internal control. Stakeholders as well as outside investors would be interested to know the firm's financial conditions. Section 4.1 of this chapter introduces the balance sheet, the income statement, and the statement of cash flows. Section 4.2 discusses how to use financial ratios to evaluate firm's liquidity, asset management, debt management, profitability, and market value.

4.1 Understanding Financial Statements

A public firm annually needs to report and communicate its financial statements to outsiders including suppliers (or material providers), customers, debtholders, and equityholders, etc. Among the four financial statements: the balance sheet, the income statement, the statement of cash flows and the statement of stockholders' equity, the balance sheet and the income statement are probably the most important statements. The balance sheet shows the economic status of capital providers (e.g., bondholders, stockholders) on a particular date, e.g., last day of each year. The income statement shows that for a period of time (e.g., a year) how the firm's operations affect different resource providers, e.g., labor, material providers, capital providers, and tax agency of a government.

The following is an example of a public firm's financial statements. Suppose the ABC company was established in the beginning of 2010 with debt: $20,000,000 and equity: $80,000,000, i.e., its total asset is: $100,000,000. The 2010 January 1 balance sheet of the company (Table 4.1) shows that the items on the left-hand side are *physical assets*, i.e., $100,000,000 invested by debtholders and equityholders is used to purchase equipment: $70,000,000 and maintain cash: $30,000,000; and those on the right-hand side are *financial assets* (*or financial claims*), which

K.-P. Chang, *Corporate Finance: A Systematic Approach*, Springer Texts in Business and Economics, https://doi.org/10.1007/978-981-19-9119-6_4

shows liabilities and equity of the company, i.e., liabilities: \$20,000,000 belongs to debtholders, and equity: \$80,000,000 belongs to equityholders.

After a whole year of operation (i.e., purchasing materials, hiring labors, and production and sales), ABC Corporation's all cash inflows and cash outflows are listed in the income statement (Table 4.2). The corporate tax rate is 40%, i.e., \$4,000,000 taxes paid to the government. The annual interest rate for the debt is 5%, i.e., debtholders receive \$1,000,000 annual interest expense. The method of straight line depreciation with no scrap value is adopted, i.e., annual depreciation expense is \$7,000,000 ($= \$70,000,000/10$). Note that \$7,000,000 depreciation expense is not a real cash outflow, i.e., the money is still in the firm and belongs to the equityholders. Payments to labor, material providers and public utilities (for supplying water, gas, and electricity, etc.) are included in 'cost of sales' and 'sales, general and administration expenses'. For 'equipment and plant', maintenance worker's salary and other maintenance expenses are included in 'cost of sales'. Among \$6,000,000 net income (which belongs to the equityholders), \$2,000,000 cash dividends were paid to the equityholders, and \$4,000,000 was kept in the company as 'increase in retained earnings'.

Table 4.1 shows that in 2010, 'fixed assets', 'long-term debt' and 'common stock' did not change. There was no short-term debt (i.e., both 'accounts payable' and 'notes payable' are zero). Thus, the company's *actual* cash outflows in 2010 were: \$67,500,000 ('cost of sales'), \$15,200,000 ('sales, general and administration expenses'), \$1,000,000 ('interest expense') and \$4,000,000 ('taxes'), and their sum is: \$87,700,000. Deduct the total actual cash outflow: \$87,700,000 from 'total sales': \$100,700,000, the residual is \$13,000,000, where $\$13,000,000 = 6,000,000$ ('net income') $+7,000,000$ ('depreciation expense') $= 2,000,000$ ('cash dividends') $+3,000,000$ ('accounts receivable') $+8,000,000$ ('cash and equivalents'). Because \$2,000,000 cash dividends were paid to the equityholders, 'retained earnings' increased from \$0 to \$4,000,000 ($= 6,000,000$ ('net income') $-2,000,000$ ('cash dividends')).

After ten years, the ABC Corporation has become a bigger company. Tables 4.3 and 4.4 show the balance sheet and the income statement of the firm in 2020 and 2021.

Common stock (in \$)	2020	2021
Common stock per share	\$25.00	\$19.00
Earnings per share (EPS)	\$ 2.652	\$ 1.968
Dividends per share (DPS)	\$ 0.600	\$ 0.648
Book value per share (BVPS)	\$15.20	\$16.52
Cash flow per share (CFPS)	\$ 4.252	\$ 3.968

Earnings per share (EPS) $= \frac{\text{Net income}}{\text{Number of shares of common stock}}$

Dividends per share (DPS) $= \frac{\text{Common stock dividends}}{\text{Number of shares of common stock}}$

Book value per share (BVPS) $= \frac{\text{Common stock holder's equity}}{\text{Number of shares of common stock}}$

Cash flow per share (CFPS)$= \frac{\text{Net income+Depreciation}}{\text{Number of shares of common stock}}$

(Note: Here cash flow is the stockholders' share calculated from the income statement)

Table 4.1 ABC corporation balance sheet 2010 (in $ million)

Assets:		2010 Jan. 1		2010 Dec. 31	Liabilities and Stockholders' Equity		2010 Jan. 1		2010 Dec. 31
Current assets					Current liabilities				
Cash and equivalents		$30		$38	Accounts payable		$0		$0
Accounts receivable		0		3	Notes payable		0		0
Total current asset		$30		$41	Total current liability		$0		$0
Fixed assets					Long-term debt		$20		$20
Equipment and plant	70		70		Common stock	80		80	
Less accumulated depreciation	0		7		Retained earnings	0		4	
Net equipment		$70		$63	Total equity		$80		$84
Total assets		$100		$104	Total liabilities and stockholders' equity		$100		$104

Table 4.2 ABC corporation income statement 2010 (in $ million)

Total sales		$100.7
Cost of sales		67.5
Gross profit		$33.2
Sales, general and administration expenses		15.2
Depreciation		7.0
Operating income		$11.0
Earnings Before Interest and Taxes (EBIT)		$11.0
Interest expense		1.0
Pretax income		$10.0
Taxes		4.0
Net income		$ 6.0
–	–	–
Dividends		$ 2.0
Increase in retained earnings		$ 4.0

1. Current assets and current liabilities
   In the income statement, 'total sales' may include both 'cash' and 'account receivable'. 'Accounts receivable' means someone (e.g., customer) owes the company, and it is a short-term debt. The numbers in 'cost of sales' and 'sales, general and administration expenses' may represent paying out cash and/or an increasing in 'accounts receivable'. 'Inventories' includes: materials, work-in-process and finished goods. In both 2020 and 2021, the company's 'total current asset' was much greater than 'total current liability'.
2. Fixed assets and long-term debt
   Between 2020 and 2021, the company's 'fixed assets', i.e., long-term assets, increased by $300,000,000 ($= 1,380,000,000 - 1,080,000,000$).
3. Liabilities and Stockholders' Equity
   The magnitude of liabilities is about the same as that of the stockholders' equity. In 2021, 'retained earnings' increased by $6,600,000 ($= 9,840,000$ ('net income') $-3,240,000$ ('cash dividends')). Like other resource providers (i.e., labor, material providers, debtholders, preferred stockholders), common stockholders also have limited liability.
4. The performance of management and the opportunity cost of common stock
   According to the corporate law (or the firm's corporate charter), common stockholders elect directors, and the board of directors (especially, the chairman) hires the CEO to organizes the management team. Thus, the management team should work and maximize wealth for common stockholders. Under no default, the income statement shows the opportunity costs of all resources: labor, material, debt, preferred stock, except common stock. Economic value added (EVA) method can be used to measure costs and benefits of all capital providers within a year:

Table 4.3 ABC corporation balance sheet, year ended December 31 (in $ million)

Assets		2020		2021	Liabilities and Stockholders' Equity		2020		2021
Current assets					Current liabilities				
Cash and equivalents		$ 15		$ 10	Accounts payable		$ 20		$ 50
Accounts receivable		310		370	Notes payable		200		230
Inventory		415		620	Total current liability		$220		$280
Total current asset		$740		$1,000					
					Long-term debt		520		854
Fixed assets									
Equipment and plant	1,080		1,380		Preferred stock		40		40
Less accumulated depreciation	280		380		Common stock	130		130	
Net equipment and plant		$800		$1,000	Retained earnings	630		696	
Total assets		$1,540		$2,000	Total equity		$760		$826
					Total liabilities and stockholders' equity		$1,540		$2,000
Number of preferred stocks	400,000 shares								
Number of common stocks	50,000,000 shares								

Table 4.4 ABC corporation income statement, year ended December 31 (in $ million)

	2020	2021
Total sales	$8,600.0	$9,742.7
Cost of sales	5,743.6	6,742.5
Gross profit	$2,856.4	$3,000.2
Sales, general and administration expenses	2,500.4	2,653.2
Depreciation	80.0	100.0
Operating income Earnings Before Interest and Taxes (EBIT)	$ 276.0 $ 276.0	$ 247.0 $ 247.0
Interest expense	50.0	78.0
Pretax income	$ 226.0	$ 169.0
Taxes	90.4	67.6
Net income before preferred stock dividends	$ 135.6	$ 101.4
Preferred stock dividends	3.0	3.0
Net income	$ 132.6	$ 98.4
Common stock dividends	$30.0	$ 32.4
Increase in retained earnings	$102.6	$ 66.0

$$\text{EVA} = (\text{EBIT})(1 - \text{Corporate Income Tax Rate}) - (\text{Operating Capital})(\text{WACC}), \tag{4.1}$$

where EBIT is: earnings before interest and taxes. '(EBIT)(1 – Corporate Income Tax Rate)' or the net operating profit after taxes (NOPAT) is the one-year after-tax revenue the common stockholders could receive if it were a totally-equity financed firm. In a year, operating capital provided by all capital providers includes: operating long-term assets and net operating working capital. Operating long-term assets are the 'net equipment and plant' in Table 4.3. Net operating working capital is the difference between 'total current asset' and 'accounts payable', where 'accounts payable' is like an interest-free loan, i.e., the firm owes someone and does not need to pay interest.

Assume that the weighted average cost of capital (WACC) of the operating capital is 9%. As shown in Table 4.5, in 2021, EVA of the company decreased by $56,1000,000. Return on invested capital (i.e., ROIC = (EBIT)(1 – Corporate Income Tax Rate)/Operating Capital) dropped from 10.89% to 7.60%. This example shows that a large increase in fixed assets could reduce both EVA and ROIC.

Table 4.5 The calculations of EVA and ROIC, year ended December 31 (in $ million)

	EBIT	(1-Corp. tax rate)	Operating capital	WACC	EVA	ROIC
2020	276.0	60%	(15 + 310 + 415)–20 + 800 = 1520	9%	28.8	10.89%
2021	247.0	60%	(10 + 370 + 620)–50 + 1000 = 1950	9%	−27.3	7.60%

Suppose that we are using the stock price to evaluate the firm's performance. The market value add (MVA) method is:

$$\text{MVA} = (\text{Number of shares})(\text{Market price of stock per share}) - \left(\text{Stockholders}'\text{equity}\right). \quad (4.2)$$

In 2020 to 2021, the MVA of the firm decreased from $490,000,000 to $124,000,00.

5. Statement of cash flows

   In a year the firm may produce & sell goods, invest and finance. These activities generate cash inflows or cash outflows which affect 'cash and equivalents' in the balance sheet. From the balance sheet and the income statement, we can construct the statement of cash flows for the ABC corporation in 2021 (Table 4.6).

   'Cash from operating activities' is negative. It is a bad signal. 'Cash from investing activities' is close to 'cash from financing activities'. Comparing with 2020, 'cash and equivalents' in 2021 decreased by $5,000,000.

4.2 Financial Ratios Analysis

Financial statements can be used to analyze the effectiveness of the firm's liquidity, asset management, debt management, profitability, and market value.

Liquidity Indexes

1. Current ratio

$$\text{Current ratio} = \frac{\text{Current assets}}{\text{Current liabilities}} \quad (4.3)$$

Current assets are cash, accounts receivable and inventory. Current liabilities are accounts payable and notes payable. Thus, the current ratio measures the firm's capability to pay its short-term debt. The ABC company's current ratio is: $3.36 = 740/220$ in 2020 and $3.57 = 1,000/280$ in 2021. Higher current ratio gives more protection to loaners (e.g., upstream suppliers), but it also means that much idle fund in the firm which is bad to stockholders.

Table 4.6 ABC corporation statement of cash flows, December 31, 2021 (in $ million)

Operating activities:	
Net income before preferred stock dividends	$101.4
Adjustments Non-cash effect of changes in	
Depreciation	100.0
Cash effect of changes in	
Accounts receivable	(60.0)
Inventories	(205.0)
Accounts payable	30.0
Cash from operating activities	($33.6)
Investment activities:	
Capital expenditures	($300.0)
Cash from investing activities	($300.0)
Financing activities:	
Notes payable	$30
Long-term deb	334
Preferred stock and common stock dividends	(35.4)
Cash from financing activities	$328.6
Change in cash (on the balance sheet)	($5.0)
Cash in the beginning of 2021	15.0
Cash at the end of 2021	$10.0

2. Quick ratio

$$\text{Quick ratio} = \frac{\text{Current assets} - \text{Inventory}}{\text{Current liabilities}} \tag{4.4}$$

Inventory may not be easy to transform into cash. This implies that the quick ratio is more conservative than the current ratio. Between 2020 and 2021, the company's quick ratio decreased from 1.48 (= 325/220) to 1.36 (= 380/280) which implies that the company's inventory was increasing.

Asset Management Indexes

3. Inventory turnover ratio

$$\text{Inventory turnover ratio} = \frac{\text{Gross profit}}{\text{Inventory}} \tag{4.5}$$

Higher inventory turnover ratio means shorter cycle of production and sales and less idle cash. Between 2020 and 2021, the company's inventory turnover ratio decreased from 6.68 (= 2, 856.4/415) to 4.84 (= 3, 000.2/620) which indicates that the company's inventory and idle cash were increasing.

4. Days sales outstanding

$$\text{Days sales outstanding} = \frac{\text{Accounts receivable}}{\text{Gross profit per day}} = \frac{\text{Accounts receivable}}{\text{Gross profit}/365} \tag{4.6}$$

Divide gross profit by accounts receivable to calculate: receivables turnover ratio, which measures the company's effectiveness in collecting its accounts receivable. Higher receivables turnover ratio means less days sales outstanding. During 2020–2021, the company's inventory turnover ratio increased from 39.61 $(= 310/(2,856.4/365))$ to 45.01 $(= 370/(3,000.2)/365))$ which indicates that the company needed more time to collect its accounts receivable.

5. Fixed assets turnover ratio

$$\text{Fixed assets turnover ratio} = \frac{\text{Gross profit}}{\text{Net equipment and plant}} \tag{4.7}$$

Fixed assets turnover ratio quantifies the company's effectiveness in using its fixed assets to make profit. Higher Fixed assets turnover ratio indicates less idle properties. Between 2020 and 2021, the company's fixed assets turnover ratio decreased from 3.57 $(= 2,856.4/800)$ to 3.00 $(= 3,000.2/1,000)$ which indicates that the company was less effectiveness in using fixed assets to generate cash inflows.

6. Total asset turnover ratio

$$\text{Total asset turnover ratio} = \frac{\text{Gross profit}}{\text{Total assets}} \tag{4.8}$$

Fixed assets turnover ratio is useful for capital-intensive companies. For service industry, total asset turnover ratio makes more sense. Between 2020 and 2021, the company's total asset turnover ratio decreased from 1.85 $(= 2,856.4/1,540)$ to 1.50 $(= 3,000.2/2,000)$ which indicates that the company was less effectiveness in using total assets to make profit.

Debt Management

7. Debt ratio

$$\text{Debt ratio} = \frac{\text{Total liabilities}}{\text{Total assets}} = \frac{\text{Current liabilities} + \text{long term debt}}{\text{Total assets}} \tag{4.9}$$

High debt ratio indicates less taxes paid to the government but also higher probability of bankruptcy. During 2020–2021, the company's debt ratio increased from 48.05% $(= (220 + 520)/1,540)$ to 56.70% $(= (280 + 854)/2,000)$.

8. Times-interest-earned ratio

$$\text{Times} - \text{interest} - \text{earned ratio} = \frac{\text{EBIT}}{\text{Interest expense}} \tag{4.10}$$

Higher times-interest-earned ratio means debtholders' interest has more protection. Between 2020 and 2021, the company's times-interest-earned ratio decreased from 5.52 ($= 276/50$) to 3.17 ($= 247/78$).

9. EBITDA coverage ratio

$$\text{EBITDA coverage ratio} = \frac{\text{EBITDA} + \text{Leasing expense}}{\text{Interest} + \text{Amortization} + \text{Leasing expense}} \tag{4.11}$$

EBITDA denotes earnings before interest, taxes, depreciation and amortization. Short-term debtholders may pay attention to EBITDA coverage ratio. Long-term debtholders (e.g., corporate bondholders) care more about times-interest-earned ratio. During 2020–2021, the company's EBITDA coverage ratio decreased from 5.08 ($= (276 + 80)/(50 + 20)$) to 3.54 ($= (247 + 100)/(78 + 20)$).

Profitability Indexes

10. Profit margin on sale

$$\text{Profit margin on sale} = \frac{\text{Net income for common stockholders}}{\text{Gross profit}} \tag{4.12}$$

The company's debt policy could affect the net income in the income statement. During 2020–2021, the company's Profit margin on sale decreased from 4.64% ($= 132.6/2,856.4$) to 3.28% ($= 98.4/3,000.2$).

11. Basic earning power ratio

$$\text{Basic earning power ratio} = \frac{\text{EBIT}}{\text{Total assets}} \tag{4.13}$$

Basic earning power ratio can compare the earning power under different capital structures and tax policies. Between 2020 and 2021, the company's basic earning power ratio decreased from 17.92% ($= 276/1,540$) to 12.35% ($= 247/2,000$).

12. Return on assets (ROA)

$$\text{Return on assets} = \frac{\text{Net income for common stockholders}}{\text{Total assets}} \tag{4.14}$$

Between 2020 and 2021, the company's return on assets decreased from 8.61% ($= 132.6/1,540$) to 4.92% ($= 98.4/2,000$).

13. Return on common equity (ROE)

$$\text{Return on common equity} = \frac{\text{Net income for common stockholders}}{\text{Common stockholders}' \text{equity}} \quad (4.15)$$

Between 2020 and 2021, the company's return on common equity decreased from 17.45% (= 132.6/760) to 11.91% (= 98.4/826).

Market Value Indexes

14. Price/earnings ratio

$$\begin{aligned}\text{Price/earnings ratio} &= \frac{\text{Market price per share}}{\text{Earnings per share}} \\ &= \frac{\text{Market price per share}}{\text{Net income/Number of common stocks}}\end{aligned} \quad (4.16)$$

Price/earnings ratio represents investors' expectations about the firm's future. Between 2020 and 2021, the company's price/earnings ratio increased from 9.43 (= 25/2.652) to 9.65 (= 19/1.968).

15. Price/cash flow ratio

$$\begin{aligned}\text{Price/cash flow ratio} &= \frac{\text{Market price per share}}{\text{Cash flow per share}} \\ &= \frac{\text{Market price per share}}{(\text{Net income} + \text{depreciation})/\text{Number of shares}}\end{aligned} \quad (4.17)$$

Between 2020 and 2021, the company's price/cash flow ratio decreased from 5.88 (= 25/4.252) to 4.79 (= 19/3.968).

16. Market/book ratio

$$\begin{aligned}\text{Market/book ratio} &= \frac{\text{Market price per share}}{\text{Book value per share}} \\ &= \frac{\text{Market price per share/Common stock holders' equity}}{\text{Number of shares}}\end{aligned} \quad (4.18)$$

Market/book ratio reveals investors' expectations about the firm's future. Between 2020 and 2021, the company's market/book ratio decreased from 1.64 (= 25/15.20) to 1.15 (= 19/16.52).

Suppose the company's objective is to maximize the shareholders' wealth. Then the Du Pont equation may show where the firm should make efforts: Let Equity Multiplier = Total assets/Stockholders' equity,

$$\text{ROA} = \text{Profit margin on sale} \times \text{Total asset turnover ratio}$$

$$= \frac{\text{Net income for common stockholders}}{\text{Gross profit}} \times \frac{\text{Gross profit}}{\text{Total assets}} \quad (4.19)$$

and

$$\text{ROE} = \text{Profit margin on sale} \times \text{Total asset turnover ratio} \times \text{Equity Multiplier}$$
$$= \frac{\text{Net income for common stockholders}}{\text{Gross profit}} \times \frac{\text{Gross profit}}{\text{Total assets}} \times \frac{\text{Total assets}}{\text{Stockholders' equity}}. \quad (4.20)$$

Summary and Conclusions

Financial statements of a company can help the management team to discover potential problems of the firm and internal control. Stakeholders as well as outside investors would also be interested to know the firm's financial conditions and form their expectations about it.

- The most important two financial statements are the balance sheet and the income statement. Firms use these two financial statements to construct the statement of cash flows. The balance sheet shows the shares, i.e., the financial/legal claims, the capital providers (e.g., debtholders and equityholders) have on a particular day. The income statement shows within one year, cash inflows and outflows of all resource providers. The statement of cash flows indicates within one year how the firm's cash affected by its operating activities, investment activities and financing activities.
- Economic value added (EVA) method measures costs and benefits of all capital providers within a year.
- Financial statements can be used to construct sixteen financial ratios to analyze the effectiveness of the firm's liquidity, asset management, debt management, profitability, and market value.

Problems

1. Explain the difference between balance sheet and income statement.
2. Explain the difference between free cash flow and cash flows statement.
3. What is economic value added (EVA) method? What are the limitations of this method?
4. In the income statement, is the depreciation expense a real expenditure?
5. What are the limitations of using financial ratios?

5 Opportunity Cost and Investment Criteria

In corporate finance or investment, cost–benefit analysis is the main theme. Investors will benefit if revenue is greater than cost. Section 5.1 of this chapter emphasizes that cost is ex-ante and hence, relevant to decision making. Budgeting and accounting expenses on the other hand are ex-post and irrelevant to decision making. Section 5.2 shows how to draw information from the forecasted income statement to calculate forecasted cash inflows and outflows. The forecasted cash inflows and cash outflows of investment are used in the net present value (NPV) analysis in Sect. 5.3. This section also shows that in the multi-period case, the opportunity cost of capital, the discount rate, is the reinvestment rate. Section 5.4 examines the serious consequence of incorporating sunk expense into cost–benefit analysis.

5.1 Cost, Budgeting, and Accounting Numbers

In the previous chapter of accounting, the words: 'cost', 'expenses', 'expenditure', and 'budgeting' are often used freely and interchangeably. However, in economics and management, when we invoke decision making or cost–benefit analysis, cost must be opportunity cost, i.e., *you still have a choice to spend or not to spend*. An opportunity cost is defined as: "the evaluation placed on the most highly valued of the rejected alternatives or opportunities" (Buchanan, 2008). Buchanan (1969, p. 43) emphasizes that "cost is based on anticipations; it is necessarily a forward-looking or *ex-ante* concept".[1] Thirlby (1946) argues that "cost occurs only when

[1] Buchanan (1969, p. 28) introduces Ronald Coase's definition of opportunity cost as: "Any profit opportunity that is within the realm of possibility but which is rejected becomes a cost of undertaking the preferred course of action".

K.-P. Chang, *Corporate Finance: A Systematic Approach*, Springer Texts in Business and Economics, https://doi.org/10.1007/978-981-19-9119-6_5

decisions are made, that is, in planning stages" (p. 259). Thirlby clarifies the distinction between decision, budget, and accounting levels of calculation (Buchanan, 1969, p. 32):

(1) Cost is relevant to decision, and it must reflect the value of foregone alternatives.
(2) A budget reflects the prospective or anticipated revenue and outlay sides of a decision that *has been made*. It is erroneous to consider such prospective outlays as appear in a budget as costs. The budget must, however, also be distinguished from the account, which measures realized revenues and outlays that result from a particular course of action.

In summary, opportunity cost is ex-ante, implying that you still have the opportunity to make a choice. Thus, the timeline for opportunity cost, budgeting, and accounting numbers (e.g., realized expense and revenues) can be shown as:

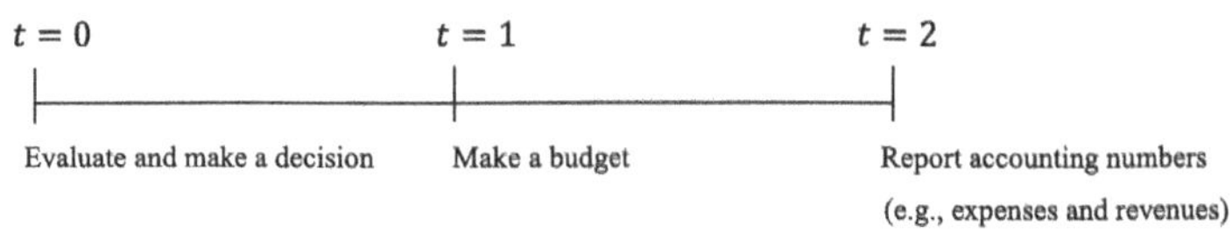

Between $t = 0$ and $t = 1$, opportunity cost occurs when the firm evaluates different alternatives and makes a choice. At $t = 1$, after a choice has been made, the firm makes a budget. At $t = 2$, the financial statements show all realized expense and revenues. Thus, cost (i.e., opportunity cost) is ex-ante, i.e., related to make a choice. Budgeting and accounting numbers are ex-post, i.e., unrelated to make a choice. These important concepts will be used to examine the issues and problems in behavioral economics and behavioral finance in Chap. 11.

Suppose that the firm has a production opportunity to invest \$1,000 at $t = 0$, and will obtain \$1,200 at $t = 1$. Assume that the opportunity cost of capital for one-period is 10%, i.e., if the firm does not have this production opportunity, the most the firm can get by investing \$1,000 is \$1,100 (= 1000 × (1 + 10%)). At $t = 1$, the excess profit of owning the property rights of the production opportunity is:

$$NFV = -1,000 \times (1 + 10\%) + 1,200 = \$100 \tag{5.1}$$

where \$100, the excess profit, is the net future value (NFV), and \$1,100 (= 1000 × (1 + 10%)) is the opportunity cost of the investment. An investment is feasible only when it can generate more than its opportunity cost, i.e., marginal revenue (\$1,200) must be greater than marginal cost (\$1,100).

Divide both sides of Eq. (5.1) by (1 + 10%), we have:

$$NPV = -1,000 + \frac{1,200}{(1 + 10\%)} = \$90.91 \tag{5.2}$$

where 10% is termed as the discount rate, and \$90.91 is the net present value (NPV) or the market (present) value of the production opportunity. On the other hand, with 10% interest rate, if the firm does not have the production opportunity and wants to receive \$1,200 at $t = 1$, it needs to deposit \$1,090.91 (= 1000 + 90.91) at a bank at $t = 0$. This indicates that the market value of the investment is \$1,090.91. Also, by dividing the present value of the final payoff by the present value of initial cost we can calculate the profitability index of the investment: $\frac{1{,}200/(1+10\%)}{1{,}000} = 1.091 > 1$. The profitability index method is equivalent to the NPV method, and the index is just a relative price ratio.

In the above one-period problem, divide the final payoff \$1,200 by the initial cash outflow \$1,000 and minus one, we can obtain the internal rate of return (IRR): $IRR = \left[\frac{1{,}200}{1{,}000} - 1\right] \times 100 = 20\%$. Since 20% (the IRR) is greater than 10% (the discount rate), the investment is feasible, profitable. This result shows that in the one-period case, both the NPV method and the IRR method give the same conclusion: the NPV is positive if and only if the IRR is greater than the discount rate.

In Eq. (5.2), if we adjust the discount rate until the NPV becomes zero, we can also derive the IRR:

$$0 = -1,000 + \frac{1,200}{(1 + IRR)} \text{ implies } IRR = 20\%. \tag{5.3}$$

However, in the next chapter, we will find that in the multi-period case, calculating the IRR by adjusting the discount rate until the NPV becomes zero may have serious problems.

5.2 From Financial Statements to Cash Flows

As explained in the Robin Hood's story in Chap. 2, each resource provider (gangster) provides resource to the gang to produce (to rob). After each 'production', each resource provider gets a share of the production according to the ex-ante contract. In a company, capital providers (e.g., debtholders and equityholders), labors and material providers provide resources to the company to produce and sell. In the one-period case, after paying to labors and material providers, the rest that belongs to capital providers is the cash flow (and the present value of this cash flow is the market value of the firm). In the multi-period case, in each period, after paying to labors and material providers, the company will keep some resource to continue production and the rest distributed to capital providers is the free cash flow (FCF). The present value of all future free cash flows is the market value of the firm. The following example explains how to use the forecasted income statements to calculate each year's free cash flow.

Suppose that a company plans to produces a new product for five years. The cost of the equipment is \$5,000,000 provided by equityholders: \$4,000,000 and debtholders: \$1,000,000 (at 10% annual interest rate). The tax agency stipulates the

Table 5.1 Forecasted income statements, year ended December 31 (in $ million)

	First year	Second year	Third year	Fourth year	Fifth year
(1) Total sales	5.00	5.60	6.60	5.00	2.00
(2) Cost of sales	1.60	1.50	2.20	2.00	0.70
(3) Sales, general and administration expenses	0.10	0.18	0.25	0.28	0.10
(4) Depreciation	0.96	0.96	0.96	0.96	0.96
(5) Interest expense	0.10	0.10	0.10	0.10	0.10
(6) Pretax income [(1)−(2)−(3)−(4)−(5)]	2.24	2.86	3.09	1.66	0.14
(7) Taxes [(6) × 30%]	0.672	0.858	0.927	0.498	0.042
(8) Net income	1.568	2.002	2.163	1.162	0.098

straight line depreciation method with scrap value of the equipment: $200,000, i.e., the annually depreciation expense of the equipment is $960,000 ($= (5,000,000 - 200,000)/5)$). The company predicts the scrap value of the equipment: $300,000 and working capital: $100,000 (to meet temporary shortfalls in cash flow). The corporate income tax rate is 30%. The five year forecasted income statements are shown in Table 5.1.

In Table 5.1, every expense goes to a particular resource provider except the depreciation expense. The depreciation expense listed in Table 5.1 is not a real cash outflow. The *real* depreciation expenses (e.g., lubricating oil, replacement of parts and maintenance labor's wages) are included in 'cost of sales' and 'sales, general and administration expenses'.

Suppose that for this investment project, the company wants to do a cost–benefit analysis for capital providers (i.e., both equityholders and debtholders). The forecasted cash flows of the project are calculated and listed in Table 5.2. Negative number means cash outflow, and positive number cash inflow. The cash outflow at the beginning of the first year is: $5,100,000 $= (5,000,000 + 100,000)$. The cash inflow at the end of fifth year is: $1,528,000 $= 270,000$ (after-tax scrap value) $+98,000$ (net income) $+100,000$ (interest expense) $+960,000$ (depreciation expense) $+100,000$ (working capital).

5.3 Fundamental Cost and Benefit Analysis: Net Present Value Method

As mentioned previously, the NPV method is to measure the difference (the excess profits) between the present value of the future payoffs and the present value of initial cost. The basic idea is very simple: As long as the revenue is greater than the cost, it is worthwhile to go ahead. Using the forecasted cash flows in Table 5.3 we can do the following multi-period NPV analysis.

Table 5.2 Forecasted cash flows for capital providers (in $ million)

	Beginning of first year	End of first year	End of second year	End of third year	End of fourth year	End of fifth year
(1) Scrap value						0.30
(2) After-tax scrap value						0.27(= 0.3(1 – 0.3))
(3) Net income		1.568	2.002	2.163	1.162	0.098
(4) Interest expense		0.10	0.10	0.10	0.10	0.10
(5) Depreciation expense		0.96	0.96	0.96	0.96	0.96
(6) Working capital	−0.10					0.10
(7) Cost of equipment	−5.00					
(8) Cash flow [(2) + (3) + (4) + (5) + (6) + (7)]	– 5.10	2.628	3.062	3.223	2.222	1.528

Table 5.3 Cash flows for capital providers (in $ million)

	Beginning of first year	End of first year	End of second year	End of third year	End of fourth year	End of fifth year
Cash flow	−5.10	2.628	3.062	3.223	2.222	1.528

Example 5.1 Suppose that the weighted average cost of capital (or the discounted rate) of the five-year investment project is 10%. The forecasted cash flows are in Table 5.3.

With 10% discount rate (i.e., 10% reinvestment rate), the final values of these five cash flows are:

$t = 0$	$t = 1$	$t = 2$	$t = 3$	$t = 4$	$t = 5$	
-5.10	$-5.10(1+0.1)$	$-5.10(1+0.1)^2$	$-5.10(1+0.1)^3$	$-5.10(1+0.1)^4$	$-5.10(1+0.1)^5$	Opportunity cost of investing after 5 years
	2.682	$2.682(1+0.1)$	$2.682(1+0.1)^2$	$2.682(1+0.1)^3$	$2.682(1+0.1)^4$	Reinvest the 1st year cash flow for 4 years
		3.062	$3.062(1+0.1)$	$3.062(1+0.1)^2$	$3.062(1+0.1)^3$	Reinvest the 2nd year cash flow for 3 years
			3.223	$3.223(1+10\%)$	$3.223(1+0.1)^2$	Reinvest the 3rd year cash flow for 2 year
				2.222	$2.222(1+0.1)$	Reinvest the 4th year cash flow for 1 year
					1.528	The 5th year cash flow

At the end of the fifth year, the future value of the opportunity cost of investing is: $5.10(1+0.1)^5$, and the future value of the revenue is: $2.682(1+0.1)^4 + 3.062(1+0.1)^3 + 3.223(1+0.1)^2 + 2.222(1+0.1) + 1.528$. Hence, the net future value (NFV) of the investment is:

$$\begin{aligned} NFV &= -5.10(1+10\%)^5 + 2.682(1+10\%)^4 + 3.062(1+10\%)^3 \\ &+ 3.223(1+10\%)^2 + 2.222(1+10\%) + 1.528 \\ &= 7.5816 = (4.7076)(1+10\%)^5, \end{aligned} \tag{5.4}$$

where \$4,707,600 is the net present value (NPV), i.e., the excess profits, of the investment. Divide both sides of Eq. (5.4) by $(1+10\%)^5$, we can get:

$$\begin{aligned} NPV &= -5.10 + \frac{2.628}{(1+10\%)} + \frac{3.062}{(1+10\%)^2} + \frac{3.223}{(1+10\%)^3} \\ &+ \frac{2.222}{(1+10\%)^4} + \frac{1.528}{(1+10\%)^5} \\ &= 4.7076. \end{aligned} \tag{5.5}$$

Since the present value of the final payoff is greater the present value of initial cost, the investment is feasible, worthwhile. Equation (5.5) also shows that in the multi-period case, under the NPV method, the reinvestment rate (or the opportunity cost of capital (WACC) or the discount rate) is assumed to be a constant. This is a very strong assumption. In Chap. 7, we will discuss how to calculate the discount rate.

Equation (5.5) can also be stated as:

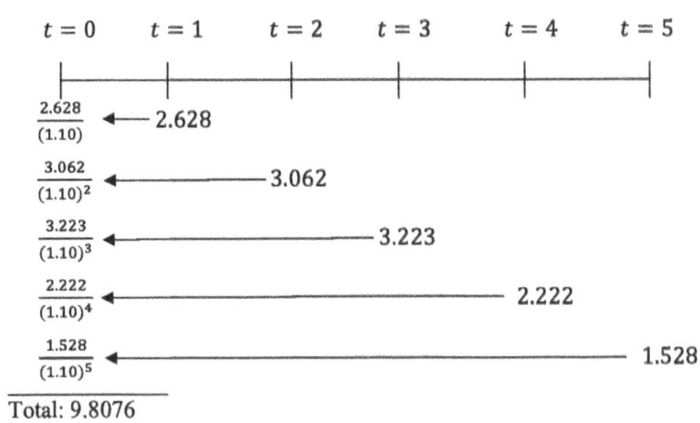

That is, at $t = 0$, the market value of the investment is: \$9,807,600 ($= 5,100,000 + 4,707,600$), where \$4,707,600 is the market value of the production opportunity (the patent). It indicates that if the firm does not have the property rights of the production opportunity (the patent), to have the cash inflows in Table 5.3, the firm needs to invest \$9,807,600 in other place (with 10% interest rate) in the beginning of the first year.

Three things needed to take into consideration when using the NPV method, e.g., Eq. (5.4) or Eq. (5.5). First, plant and equipment will incur three different expenses: (a) lubricating oil, replacement of parts and maintenance labor's wages; (b) as time goes by, the market value of equipment/machine decreases; (c) money can be earned by investing $5,100,000 in another place, i.e., opportunity cost. Lubricating oil, replacement of parts and maintenance labor's wages are included in 'cost of sales' and 'sales, general and administration expenses' when calculating the net income in the income statement. In Eq. (5.4)'s '$5.10(1+10\%)^5$', the reinvestment rate (i.e., the opportunity cost of capital) '10%' considers: the money can be earned by investing $5,100,000 in other place, and '1' considers: the decreasing in the market value of equipment/machine.

Second, who can own the NPV (i.e., the excess profits) of the investment? Eq. (5.4) or Eq. (5.5) assumes the capital providers (debtholders and equityholders) own the property rights of the excess profits. If the equityholders own the property rights of the excess profits, then their NPV is:

$$\begin{aligned} NPV_{equityholders} &= -4.10 + \frac{2.528}{(1+10\%)} + \frac{2.962}{(1+10\%)^2} + \frac{3.123}{(1+10\%)^3} \\ &\quad + \frac{2.122}{(1+10\%)^4} + \frac{0.428}{(1+10\%)^5} \\ &= 4.7076 \end{aligned} \tag{5.6}$$

where the debtholders can only earn the opportunity cost of debt (10%), i.e., no excess profit:

$$\begin{aligned} NPV_{debtholders} &= -1.00 + \frac{0.10}{(1+10\%)} + \frac{0.10}{(1+10\%)^2} + \frac{0.10}{(1+10\%)^3} \\ &\quad + \frac{0.10}{(1+10\%)^4} + \frac{1.10}{(1+10\%)^5} \\ &= 0. \end{aligned} \tag{5.7}$$

This shows that except the equityholders who can own both $4,100,000 and the NPV ($4,707,600), all other resource providers can only earn the opportunity costs of the resources they provide, i.e., no excess profit.

Since (according to the corporate law) the equityholders own the property rights of production opportunity and hence, can have excess profits (positive NPV), when financing a new investment, the firm usually first uses its internal fund (e.g., retained earnings and/or new funds from the existing equityholders), and then debt financing. If the firm wants to finance a new investment by issuing new stocks to outside investors, its current stock price may decrease because people will think this must be a negative NPV investment, and the firm wants to use new stockholders' wealth to subsidize the existing stockholders. This is the pecking order theory in corporate finance.

When use the NPV method, we can also change discount rate to see how the NPV of an investment project changes (i.e., the sensitivity analysis). If we change

Table 5.4 Cash flows for capital providers (in $ million)

	Beginning of the 1st year	End of 1st year	End of 2nd year	......	End of 10th year
Department Store	100	18	18	......	18
Theater	76	14	14	......	14

both discount rate and cash flows, this is the scenario analysis. In Eq. (5.4) or Eq. (5.5) increase the discount rate from 10 to 15%, the NPV will decrease. Higher discount rate means future cash inflows are less valuable.

Example 5.2 (Mutually Exclusive Projects) Suppose that the firm has a piece of land and plans to build a department store or a theater lasting for ten years. The weighted average cost of capital (or the discounted rate or the reinvestment rate) of both investments is 10%. The forecasted cash flows are: (Table 5.4).

$$NPV_{\text{department store}} = -100 + \frac{18}{(1+10\%)} + \frac{18}{(1+10\%)^2} + \cdots\cdots + \frac{18}{(1+10\%)^{10}} = 10.602$$

$$NPV_{\text{theater}} = -76 + \frac{14}{(1+10\%)} + \frac{14}{(1+10\%)^2} + \cdots\cdots + \frac{14}{(1+10\%)^{10}} = 16.024$$

Investing in the theater can obtain higher NPV, i.e., $16,024,000. This shows that the opportunity cost of investing in the department store is: $16,024,000, and the opportunity cost of investing in the theater is: $10,602,000.

5.4 Opportunity Cost Versus Sunk Expense

Investment analysis is about decision-making or making a choice which relates to the concept of opportunity cost. Since cost must be opportunity cost, i.e., you still have a choice/opportunity to spend or not to spend, the so-called sunk cost (it should be stated as: sunk expense) is irrelevant in decision-making.

Example 5.3 Suppose that a finance major undergraduate student will soon graduate and is thinking about applying for MS program in finance or in computer science. After finishing a two-year MS program, the student plans to work 20 years. The weighted average cost of capital (i.e., the discounted rate) of the 20-year work is 10%. The forecasted free cash flows of the two choices are (free cash flows here means savings): (Table 5.5).

Table 5.5 Free cash flows for the investor (in $ thousand)

	Beginning of the 1st year	End of 2nd year	End of 3rd year	End of 4th year	End of 5th year	......	End of 22th year
MS in finance	−50	0	10	10	10	......	10
MS in computer science	−50	0	11	11	11	......	11

The net present values of the two choices are:

$$NPV_{finance} = -50 + \frac{10}{(1+0.1)^3} + \frac{10}{(1+0.1)^4} + \frac{10}{(1+0.1)^5} + \cdots\cdots + \frac{10}{(1+0.1)^{22}} = 20.36,$$

$$NPV_{computer\ science} = -50 + \frac{11}{(1+0.1)^3} + \frac{11}{(1+0.1)^4} + \frac{11}{(1+0.1)^5} + \cdots\cdots + \frac{11}{(1+0.1)^{22}} = 27.40.$$

Since $NPV_{computer\ science} > NPV_{finance}$, the student should choose the MS program in computer science.

Now, suppose that the student feels if she pursues a MS degree in computer science, then her past four-year study of finance would be a waste. She decides that she should pursue the two-year MS degree in finance first, and then see whether a MS degree in computer science is better. Then after two years, the NPVs of the two choices are:

$$NPV_{finance} = \frac{10}{(1+0.1)} + \frac{10}{(1+0.1)^2} + \frac{10}{(1+0.1)^3} + \cdots\cdots + \frac{10}{(1+0.1)^{20}} = 85.14$$

$$NPV_{computer\ science} = -50 + \frac{11}{(1+0.1)^3} + \frac{11}{(1+0.1)^4} + \cdots\cdots + \frac{11}{(1+0.1)^{22}} = 24.56.$$

After two years, the initial cost of studying MS in finance ($50,000) is already sunk (i.e., a sunk expense) and hence, should not be considered in calculating the $NPV_{finance}$. Since $85,140 is greater than $24,560, this undergraduate student will think that choosing the MS program in finance is a correct choice. These results show that (a) incorporating sunk expense (e.g., past four-year study of finance) into decision-making is seriously wrong; and (b) making decision (choice) at a later time point can lead to error.[2]

[2] See also Appendix A of Chap. 11.

Summary and Conclusions

The main topic in corporate finance or investment is cost and benefit analysis. As long as the revenue is greater than the cost, the investment is feasible and worthwhile. For mutually exclusive projects, we should always choose the one which has the highest net present value. Cost is ex-ante and must be opportunity cost, i.e., you still have an opportunity (choice) to spend or not to spend. Budgeting and accounting expenses are ex-post and hence, are irrelevant in decision-making. Sunk expense should never be considered in cost–benefit analysis.

- In the single period case, the net present value (NPV) method, the internal rate of return (IRR) method and the profitability method give the same result.
- In the multi-period case, the opportunity cost of capital (or the discount rate) used in the NPV method is the reinvestment rate. This is a very strong assumption.
- In the firm, according to the corporate law, positive NPV (excess profits) belongs to the equityholders (stockholders). Other resource providers, such as labor, material providers and debtholders can only earn the opportunity costs of the resources they provide and have zero NPV.

Problems

1. Give an investment example to explain cost, budgeting, and accounting numbers.
2. What is cash flow? Why is the firm's depreciation expense needed to be included in cash inflows?
3. Is the net present value (NPV) analysis for equityholders equivalent to the NPV analysis for capital providers?
4. Suppose that you need to choose one project from a group of mutually exclusive investment projects which have different investment horizons. What kind of assumptions do you need to do the cost and benefit analysis?
5. With 10% annual discount rate, calculate the NPV of the following dam construction project. Explain which number(s) is opportunity cost.

	$t = 0$	$t = 1$	$t = 2$	$t = 3$	$t = 4$
Cash flow	−510	−50	700	800	400

References

Buchanan, J. (1969). *Cost and choice: An inquiry in economic theory*. The University of Chicago Press.

Buchanan, J. (2008). Opportunity cost. In N. Steven (Ed.), *The new Palgrave dictionary of economics*, 2nd ed., Durlauf and Lawrence E. Blume, Palgrave Macmillan. http://www.dictionaryofeconomics.com.

Thirlby, G. F. (1946). The ruler. *South African Journal of Economics, 14*, 253–276.

Internal Rate of Return, Profitability Index and Payback Period Methods

6

This chapter discusses several other investment criteria, and how they are related to the net present value (NPV) method. Section 6.1 analyzes the similarity of the NPV and internal rate of return (IRR) methods in the one-period case. In the multi-period case, a restatement of the NPV method, i.e., the modified internal rate of return (MIRR) method, is introduced which uses the opportunity cost of capital as the reinvestment rate. Section 6.2 shows that the profitability index (PI) is the ratio of the market value of the investment project to the initial cost of the project. Section 6.3 discusses the payback period method which considers length of time an investment takes to recover its cost. Section 6.4 reviews the investment criteria employed by practicians.

6.1 Internal Rate of Return and Modified Internal Rate of Return

When we use the net present value (NPV) method, we can change the discount rate (or the reinvestment rate) to see how the NPV changes, i.e., a sensitivity analysis. The internal rate of return (IRR) is defined as the discount rate that makes the NPV of the project equal to zero.

Example 6.1 In the one-period case, suppose that the firm invests \$1,000 at $t = 0$, and obtains \$1,200 at $t = 1$. Assume that the opportunity cost of capital for the investment is 10%. The IRR of the project is:

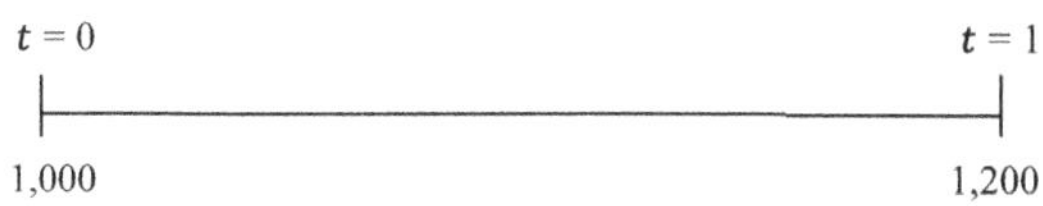

K.-P. Chang, *Corporate Finance: A Systematic Approach*, Springer Texts in Business and Economics, https://doi.org/10.1007/978-981-19-9119-6_6

Table 6.1 Cash flows for capital providers (in $ million)

	$t = 0$	$t = 1$	$t = 2$	$t = 3$
Cash flow	−100.0	57.0	25.992	44.44632

$$0 = -1,000 + \frac{1,200}{(1 + IRR)} \text{ implies } IRR = 20\%. \tag{6.1}$$

Rewrite Eq. (6.1) as:

$$1,000(1 + 20\%) = 1,200 \tag{6.2}$$

or

$$\frac{\text{Final value}}{\text{Initial cost}} = \frac{1,200}{1,000} = 1 + 20\% = 1 + IRR. \tag{6.3}$$

The rate of turn of the investment: 20% is greater than the opportunity cost of capital: 10%, i.e., the investment is profitable. The NPV of the investment is positive: $NPV = -1,000 + \frac{1,200}{(1+10\%)} = 90.91 > 0$. These results indicate that in the one-period model, the IRR method is consistent with the NPV method.

In the multi-period case, e.g., the IRR method can be shown as:

$$0 = -CF_0 + \frac{CF_1}{(1 + IRR)} + \frac{CF_2}{(1 + IRR)^2} + \cdots\cdots + \frac{CF_T}{(1 + IRR)^T} \tag{6.4}$$

where CF_t is the cash flow at $t = 0, 1, 2, \ldots, T$.

Example 6.2 Suppose that the firm invests $100,000,000 in a three-year project with annual opportunity cost of capital 10%. The forecasted cash flows are: (Table 6.1)

Based on Eq. (6.4), the IRR analysis for the investment project is:

$$0 = -100 + \frac{57.0}{(1 + IRR)} + \frac{25.992}{(1 + IRR)^2} + \frac{44.44632}{(1 + IRR)^3}. \tag{6.5}$$

By try and error, we can get: $IRR = 14\%$. Also, rewrite Eq. (6.5) as:

$$\begin{aligned} 100.0(1.481514) &= 100.0(1 + 14\%)^3 \\ &= 57.0(1 + 14\%)^2 + 25.992(1 + 14\%) + 44.44632 \\ &= 148.1544. \end{aligned} \tag{6.6}$$

Equation (6.6) shows a one-period result as Eq. (6.2), where \$100,000,000 is the cash outlay at $t = 0$, and \$148,154,400 is the future/final value (FV) of the investment at $t = 3$, i.e.,

$$FV = 57.0(1 + 14\%)^2 + 25.992(1 + 14\%) + 44.44632 = 148.1544. \quad (6.7)$$

The time line of cash flows for Eq. (6.7) is:

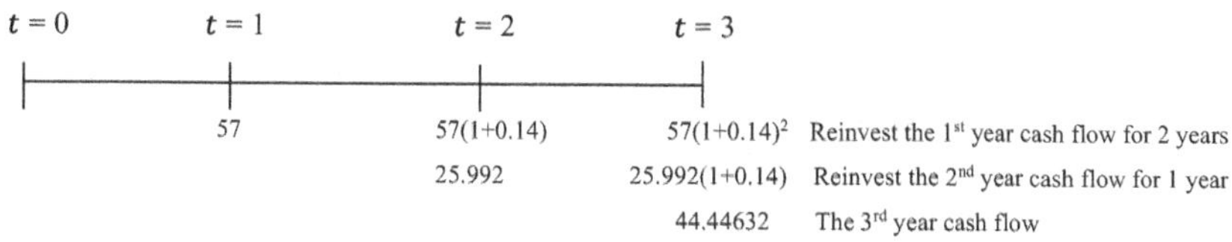

This shows that the IRR method implicitly assumes that the reinvestment rate of the project's cash flows is the discount rate which makes the NPV of the project equal to zero, i.e., 14%. This is, of course, not correct.

We can also calculate the NPV of this investment:

$$NPV = -100 + \frac{57.0}{(1 + 10\%)} + \frac{25.992}{(1 + 10\%)^2} + \frac{44.44632}{(1 + 10\%)^3} = 6.69235. \quad (6.8)$$

Rewrite Eq. (6.8) as:

$$\begin{aligned} 100.0(1.4200752) &= 100.0(1 + 12.401\%)^3 \\ &= 57.0(1 + 10\%)^2 + 25.992(1 + 10\%) + 44.44632 \\ &= 142.00752. \end{aligned} \quad (6.9)$$

It shows that Eq. (6.9) is a one-period result as Eq. (6.2), where \$100,000,000 is the cash outflow at $t = 0$, and \$142,007,520 is the future/final value (FV) of the investment at $t = 3$:

$$FV = 57.0(1 + 10\%)^2 + 25.992(1 + 10\%) + 44.44632 = 142.00752. \quad (6.10)$$

The time line of cash flows for Eq. (6.10) is:

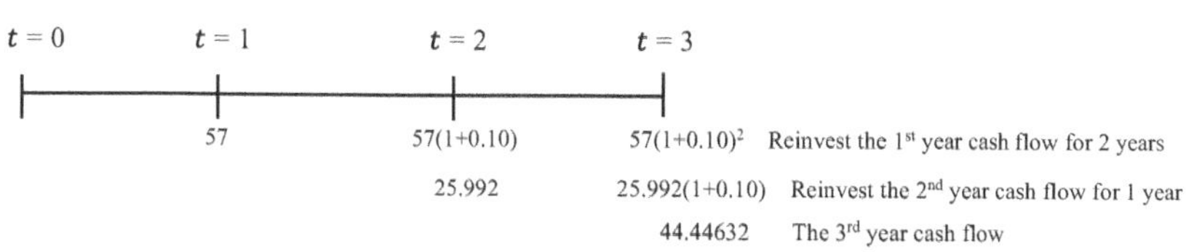

Compare Eq. (6.6) with Eq. (6.9), we know that the correct reinvestment rate (i.e., the opportunity cost of capital) of the project is 10% rather than 14%. From

Table 6.2 Cash flows for capital providers (in $ million)

	$t = 0$	$t = 1$	$t = 2$	$t = 3$	$t = 4$	$t = 5$
Cash flow	−100.0	−50.0	70.0	80.0	−10.0	90.0

Eq. (6.9), we can calculate the "modified" internal rate of return (MIRR) of the investment project: 12.401%, which is greater than the opportunity cost of capital: 10%. Also, the NPV of the investment is: $\$6,692,350 > 0$. The above results show that in the multi-period case, the MIRR method is just a restatement of the NPV method.

The MIRR method of Eq. (6.9) can be generalized as:

$$0 = -CF_0 + \frac{CF_1(1+r)^{T-1}}{(1+MIRR)^T} + \frac{CF_2(1+r)^{T-2}}{(1+MIRR)^T} + \cdots + \frac{CF_{T-1}(1+r_T)}{(1+MIRR)^T} + \frac{CF_T}{(1+MIRR)^T} \tag{6.11}$$

or

$$\frac{\text{Final value}}{\text{Initial cost}} = \frac{CF_1(1+r)^{T-1} + CF_2(1+r)^{T-2} + \cdots + CF_{T-1}(1+r_T) + CF_T}{CF_0} = (1+MIRR)^T \tag{6.12}$$

where CF_t is the cash flow at $t = 0, 1, 2, \ldots, T$; r is the opportunity cost of capital (i.e., the reinvestment rate); and MIRR is the modified internal rate of return. Comparing Eq. (6.11) with Eq. (6.4), we can find that the IRR method implicitly assumes: $r = MIRR = IRR$.

Example 6.3 Suppose that the firm invests $100,000,000 in a five-year project with annual opportunity cost of capital 10%. The forecasted cash flows are in Table 6.2.

The NPV of this investment is:

$$NPV = -100.0 + \frac{-50.0}{(1+10\%)} + \frac{70.0}{(1+10\%)^2} + \frac{80.0}{(1+10\%)^3} + \frac{-10.0}{(1+10\%)^4} + \frac{90.0}{(1+10\%)^5} = 21.55466 > 0.$$

From Eq. (6.11), the MIRR can be calculated as:

$$0 = -100.0 + \frac{-50.0(1+10\%)^4}{(1+MIRR)^5} + \frac{70.0(1+10\%)^3}{(1+MIRR)^5} + \frac{80.0(1+10\%)^2}{(1+MIRR)^5} + \frac{-10.0(1+10\%)}{(1+MIRR)^5} + \frac{90.0}{(1+MIRR)^5}$$

$$MIRR = 14.379\% > 10\%$$

Table 6.3 Cash flows for capital providers (in $ million)

	$t = 0$	$t = 1$	$t = 2$
Cash flow of project 1	−400.0	2,500.0	−2,500.0
Cash flow of project 2	−100.0	300.0	−250.0

Thus, the investment project is profitable, and the NPV is positive if and only if the MIRR is greater than the opportunity cost of capital.

Example 6.4 Suppose that a mining company has two two-year investment projects with annual opportunity cost of capital 10%. The forecasted cash flows are in Table 6.3.

The IRR for Project 1 is:

$$0 = -400.0 + \frac{2,500.0}{(1 + IRR)} + \frac{-2,500.0}{(1 + IRR)^2}, IRR = 400\% \text{ or } 25\%.$$

But multiple solutions of the IRR: 400% or 25%, are meaningless. The MIRR of Project 1 is:

$$0 = -400.0 + \frac{2,500.0(1 + 10\%)}{(1 + MIRR)^2} + \frac{-2,500.0}{(1 + MIRR)^2}, \quad MIRR = -29.94\% < 10\%.$$

Thus, Project 1 is not feasible.
The IRR for Project 2 is:

$$0 = -100.0 + \frac{300.0}{(1 + IRR)} + \frac{-250.0}{(1 + IRR)^2}, \text{ no real number solution for the IRR.}$$

The MIRR for Project 2 is:

$$0 = -100.0 + \frac{300.0(1 + 10\%)}{(1 + MIRR)^2} + \frac{-250.0}{(1 + MIRR)^2}, \quad MIRR = -10.56\% < 10\%,$$

and Project 2 is not feasible.

Example 6.5 Suppose that an investor plans to buy a 10-year 8% coupon bond with a $1,000 par value for $875.38. The interest is paid semiannually, i.e., $40 ($= 1,000(0.08)/2$). The investor expects to hold the bond for three years with the annual reinvestment rate 6%. After three years, the bond sold to the market is expected to offer a 7% yield to maturity (YTM or IRR).

At $t = 0$, the YTM (or the IRR) of the bond is:

$$0 = -875.38 + \frac{40}{(1+y)} + \frac{40}{(1+y)^2} + \cdots + \frac{40}{(1+y)^{20}} + \frac{1,000}{(1+y)^{20}} \text{ implies}$$
$$y = 5\%, \text{ i.e., } YTM = 10\%.$$

At $t = 3$, according to Eq. (3.7) of Chap. 3, the total value of reinvesting all interests in the past three years is:

$$(1+0.03)^6\left[\frac{40}{0.03} - \frac{40}{0.03}\frac{1}{(1+0.03)^6}\right] = 40\left[\frac{(1+0.03)^6 - 1}{0.03}\right] = 258.74,$$

and the market price of the bond is:

$$\left[\frac{40}{0.035} - \frac{40}{0.035}\frac{1}{(1+0.035)^{14}}\right] + \frac{1,000}{(1+0.035)^{14}} = 1,054.60.$$

Thus, based on Eq. (6.12), the MIRR (the total return) of investing in the bond for three years is:

$$\frac{\text{Final value}}{\text{Initial cost}} = \frac{258.74 + 1,054.60}{875.38} = (1+6.99\%)^6,\ MIRR = 6.99\% \times 2 = 13.98\%.$$

6.2 Profitability Index

The NPV method measures the difference between revenue and cost. The profitability index (PI) method calculates the ratio of revenue to cost. Thus, the NPV is positive if and only if the PI is greater than 1. For example, in Example 6.3, the NPV of the investment is:

$$\begin{aligned} NPV &= -100.0 + \frac{-50.0}{(1+10\%)} + \frac{70.0}{(1+10\%)^2} + \frac{80.0}{(1+10\%)^3} + \frac{-10.0}{(1+10\%)^4} + \frac{90.0}{(1+10\%)^5} \\ &= 21.55466 > 0. \end{aligned}$$

Then the PI of the investment is:

$$PI = \frac{21.55466 + 100.0}{100.0} = 1.2155466 > 1.$$

It indicates that every one dollar invested can generate \$1.2155 present value of revenue or \$0.2155 excess profits. Note that the above equation can be rewritten as:

$$\begin{aligned} PI &= 1.2155466 \\ &= \frac{-50.0(1+10\%)^4 + 70.0(1+10\%)^3 + 80.0(1+10\%)^2 - 10.0(1+10\%) + 90}{100.0(1+10\%)^5} \end{aligned}$$

$$= \frac{100.0(1 + 14.379\%)^5}{100.0(1 + 10\%)^5},$$

where 14.379% is the modified internal rate of return (MIRR), which is greater than the opportunity cost of capital 10%. Thus, in relation to Eq. (6.12), the formula of the PI of an investment project can be written as:

$$PI = \frac{CF_1(1+r)^{T-1} + CF_2(1+r)^{T-2} + \cdots + CF_{T-1}(1+r_T) + CF_T}{CF_0(1+r)^T}$$

$$= \frac{CF_0(1+MIRR)^T}{CF_0(1+r)^T}, \tag{6.13}$$

and $$NPV > 0 \text{ if and only if } PI > 1 \text{ if and only if } MIRR > r. \tag{6.14}$$

It should be noted that not every cash outflow is (opportunity) cost. For example, in Example 6.3, among the three cash outflows: −100.0, −50.0, and −10.0, probably only the first one: −100.0 is the opportunity cost, the other two: −50.0 and −10.0 are budgets (i.e., once the firm determines to invest and commits $100,000,000 at $t = 0$, the firm cannot avoid the cash outflows: $50,000,000 at $t = 1$ and $10,000,000 at $t = 4$). Thus, the following calculation of the PI is not correct:

$$PI = \frac{\text{PV of cash inflows}}{\text{PV of cash outflows}} = \frac{\frac{70.0}{(1+10\%)^2} + \frac{80.0}{(1+10\%)^3} + \frac{90.0}{(1+10\%)^5}}{100.0 + \frac{50.0}{(1+10\%)} + \frac{10.0}{(1+10\%)^4}} = 1.1415.$$

In the case of mutually exclusive projects, ratio methods such as the IRR, MIRR and PI may not be as good as the NPV because, after all, investment is for future consumption and what people can consume is the amount of money, not the ratio. The following example shows that the PI method can prioritize different projects to fast increase investors' wealth.

Example 6.5 Suppose that the firm has the following five possible investment projects.

The PI's of Projects B, C and E are greater than 1 (i.e., they are all profitable), and Project E has the highest PI and thus, should be the first to be undertaken. Suppose the firm cannot spend more 10 million dollars in investment. Then, Project B is better than the combination of Projects C and E because Project B uses less money to generate more NPV (Table 6.4).

6.3 Payback Period

The payback period method focuses on the length of time an investment takes to recover its cost. Hence, it is a safety-first investment rule. The rule of the payback

Table 6.4 NPV (in $ million) and PI ratio

Project	Cost (1)	NPV (2)	PI = [(1) + (2)]/(1)
A	6	−1	0.83
B	7	5	1.71
C	6	1.5	1.25
D	5	−1	0.80
E	4	3	1.75

Table 6.5 NPV (in $ million) and Payback Period

Project	CF_0	CF_1	CF_2	CF_3	Payback years	NPV
A	−500.0	0	500.0	0	2	−867.77
B	−500.0	250.0	250.0	0	2	−661.16
C	−500.0	250.0	250.0	250.0	2	1217.13
D	−500.0	200.0	200.0	200.0	2.5	−26.29

period method is: Accept the project if the payback period is less than or equal to some arbitrary cutoff.

Example 6.5 Suppose that the firm has the following four 3-year non-mutually exclusive projects with annual opportunity cost of capital 10% in Table 6.5.

If the cutoff date is two years, the firm will only consider Projects A, B and C, and only Project C with a positive NPV will be chosen.

The payback period method seems not to consider all cash flows and the discount rate for future cash flows. However, if the firm feels the future cash flows after the cutoff date, e.g., 2 years, are very uncertain, it may just ignore them (i.e., the discount rate employed for those cash inflows is extremely big). It will not be surprising to see the payback period method exists in an environment with high political risk and/or high inflation risk and/or very fast technology change.

6.4 Empirical Evidence of the Use of Investment Criteria

The purpose of investment is for future consumption. Since what people can consume is real money, not ratio, the NPV method should be more popular than the IRR, MIRR or Profitability Index method. However, the magnitude of a NPV depends on the discount rate (reinvestment rate) employed. The IRR method on the other hand just gives a simple number: IRR which is easier to use. For example, suppose that there are two projects with the same investment period, say, 10 years. The first project needs 10 million dollars initial cost and has 5 million dollars NPV. The second project needs one billion dollars initial cost and has 6 million dollars NPV. Although the second project generates higher NPV, investors may still prefer the first one because it has higher rate of return: $5/10 > 6/1,000$, and such a large amount of money (i.e., one billion dollars) invested in 10 years is too risky. Understand the difference between real money and rate of return (or relative price ratio) is very important in decision-making. Later in Chap. 11, we will see how this misunderstanding can result in serious errors in behavioral economics and behavioral finance.

In the literature of investment criteria, the empirical results are somewhat consistent: the payback period method is popular.[1] Klammer (1972) find that more and more US large corporation (especially, petrochemical and automobile companies) adopt both the NPV and IRR methods, but not the payback period method. Schall et al. (1978) find: the payback period method is the most popular method: 74%; the IRR is the next: 65%; the accounting rate of return (ARR) is the third: 58%; and the last is the NPV: 56%.[2] Only 16% of the firms never use the payback period method. Moore and Reichert (1983) find: the payback period method is the first: 79.9%, the NPV is the second: 68.1%, the IRR is the third: 66.4%, and the ARR is the fourth: 59.1%. Graham and Harvey (2001) find: the payback period method (including simple (56.7%) and discounted (29.5%) payback period) is the highest: 86.2%, the IRR is the second: 75.6%; and the NPV is the third: 74.9%, and the ARR is the lowest: 20.3%. Graham et al. also find that (a) the firms having higher debt ratio or paying dividends more often employ the NPV and IRR methods; (b) small size firms more often use the payback period method; (c) younger CFOs with a MBA degree would be more likely to adopt the NPV and IRR methods.

Shinoda (2010) finds that among Japanese corporations, the payback period method (including simple (50.2%) and discounted (20.4%) payback period) is the highest: 70.6%, the NPV is the second: 30.5%; the ARR is the third: 30.3%; and the IRR is the fourth: 24.5%. Shinoda also finds that first, when making simple investment plans such as investment in equipment, the firms prefer the payback period method. Second, when considering the propriety of R&D investments and investment in information system, the firms consider payback periods as the most important criterion. Third, in the case of extremely strategic and long-range investments, such as M&A or investment in foreign business, the firms use the NPV method. Fourth, the ARR method is important when investing in new products and services.

Summary and Conclusions

- In the one-period non-mutually exclusive projects case, the NPV method and the IRR method are equivalent. The IRR is the discount rate that makes the NPV of the project equal to zero, which is also the return of investment project.

---

[1] Klammer, Thomas (1972). Moore, James and Alan Reichert (1983). Schall, Lawrence, Gary Sunden and William Geijsbeek, Jr. (1978). Graham, John and Harvey Campbell (2001). Shinoda, Tomonari (2010).

[2] $ARR =$ Average Annual Profit/Initial Investment.

- In the multi-period case, the opportunity cost of capital (the discount rate) used in the NPV method is also the reinvestment rate of the project's future cash flows. The IRR is the discount rate that makes the NPV of the project equal to zero, which is also the reinvestment rate of the project's future cash flows. This is not correct since the reinvestment rate used should be the opportunity cost of capital of the project.
- The MIRR method is a restatement of the NPV method where the reinvestment rate used is the opportunity cost of capital of the project. For non-mutually exclusive projects case, the MIRR and NPV methods produce exactly the same result.
- The profitability index (PI) is greater than one if and only if the NPV is positive. Higher PI means higher profit for each invested dollar.
- The relation between NPV, PI and MIRR is: $NPV > 0$ if and only if $PI > 1$ if and only if $MIRR > r$.
- The payback period method, though does not consider all cash flows and/or the discount rate for future cash flows, is still popular among practicians. The payback period method is a kind of safety-first rule method, which exists in an environment with high political/inflation risk and fast technology change.

Problems

1. With 10% annual discount rate, calculate the NPV, IRR and MIRR of the following mining project. Explain which number(s) is opportunity cost.

	$t = 0$	$t = 1$	$t = 2$	$t = 3$	$t = 4$
Cash flow	–400	−100	300	360	–50

2. In the profitability index analysis, what is its denominator? Is the denominator of the profitability index analysis an opportunity cost or accounting expense?
3. In the one-period model, the internal rate of return (IRR) analysis is consistent with the net present value (NPV) analysis. But in the multiperiod model, the internal rate of return (IRR) analysis is inconsistent with the net present value (NPV) analysis. Explain why?
4. Some investors suggest choosing stocks with low price-earning ratios. Do they use high or low discount rate?
5. Explain why the payoff period method is very popular in high-tech industry.

References

Graham, J., & Campbell, H. (2001). The theory and practice of corporate finance: evidence from the field. *Journal of Financial Economics, 60*, 187-243.

Klammer, T. (1972). Empirical evidence of the adoption of sophisticated capital budgeting techniques. *Journal of Business, 45*, 387-397.

Moore, J., & Reichert, A. (1983). An analysis of the financial management techniques currently employed by large U.S. corporations. *Journal of Business Finance and Accounting, 10*, 623-645.

Schall, L., Sunden, G., & Geijsbeek, W., Jr. (1978). Survey and analysis of capital budgeting methods. *Journal of Finance, 33*, 281-287.

Shinoda, T. (2010). Capital budgeting management practices in Japan: A focus on the use of capital budgeting methods. *Economic Journal of Hokkaido University, 39*, 39-50.

Risk and Return

7

Under uncertainty the discount rate for an asset's future cash flows needs incorporate risk. Using higher discount rate means adopting the safety-first investment rule. This chapter discusses how risk affects an asset's opportunity cost of capital. Section 7.1 analyzes the investor's preference toward risk in the framework of the expected utility function. Mean–variance portfolio analysis is introduced in Sect. 7.2. Section 7.3 discusses the measure of risk (beta) in the capital asset pricing model and the two-factor model. Section 7.4 introduces some alternative models for measuring the risk-return relationship.

7.1 Risk-Averse, Risk-Love and Risk-Neutral

In the early days, mean or expected value was used to evaluate investment under uncertainty. However, Bernoulli's (1738/1954) St. Petersburg Paradox shows that the decision criterion based only on the expected value is not plausible. The St. Petersburg game is played as follows: A fair coin is flipped until it comes up heads the first time where the initial stake begins at 2 dollars and is doubled every time tail appears. Thus, the expected value for getting the head on the first flip is: $\left(\frac{1}{2}\right)(2)$. The expected value for getting the head on the second flip is: $\left(\frac{1}{2}\right)\left(\frac{1}{2}\right)\left(2^2\right)$. The expected value for getting the head on the third flip is: $\left(\frac{1}{2}\right)^2\left(\frac{1}{2}\right)\left(2^3\right)$. This shows that the expected value from the St. Petersburg game is infinite: $\left(\frac{1}{2}\right)(2) + \left(\frac{1}{2}\right)\left(\frac{1}{2}\right)\left(2^2\right) + \left(\frac{1}{2}\right)^2\left(\frac{1}{2}\right)\left(2^3\right) + \left(\frac{1}{2}\right)^3\left(\frac{1}{2}\right)\left(2^4\right) + \cdots = +\infty$. However, no one will pay a huge amount of money (not to mention infinite amount of money) to obtain the right to join this game. Bernoulli argues that the marginal utility of increasing wealth is decreasing, i.e., the marginal utility of increasing from \$4 to \$8 is greater than the marginal utility of increasing from \$8 to \$12. Hence, the value of the game should be finite, not infinite.

K.-P. Chang, *Corporate Finance: A Systematic Approach*, Springer Texts in Business and Economics, https://doi.org/10.1007/978-981-19-9119-6_7

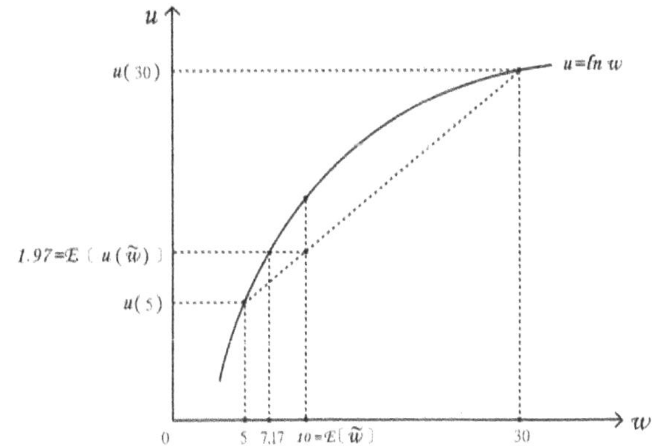

Fig. 7.1 Risk premium and expected utility of a concave utility function

In 1947, von Neumann and Morgenstern developed the expected utility theory to analyze how people make decision under uncertainty. For example, suppose Peter is a feudal lord owning \$10. A war just broke out and the king wants Peter to join the war. From this war, Peter has 20% chance to increase his wealth from \$10 to \$30, and 80% chance to decrease his wealth to \$5. The expected value (mean) of this war is: $\$10 = E[\tilde{w}] = 0.8(5) + 0.2(30)$. Assume that Peter's utility function is: $u(w) = \ln w$, where w is the wealth, and there exists an expected utility function. Then, Peter's expected utility of joining the war is: $E[u(\tilde{w})] = (0.8) \cdot u(5) + (0.2) \cdot u(30) = (0.8)(\ln 5) + (0.2)(\ln 30) = 1.97$. As shown in Fig. 7.1, Peter will think the value of this gamble is worth only \$7.17 (i.e., let $u(w') = \ln w' = 1.97$, and hence, $w' = \$7.17$). This indicates that Peter is willing to pay the king at most \$2.83 ($= 10 - 7.17$) to avoid joining the war and \$2.83 is the risk premium. Since Peter's utility function is concave in w, there is a positive risk premium, i.e., Peter is risk averse.

Suppose that John is another feudal lord who has a convex utility function. This implies that John will be willing to buy the right to join the war. As shown in Fig. 7.2, if John's initial wealth is \$10, and his utility function is: $u(w) = w^{3/2}$, John will think the value of joining the war is: $w' = \$12.046$ (and w' is calculated from: $(0.8)(5)^{3/2} + (0.2)(30)^{3/2} = (w')^{3/2}$), which is larger than \$10, the wealth of not joining the war. Thus, the maximum amount of money that John is willing to pay to the king to join the war is: $X = \$2.61072$, where X is estimated from: $(0.8)(5 - X)^{3/2} + (0.2)(30 - X)^{3/2} = (10)^{3/2}$.

In sum, in the framework of the expected utility function, when facing uncertainty, e.g., a gamble, people's attitudes toward risk are defined as follows.

Risk averse

(a) Utility function is concave in wealth;
(b) Prefer the expected value of the gamble to the gamble itself, e.g., prefer receiving \$10 for sure to a gamble which provides: $E[\tilde{w}] = \$10$.

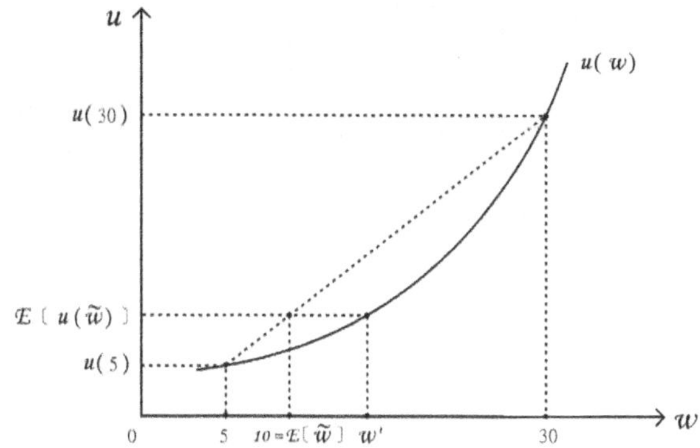

Fig. 7.2 Expected utility of a convex utility function

Risk neutral

(a) Utility function is linear in wealth;
(b) Indifferent between the expected value of the gamble and the gamble itself.

Risk love

(a) Utility function is convex in wealth;
(b) Prefer the gamble itself to the expected value of the gamble.

7.2 Mean–Variance Portfolio Analysis

In the mean–variance portfolio analysis, investors are assumed to *prefer high expected rate of return and low variance of rate of return.* Suppose there are two assets providing uncertain rates of return: $\tilde{R}_1$ and $\tilde{R}_2$, respectively (where tilde "~" denotes a random variable). An investor invests her wealth \$120 in the two assets: \$80 in $\tilde{R}_1$, and \$40 in $\tilde{R}_2$. The return of this portfolio is: $120\tilde{R}_P \equiv 80\tilde{R}_1 + 40\tilde{R}_2$, and the rate of the return of the portfolio is: $\tilde{R}_p = (80/120)\tilde{R}_1 + (40/120)\tilde{R}_2$. That is, the weight of investing in $\tilde{R}_1$ is 2/3, and the weight of investing in $\tilde{R}_2$ is1/3. If the investor short-sells the second asset whose current value is \$70 and invests \$190 (= 120 + 70) into the first asset, then the return of this portfolio is: $120\tilde{R}_P \equiv 190\tilde{R}_1 + (-70)\tilde{R}_2$, and the rate of return of the portfolio is: $\tilde{R}_P = (190/120)\tilde{R}_1 + (-70/120)\tilde{R}_2$. That is, the investor short-sells the second asset with a ratio: $-7/12$, and has a long position in the first asset with a ratio: $19/12$, where $19/12 + (-7/12) = 1$.

The rate of return of a portfolio with two assets is:

$$\tilde{R}_P \equiv a\tilde{R}_1 + (1-a)\tilde{R}_2 \tag{7.1}$$

The portfolio's expected rate of return and variance of rate of return are:

$$E\left[\tilde{R}_P\right] \equiv \mu = E\left[a\tilde{R}_1 + (1-a)\tilde{R}_2\right] = a \cdot E\left[\tilde{R}_1\right] + (1-a) \cdot E\left[\tilde{R}_2\right] \quad (7.2)$$

$$\begin{aligned} Var\left(\tilde{R}_P\right) &\equiv \sigma_P^2 = E\left[\left[a\tilde{R}_1 + (1-a)\tilde{R}_2\right] - E\left[a\tilde{R}_1 + (1-a)\tilde{R}_2\right]\right]^2 \\ &= E\left[a\left(\tilde{R}_1 - E\left[\tilde{R}_1\right]\right) + (1-a)\left(\tilde{R}_2 - E\left[\tilde{R}_2\right]\right)\right]^2 \\ &= a^2\sigma_1^2 + (1-a)^2\sigma_2^2 + 2a(1-a)\sigma_{12} \\ &= a^2\sigma_1^2 + (1-a)^2\sigma_2^2 + 2a(1-a) \cdot \gamma_{12} \cdot \sigma_1 \cdot \sigma_2 \end{aligned} \quad (7.3)$$

where $\sigma_{12} \equiv Cov\left(\tilde{R}_1, \tilde{R}_2\right) = E[(\tilde{R}_1 - E[\tilde{R}_1])(\tilde{R}_2 - E[\tilde{R}_2])]$ is the covariance between $\tilde{R}_1$ and $\tilde{R}_2$, $\gamma_{12} \equiv Cov(\tilde{R}_1, \tilde{R}_2)/\sigma_1\sigma_2$ is the correlation, and $-1 \leq \gamma_{12} \leq 1$. Note that by changing the weights (i.e., a and $(1-a)$), $E\left[\tilde{R}_P\right]$ and $Var\left(\tilde{R}_P\right)$ may change, but the market value of the portfolio will not change. That is, the market value of a portfolio is just the summation of the market value of the assets it contains, i.e., adding up assets does not create value. We may call it: *financial diversification irrelevancy*.

In Eq. (7.3), by changing a, the global minimum variance is:

$$\underset{a}{Min} \ \sigma_p^2 = a^2 \cdot \sigma_1^2 + (1-a)^2 \cdot \sigma_2^2 + 2a(1-a) \cdot \gamma_{12} \cdot \sigma_1 \cdot \sigma_2$$

First-order condition: $\frac{d\sigma_P^2}{da} = 2a\sigma_1^2 - 2(1-a)\sigma_2^2 + 2\gamma_{12}\sigma_1\sigma_2 - 4a\gamma_{12}\sigma_1\sigma_2 \equiv 0$

$$\text{and} \qquad a^* = \frac{\sigma_2^2 - \gamma_{12}\sigma_1\sigma_2}{\sigma_1^2 + \sigma_2^2 - 2\gamma_{12}\sigma_1\sigma_2}. \quad (7.4)$$

Substitute a^* into σ_P^2 (i.e., $[\sigma_P^2]_{a=a*}$), we can derive the global minimum variance portfolio.

In Eq.'s (7.2) and (7.3), by changing a, we can estimate the portfolio's μ (the expected rate of return) and σ (the standard deviation of rate of return).

Case 1: $\gamma_{12} = 1$.

$$E[\tilde{R}_P] \equiv \mu = aE[\tilde{R}_1] + (1-a)E[\tilde{R}_2]$$

$$\sigma_P^2 = a^2\sigma_1^2 + (1-a)^2\sigma_2^2 + 2a(1-a)\sigma_1\sigma_2 = [a\sigma_1 + (1-a)\sigma_2]^2$$

With no short-selling (i.e., $0 \leq a \leq 1$), $\sigma_P = a\sigma_1 + (1-a)\sigma_2 > 0$,

$$\frac{dE[\tilde{R}_P]}{da} = E[\tilde{R}_1] - E[\tilde{R}_2]$$

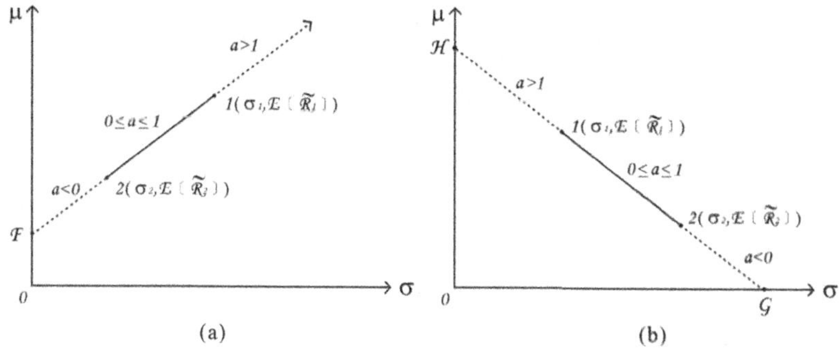

Fig. 7.3 Perfectly positively correlated ($\gamma_{12} = 1$) two uncertain assets

$$\frac{d\sigma_P}{da} = \sigma_1 - \sigma_2$$

Thus, $\frac{dE[\tilde{R}_P]}{d\sigma_P} = \frac{dE[\tilde{R}_P]/da}{d\sigma_P/da} = \frac{E[\tilde{R}_1]-E[\tilde{R}_2]}{\sigma_1-\sigma_2}$.

Since the slope: $\frac{dE\left[\tilde{R}_P\right]}{d\sigma_P}$ does not depend on a, portfolios organized by the two assets must lie on a straight line. Substitute $\gamma_{12} = 1$ into Eq. (7.4), we get: $a^* = \sigma_2/(\sigma_2 - \sigma_1)$. In Fig. 7.3a, global minimum variance portfolio F implies $\sigma_P = 0$, and short-selling the first asset: $a^* = \sigma_2/(\sigma_2 - \sigma_1) < 0$. In Fig. 7.3b, portfolio G means short-selling the first asset so that $E[\tilde{R}_P] = 0$ (i.e., $a = E[\tilde{R}_2]/(E[\tilde{R}_2] - E[\tilde{R}_1]) < 0$), and global minimum variance portfolio H means $\sigma_P = 0$, and short-selling the second asset: $1 - a^* = -\sigma_1/(\sigma_2 - \sigma_1) < 0$. Portfolio H dominates all other portfolios, and portfolio G is the worst.

Case 2: $\gamma_{12} = -1$.

$$E[\tilde{R}_P] \equiv \mu = a \cdot E[\tilde{R}_1] + (1-a) \cdot E[\tilde{R}_2]$$

$$\sigma_P^2 = a^2\sigma_1^2 + (1-a)^2\sigma_2^2 - 2a(1-a)\sigma_1\sigma_2 = [a\sigma_1 - (1-a)\sigma_2]^2$$

$$\sigma_P = a\sigma_1 - (1-a)\sigma_2 \ \text{ if } \ a\sigma_1 - (1-a)\sigma_2 > 0$$

$$\text{or} \quad \sigma_P = -[a\sigma_1 - (1-a)\sigma_2] \ \text{ if } \ a\sigma_1 - (1-a)\sigma_2 < 0.$$

Thus, $$\frac{dE[\tilde{R}_P]}{d\sigma_P} = \frac{dE[\tilde{R}_P]/da}{d\sigma_P/da} = \frac{E[\tilde{R}_1] - E[\tilde{R}_2]}{\sigma_1 + \sigma_2} \quad \text{if} \ \ a\sigma_1 - (1-a)\sigma_2 > 0$$

$$\text{or} \quad = \frac{E[\tilde{R}_1] - E[\tilde{R}_2]}{-(\sigma_1 + \sigma_2)} \quad \text{if} \ \ a\sigma_1 - (1-a)\sigma_2 < 0.$$

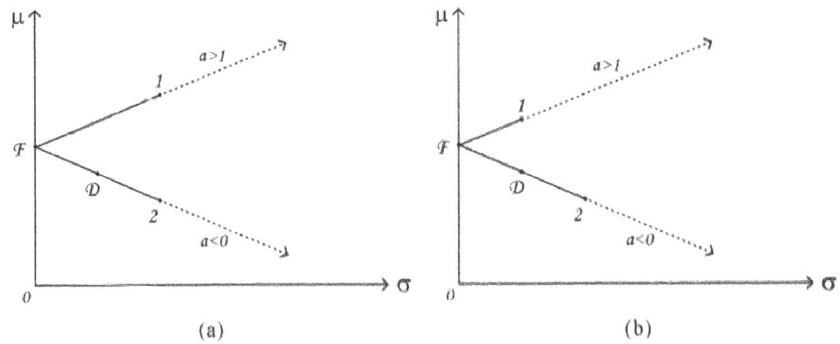

Fig. 7.4 Perfectly negatively correlated ($\gamma_{12} = -1$) two uncertain assets

The slope: $\frac{dE\left[\tilde{R}_P\right]}{d\sigma_P}$ can be positive or negative and does not depend on a, and hence, the portfolios are on two straight lines connecting the first and the second assets. Substitute $\gamma_{12} = -1$ into Eq. (7.4), we get: $a^* = \sigma_2/(\sigma_2 + \sigma_1) > 0$, i.e., no short-sell in the global minimum variance portfolio. Substitute $a^* = \sigma_2/(\sigma_2 + \sigma_1)$ into Eq.'s (7.2) and (7.3), the coordinates of the global minimum variance portfolio are: $\left(E\left[\tilde{R}_P\right], \sigma_P\right) = (0, (\sigma_2 E[\tilde{R}_1] + \sigma_1 E[\tilde{R}_2])/(\sigma_1 + \sigma_2))$, i.e., point F in Fig. 7.4a, b.

Case 3: $-1 < \gamma_{12} < 1$ and no short-sell ($0 \leq a \leq 1$). From Eq. (7.3) we have:

$$[a\sigma_1 - (1-a)\sigma_2]^2 < [a^2\sigma_1^2 + 2a(1-a)\gamma_{12}\sigma_1\sigma_2 + (1-a)^2\sigma_2^2] < [a\sigma_1 + (1-a)\sigma_2]^2 \quad (7.5)$$

As shown in Fig. 7.5a, b, the ratios of investing in the first and second assets are: 0.5 and 0.5. The coordinates of portfolio A (where $\gamma_{12} = 1$) are: $(\sqrt{0.16}, 0.4)$, the coordinates of portfolio C (where $\gamma_{12} = -1$) are: $(\sqrt{0.04}, 0.4)$, and the coordinates of portfolio B (where $\gamma_{12} = 0.5$) are: $(\sqrt{0.13}, 0.4)$. Portfolios A, B and C have the same expected rate of return: $E\left[\tilde{R}_P\right] = 0.4$, and portfolio B must lie between portfolio C and portfolio A because: $\sqrt{0.04} < \sqrt{0.13} < \sqrt{0.16}$. The following table shows that with $a = 1 - a = 0.5$, when the correlation γ_{12} increases, point B moves close to point A; and when γ_{12} decreases, point B moves close to point C. That is, *any portfolio organized by the two assets must lie inside the dashed-lined triangular.*

Correlation	σ	μ
$\gamma_{12} = 1$(Point A)	$\sqrt{0.16}$	0.4
$\gamma_{12} = 0.9$	$\sqrt{0.154}$	0.4
$\gamma_{12} = 0.5$	$\sqrt{0.13}$	0.4
$\gamma_{12} = -0.6$	$\sqrt{0.064}$	0.4
$\gamma_{12} = -1$(Point C)	$\sqrt{0.04}$	0.4

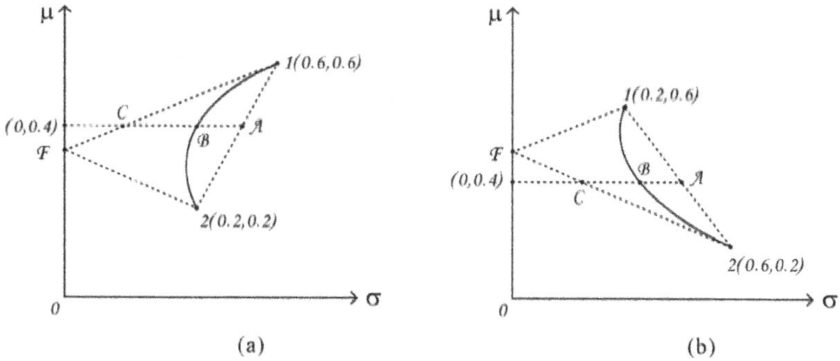

Fig. 7.5 Portfolios with $\gamma_{12} = 0.5$ and $0 \leq a \leq 1$ (the solid curves)

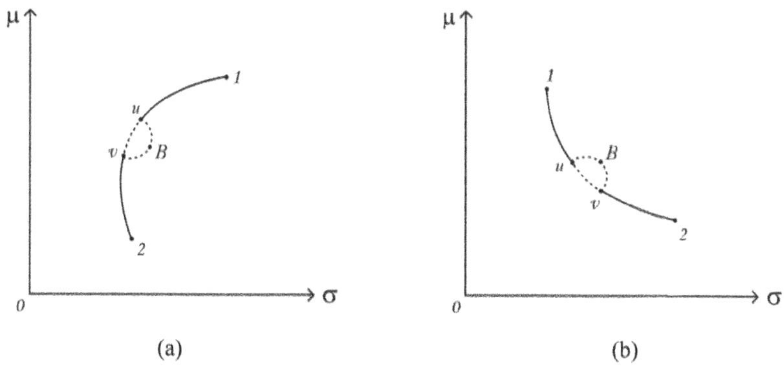

Fig. 7.6 A smooth function (curve) of minimum variance portfolios

Suppose there are only two assets, i.e., asset 1 and asset 2, as shown in Fig. 7.6a, b where $-1 < \gamma_{12} < 1$. Is it possible that portfolio B is organized by asset 1 and asset 2? The answer is no. This is because both portfolios u and v are organized by the two assets and the correlation between u and v must be less than $+1$ and greater than -1, any portfolio (including portfolio B) organized by u and v must lie within *the dashed-lined triangular* as in Fig. 7.5. Hence, the two curves of the portfolios organized by the two assets in Fig. 7.6a, b must be smooth, i.e., the two functions are twice differentiable. In Fig. 7.6a, if asset 2 is not the global minimum variance portfolio (where $a = 0$), then the curve of the portfolios whose expected rates of return are greater than that of the global minimum variance portfolio must be concave; and the curve of the portfolios whose expected rates of return are less than that of the global minimum variance portfolio must be concave. In Fig. 7.6b, the curve of the portfolios must be convex.

Similarly, suppose there are three assets, i.e., asset 1, asset 2 and asset 3, as shown in Fig. 7.7a, b where $-1 < \gamma_{ij} < 1, i, j = 1, 2, 3$. Portfolio u is organized by asset 1 and asset 2, and portfolio v is organized by asset 2 and asset 3. Hence,

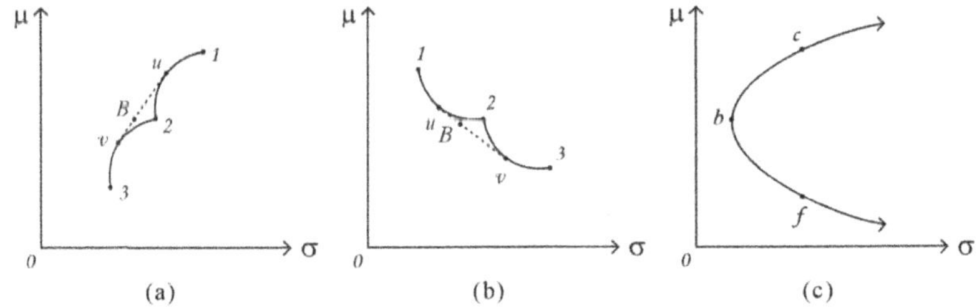

Fig. 7.7 Efficient and minimum variance portfolios

there must exist a minimum variance portfolio B, organized by portfolio u and portfolio v, which has the same expected rates of return as asset 2 but has less standard deviation of rate of return (σ_P).

For the case of n uncertain assets, we can use the method suggested above to construct the curve of minimum variance portfolios of the assets, e.g., the $c$bf curve in Fig. 7.7c. Note that every asset or portfolio will be on the right side of the $c$bf curve, i.e., it is enveloped by the $c$bf curve. Point b is the global minimum variance portfolio. The bc segment of the $c$bf curve is concave and is the curve of *efficient portfolios*,[1] e.g., portfolio c dominates portfolio f because although both portfolios provide the same standard deviation of rate of return, portfolio c has higher expected rate of return than that of portfolio f.

We can also use mathematical programming methods to derive efficient and minimum variance portfolios. In the following maximizing expected rate of return problem, i.e., Eq. (7.6), by changing the constraint of standard deviation of rate of return $\overline{\sigma}$, we can derive efficient portfolios (i.e., the bc segment in Fig. 7.7c):

$$\underset{w_1,\ldots,w_n}{Max} \quad E[\tilde{R}_P] = \sum\nolimits_{i=1}^{n} w_i \cdot E[\tilde{R}_i]$$

$$\text{subject to } \sum\nolimits_{i=1}^{n} w_i = 1,$$

$$\sum\nolimits_{i=1}^{n} \sum\nolimits_{j=1}^{n} w_i w_j \sigma_{ij} = \overline{\sigma}^2, \tag{7.6}$$

where w_i is the weight for asset $i = 1, 2, \ldots, n$.

When minimizing the standard deviation of rate of return, i.e., Eq. (7.7), by changing the constraint of expected rate of return $\overline{\mu}$, we can derive minimum variance portfolios (i.e., the $c$bf curve):

$$\underset{w_1,\ldots,w_n}{Min} \quad \sigma_P^2 = \sum\nolimits_{i=1}^{n} \sum\nolimits_{j=1}^{n} w_i w_j \sigma_{ij}$$

[1] Or, Markowitz efficient portfolio.

$$\text{subject to } \sum\nolimits_{i=1}^{n} w_i = 1,$$

$$\sum\nolimits_{i=1}^{n} w_i \cdot E\left[\tilde{R}_i\right] = \overline{\mu}. \tag{7.7}$$

where w_i is the weight for asset $i = 1, 2, \ldots, n$.

In Fig. 7.8a, Eq. (7.7) is used to derive the minimum variance portfolio curve of the ten largest market capitalization US firms listed in the NYSE in 2018.[2] Figure 7.8b is the minimum variance portfolio curve for the ten largest market capitalization Chinese firms listed in Shanghai Stock Exchange (SSE) in 2018. These two figures show that the curve of the efficient portfolios whose expected rates of return are greater than that of the global minimum variance portfolio is concave; and the curve of the portfolios whose expected rates of return are less than that of the global minimum variance portfolio is convex.

Markowitz's (1952) mean–variance portfolio analysis defines decision rules for a portfolio are: (a) for a given standard deviation of rate of return, maximize the expected rate of return (i.e., find efficient portfolios); and (b) for a given expected rate of return, minimize the standard deviation of rate of return (i.e., find minimum variance portfolios). Thus, variance of rate of return is termed as the measure for risk. Also, Markowitz's risk (variance) is defined as the summation of nonsystematic risk and systematic risk. Nonsystematic risk is specific to individual asset, which can be diversified away by organizing a portfolio. Systematic risk is the risk of the whole economy. Because systematic risk is common to all assets, and hence, it cannot be diversified away by organizing a portfolio.

The following example of equally-weighted portfolio shows that in a well-diversified portfolio, the variance of rate of return of an asset has little effect on the variance of rate of return of a portfolio. As the number of assets increases, it is the covariance between assets affects the variance of rate of return of the portfolio:

Assume an equally-weighted portfolio:

Let $\tilde{R}_P = \sum_{i=1}^{n} w_i \tilde{R}_i$ and $\sum_{i=1}^{n} w_i = 1$.

Then, $\sigma_P^2 = \sum_{i=1}^{n} \sum_{j=1}^{n} w_i w_j \sigma_{ij} = \sum_{i=1}^{n} w_i^2 \sigma_i^2 + \sum_{i=1}^{n} \sum_{\substack{j=1 \\ j \neq i}}^{n} w_i w_j \sigma_{ij}$.

With equal weights: $w_1 = w_2 = \cdots = w_n = \frac{1}{n}$,

$$\sigma_P^2 = \frac{1}{n^2} \sum\nolimits_{i=1}^{n} \sigma_i^2 + \frac{1}{n^2} \sum\nolimits_{i=1}^{n} \sum\nolimits_{\substack{j=1 \\ i \neq j}}^{n} \sigma_{ij} \tag{7.8}$$

[2] In Eq. (7.7), the i-th company stock's monthly rate of return at the t-th month is calculated as: $R_{it} = \frac{(\text{the } i-\text{th stock price at the end of the } t-\text{th month}) - (\text{the } i-\text{th stock price in the beginning of the } t-\text{th month})}{\text{the } i-\text{th stock price in the beginning of the } t-\text{th month}}$, $i = 1, 2, \ldots, 10$; $t = 1, 2, \ldots, 12$. $\overline{R}_i$ is used for $E[\tilde{R}_i]$ where $\overline{R}_i = \sum_{t=1}^{12} R_{it}/12$.

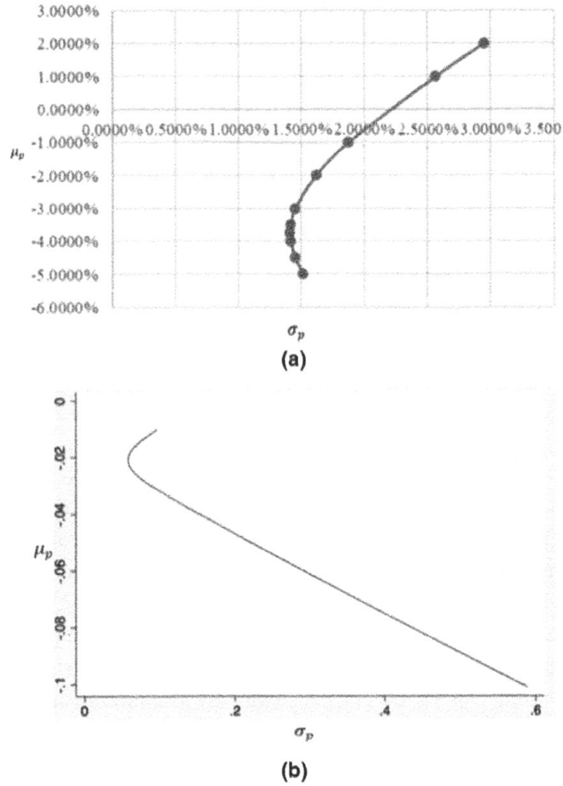

Fig. 7.8 **a** The minimum variance portfolio curve of the ten largest capitalization US firms in the NYSE in 2018. **b** The minimum variance portfolio curve for the ten largest capitalization Chinese firms in the SSE in 2018

Let $x_{max} = Max\{\sigma_1^2, \sigma_2^2, \ldots, \sigma_n^2\}$, the first term of the right-hand-side of Eq. (7.8) becomes:

$$\frac{1}{n^2}\sum_{i=1}^{n}\sigma_i^2 < \frac{1}{n^2}\sum_{i=1}^{n}x_{max} = \frac{x_{max}}{n}$$

When n becomes very large, $\frac{1}{n^2}\sum_{i=1}^{n}\sigma_i^2$ will approach zero. That is, when the portfolio is well-diversified, the variance of individual asset's rate of return has no effect on the portfolio's variance. For the second term of the right-hand-side of Eq. (7.8),

let $\tilde{\sigma}_{ij} = \frac{1}{n^2-n}\sum_{i=1}^{n}\sum_{\substack{j=1 \\ j\neq i}}^{n}\sigma_{ij}$,

when n becomes very large, $\frac{1}{n^2}\sum_{i=1}^{n}\sum_{\substack{j=1 \\ j\neq i}}^{n}\sigma_{ij} = \frac{1}{n^2}(n^2-n)\tilde{\sigma}_{ij}$ will approach to $\tilde{\sigma}_{ij}$.

In sum, when n becomes very large, σ_P^2 approaches $\tilde{\sigma}_{ij}$, i.e., the portfolio's risk (variance) is only related to the covariances of assets' rates of return, and individual assets' variances of rate of return have no effect on σ_P^2. We may say that the covariances of assets' rates of return are systematic risk, and individual assets' variances of rate of return are nonsystematic risk.

7.3 Capital Asset Pricing Model and Two-Factor Model

In the Markowitz mean–variance portfolio analysis, there are only uncertain assets. Sharpe (1964) and Lintner (1965) expand the Markowitz mean–variance portfolio analysis by adding a risk-free asset which provides risk-free rate of return: R_f. The result is the capital asset pricing model (CAPM).

Suppose there are two assets: a risk-free asset provides R_f, and an uncertain portfolio N. Then, the rate of return of the portfolio organized by the two assets is:

$$\tilde{R}_{p'} = a'\tilde{R}_N + (1 - a')R_f$$

and its mean and variance are:

$$E[\tilde{R}_{P'}] = a' \cdot E[\tilde{R}_N] + (1 - a') \cdot R_f$$

$$\sigma_{P'}^2 = (a')^2 \cdot \sigma_N^2$$

and

$$\frac{\partial E\left[\tilde{R}_{P'}\right]/\partial a'}{\partial \sigma_{P'}/\partial a'} = \frac{E\left[\tilde{R}_N\right] - R_f}{\sigma_N} \tag{7.9}$$

Since the slope: $\frac{\partial E\left[\tilde{R}_{P'}\right]/\partial a'}{\partial \sigma_{P'}/\partial a'}$ does not depend on a', portfolios organized by the two assets must lie on a straight line, i.e., $R_f N$ is a straight line in Fig. 7.9. Under the assumption that people prefer high expected rate of return and low variance of rate of return, investors may invest in a portfolio with no short-sell (i.e., $0 \le a' \le 1$) or a portfolio which short-sells the risk-free asset R_f (i.e., $a' \ge 1$). But no one will invest in a portfolio which short-sells the uncertain asset N (i.e., $a' < 0$).

Suppose there are n uncertain assets and a risk-free asset R_f. With n uncertain assets only, as shown in Fig. 7.10, the curve of minimum variance portfolios organized by the uncertain assets is the $c$bf curve in Fig. 7.7c. All uncertain assets and the portfolios organized by the uncertain assets are enveloped by the $c$bf curve. When a risk-free asset R_f is added as in Fig. 7.10, Sharpe and Lintner find that every investor's portfolio will be a combination of the uncertain portfolio M and the risk-free asset R_f. In Fig. 7.10, every portfolio on the line connected by R_f and

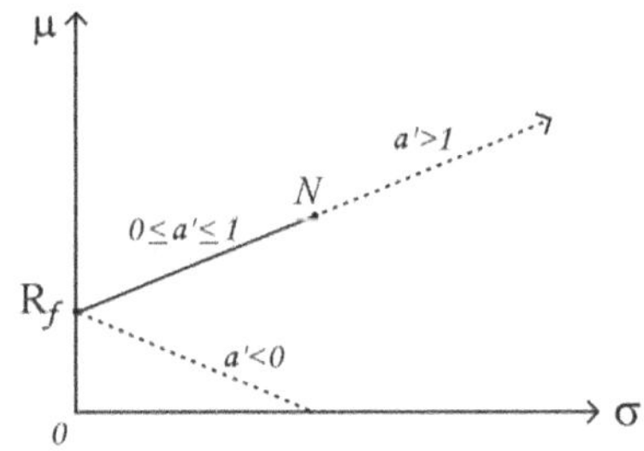

Fig. 7.9 Portfolios organized by a risk-free asset R_f and an uncertain asset N

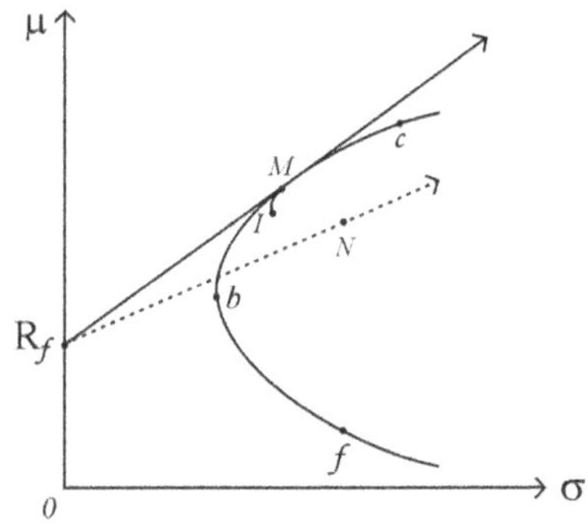

Fig. 7.10 The CAPM with a risk-free asset which provides a risk-free interest rate R_f

N will be dominated by a portfolio on the line connected by R_f and M.[3] Therefore, point M must be an efficient portfolio, i.e., it is on the bc segment of the $c$bf curve. Also, since all investors have the same expectation about Fig. 7.10 (i.e., homogenous expectation), everyone will choose the same R_f and M to invest. The portfolio M has no short-selling and is called the *market portfolio* which includes all uncertain assets. If an asset, e.g., an IBM stock, is not included in the market portfolio M, then this asset cannot exist (because no one will own it). By summing up all the investors' investments in M, we can get the rate of turn of the whole n assets:

$$\tilde{R}_M = \frac{\sum_{i=1}^{n} \tilde{X}_i}{\sum_{i=1}^{n} V_i} = \sum_{i=1}^{n} \left[\frac{V_i}{\sum_{i=1}^{n} V_i} \cdot \frac{\tilde{X}_i}{V_i} \right] = \sum_{i=1}^{n} w_i \cdot \tilde{R}_i \tag{7.10}$$

where $\tilde{X}_i$ is the ith asset's cash flow, V_i is the ith asset's market value, and $w_i = V_i / \sum_{i=1}^{n} V_i$ is the weight of the ith asset in the market portfolio M. Hence, the market portfolio M is a value-weighted portfolio.

[3] Note that N can be any other point (except M) enveloped by the $c$bf curve.

Derivation of the Capital Asset Pricing Model

Suppose that in Fig. 7.10, there exists a portfolio (or an asset) I, the portfolio combined by I and the market portfolio M is: $\tilde{R}_P = a \cdot \tilde{R}_I + (1-a) \cdot \tilde{R}_M$. Then

$$E[\tilde{R}_P] = a \cdot E[\tilde{R}_I] + (1-a) \cdot E[\tilde{R}_M]$$

$$\sigma_P^2 = a^2\sigma_I^2 + (1-a)\sigma_M^2 + 2a(1-a)\sigma_{IM}$$

$$\frac{\partial E[\tilde{R}_P]}{\partial a} = E[\tilde{R}_I] - E[\tilde{R}_M]$$

$$\frac{\partial \sigma_P}{\partial a} = \frac{1}{2}[a^2\sigma_I^2 + (1-a)^2\sigma_M^2 + 2a(1-a)\sigma_{IM}]^{\frac{-1}{2}} \cdot \left[2a\sigma_I^2 - 2(1-a)\sigma_M^2 + 2\sigma_{IM} - 4a\sigma_{IM}\right].$$

When $a < 0$ (i.e., short-sell portfolio I), the IM curve will extend to right, but it will not break through the bMc curve. Otherwise, the portfolios on the bMc curve will not be efficient portfolios. The slope of tangent line at M of the bMc curve is: $\frac{\partial E[\tilde{R}_P]}{\partial \sigma_P}$ evaluated at $a = 0$, that is,

$$\left[\frac{\partial E\left[\tilde{R}_P\right]}{\partial \sigma_P}\right]_{a=0} = \left[\frac{\partial E\left[\tilde{R}_P\right]/\partial a}{\partial \sigma_P/\partial a}\right]_{a=0} = \frac{E[\tilde{R}_I] - E[\tilde{R}_M]}{\left(\sigma_{IM} - \sigma_M^2\right)/\sigma_M}. \tag{7.11}$$

Combining Eq. (7.11) with Eq. (7.9) where the portfolio N is replaced by the market portfolio M, we have:

$$\frac{E[\tilde{R}_M] - R_f}{\sigma_M} = \frac{E[\tilde{R}_I] - E[\tilde{R}_M]}{(\sigma_{IM} - \sigma_M^2)/\sigma_M} \tag{7.12}$$

or $$E\left[\tilde{R}_I\right] = R_f + \left(E\left[\tilde{R}_M\right] - R_f\right) \cdot \beta_I, \text{ where } \beta_I = Cov\left(\tilde{R}_I, \tilde{R}_M\right)/\sigma_M^2. \tag{7.13}$$

Equation (7.13) is the capital asset pricing model (the CAPM). $E[\tilde{R}_I]$ is the opportunity cost of capital (i.e., the discount rate or the reinvestment rate) of the uncertain ith asset, and hence, it can be used to discount the ith asset's future cash flows. Under the CAPM framework, every asset has the same risk-free interest rate: R_f and market risk premium: $E\left[\tilde{R}_M\right] - R_f$. Beta for the ith asset, i.e., β_I, is a unitless risk measure for the ith asset, which depends on the covariance between $\tilde{R}_I$ and $\tilde{R}_M$. If the ith asset's β_I is greater than 1.0, it will mean that the ith asset is more volatile than the market portfolio. In Fig. 7.11 (where rate of return is the vertical axis and beta is the horizon axis), Eq. (7.13) is called the *security market line* (SML), and all assets must lie on this line. Notice that higher beta (risk) means

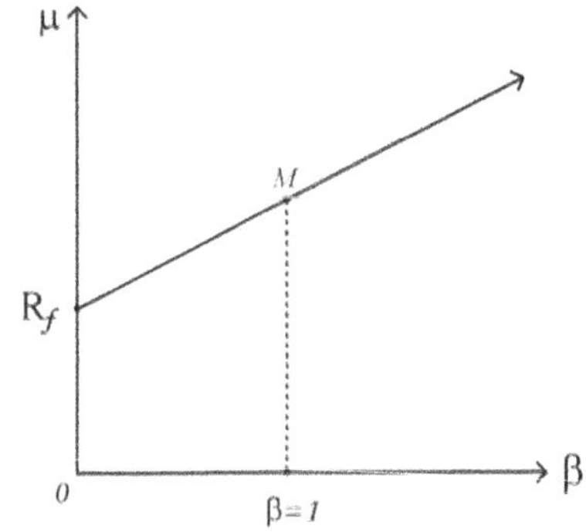

Fig. 7.11 Security market line (SML)

higher discount rate for the asset's future cash flows. When we find someone who suddenly becomes very rich, we know that, except by pure luck (e.g., receiving a huge endowment from her uncle), this person must have taken a great risk before. But we can never say: Higher beta (risk) brings higher rate of return.

There are three properties about the CAPM's beta:

(a) Higher covariance $Cov(\tilde{R}_i, \tilde{R}_M)$ means higher beta β_i:

$$\beta_i = \frac{Cov\left(\tilde{R}_i, \tilde{R}_M\right)}{\sigma_M^2} = \frac{Cov\left(\tilde{R}_i, \tilde{R}_M\right)}{\sum_{i=1}^{n} w_i \cdot Cov\left(\tilde{R}_i, \tilde{R}_M\right)}, \quad \text{where } w_i = V_i / \sum_{i=1}^{n} V_i. \tag{7.14}$$

(b) Individual asset's variance of rate of return has little effect on the portfolio's beta:

$$\begin{aligned} \beta_i &= \frac{Cov\left(\tilde{R}_i, \tilde{R}_M\right)}{\sigma_M^2} = \frac{\sum_{j=1}^{n} w_j \cdot Cov\left(\tilde{R}_i, \tilde{R}_j\right)}{\sigma_M^2} \\ &= w_i \cdot \frac{\sigma_i^2}{\sigma_M^2} + \sum_{\substack{j=1 \\ j \neq i}}^{n} w_j \frac{Cov\left(\tilde{R}_i, \tilde{R}_j\right)}{\sigma_M^2}. \end{aligned} \tag{7.15}$$

If n is large and w_i is quite small, $w_i\left(\sigma_i^2/\sigma_M^2\right)$ will approach zero. The covariance between the individual asset's rate of return and other asset's rate of return will affect the portfolio's beta.

(c) The beta of a portfolio is a linear combination of individual assets' betas. That is,

$$E\left[\tilde{R}_P\right] = a \cdot E\left[\tilde{R}_1\right] + (1 - a) \cdot E\left[\tilde{R}_2\right]$$

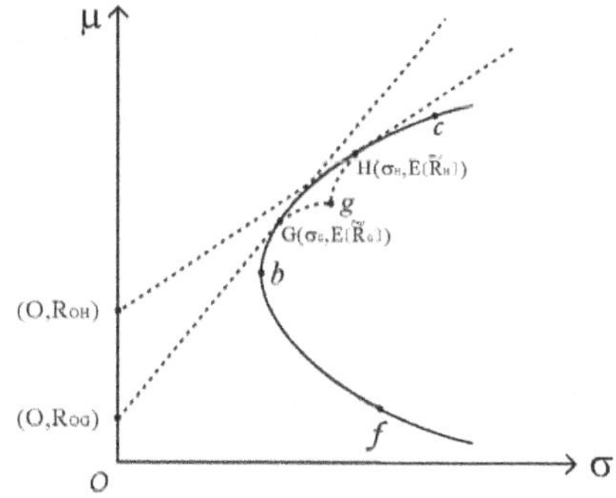

Fig. 7.12 The two-factor model without the existence of a risk-free asset

$$= R_f + \left(E\left[\tilde{R}_M\right] - R_f\right) \cdot (a\beta_1 + (1-a)\beta_2)$$

$$= R_f + \left(E\left[\tilde{R}_M\right] - R_f\right) \cdot \beta_P \tag{7.16}$$

where $\beta_P = a\beta_1 + (1-a)\beta_2$. For a portfolio organized by n' uncertain assets:

$$E\left[\tilde{R}_{P'}\right] = \sum\nolimits_{i=1}^{n'} w_i \cdot R_f + \left(E\left[\tilde{R}_M\right] - R_f\right) \cdot \sum\nolimits_{i=1}^{n'} w_i\beta_i. \tag{7.17}$$

If $\sum_{i=1}^{n'} w_i = 1$ and $\sum_{i=1}^{n'} w_i\beta_i = 0 = \beta_{P'}$, then $E\left[\tilde{R}_{P'}\right] = R_f$. Thus, R_f can be interpreted as the expected rate of return of a portfolio with zero beta. If $\sum_{i=1}^{n'} w_i = 0$ (i.e., zero investment) and $\sum_{i=1}^{n'} w_i\beta_i = 1$, then $E\left[\tilde{R}_{P'}\right] = E\left[\tilde{R}_M\right] - R_f$. Thus, $(E\left[\tilde{R}_M\right] - R_f)$ can be interpreted as the expected rate of return of a portfolio with $\beta_{P'} = 1$ and zero investment.

Derivation of the Two-factor Model

The CAPM needs the existence of a risk-free asset. Empirical studies, however, show that the security market line (SML) for US stocks is too flat relative to the CAPM. Black (1972) proposes the two-factor model which does not need the existence of a risk-free asset but needs short-sell.[4]

In Fig. 7.12, the *c*bf curve is the same as that in Fig. 7.10. Under the assumption that investors prefer high expected rate of return and low variance of rate of return, investors will always choose efficient portfolios, i.e., the bc segment of the *c*bf curve. Suppose the efficient portfolio G is chosen. Then, we can create a new portfolio organized by G and an asset g:

$$\tilde{R}_P = a\tilde{R}_g + (1-a)\tilde{R}_G$$

---

[4] Black, Fischer (1972) Capital market equilibrium with restricted borrowing. *Journal of Business* 45: 444-455.

and hence, $E[\tilde{R}_P] = a \cdot E[\tilde{R}_g] + (1-a) \cdot E[\tilde{R}_G]$

$$\sigma_P^2 = a^2\sigma_g^2 + (1-a)^2\sigma_G^2 + 2a(1-a)\sigma_{gG}.$$

The slope of the tangent line at point G of the $bGHc$ curve is: $\frac{\partial E[\tilde{R}_P]}{\partial \sigma_P}$ evaluated at $a = 0$, that is,

$$\left[\frac{\partial E[\tilde{R}_P]}{\partial \sigma_P}\right]_{a=0} = \left[\frac{\partial E[\tilde{R}_P]/\partial a}{\partial \sigma_P/\partial a}\right]_{a=0} = \frac{E[\tilde{R}_g] - E[\tilde{R}_G]}{(\sigma_{gG} - \sigma_G^2)/\sigma_G} \tag{7.18}$$

Also, as shown in Fig. 7.12, the tangent line connects the two points: $(0, R_{OG})$ and $(\sigma_G, E[\tilde{R}_G])$, and hence, its slope is:

$$\frac{R_{0G} - E\left[\tilde{R}_G\right]}{0 - \sigma_G} = \frac{E\left[\tilde{R}_G\right] - R_{0G}}{\sigma_G}. \tag{7.19}$$

The slope of the tangent line at point G (i.e., Eq. (7.18)) and the slope of the tangent line (i.e., Eq. (7.19)) should be the same:

$$\frac{E\left[\tilde{R}_G\right] - R_{0G}}{\sigma_G} = \frac{E\left[\tilde{R}_g] - E[\tilde{R}_G\right]}{(\sigma_{gG} - \sigma_G^2)/\sigma_G}$$

or $$E\left[\tilde{R}_g\right] = R_{0G} + \left(E\left[\tilde{R}_G\right] - R_{0G}\right) \cdot \beta_{gG}, \quad \text{where } \beta_{gG} = \frac{Cov\left(\tilde{R}_g, \tilde{R}_G\right)}{\sigma_G^2}. \tag{7.20}$$

Comparing Eq. (7.20) with the CAPM's Eq. (7.13), we know that Eq. (7.20) is also a linear function of beta (β_{gG}) and the expected rate of return of a zero-beta portfolio (R_{0G}), i.e., a two-factor model. With short-selling, the zero-beta portfolio having R_{0G} can be constructed by any two assets (asset 1 and asset 2):

Let $$E\left[\tilde{R}_1\right] = R_{0G} + \left(E\left[\tilde{R}_G\right] - R_{0G}\right) \cdot \beta_{1G}$$
$$E\left[\tilde{R}_2\right] = R_{0G} + \left(E\left[\tilde{R}_G\right] - R_{0G}\right) \cdot \beta_{2G}$$

and the expected rate of return of a zero-beta portfolio is:

$$E\left[\tilde{R}_P\right] = a \cdot E\left[\tilde{R}_1\right] + (1-a) \cdot E\left[\tilde{R}_2\right] = R_{0G} + \left(E\left[\tilde{R}_G\right] - R_{0G}\right) \cdot \beta_{PG} = R_{0G},$$

where $\beta_{PG} = 0 = a \cdot \beta_{1G} + (1-a) \cdot \beta_{2G}$,

and hence, $a = \beta_{2G}/(\beta_{2G} - \beta_{1G}), 1 - a = -\beta_{1G}/(\beta_{2G} - \beta_{1G})$. (7.21)

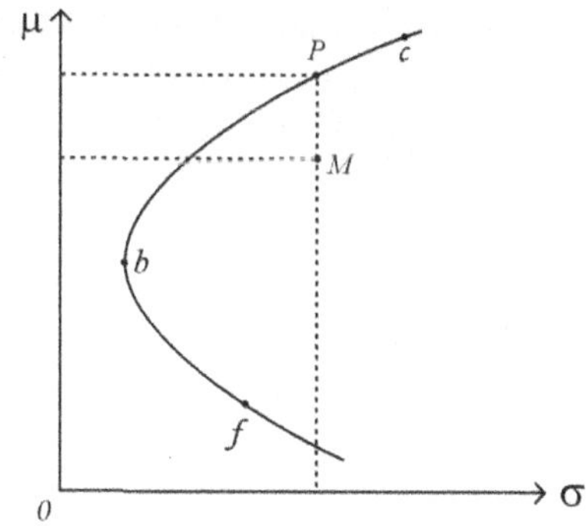

Fig. 7.13 Market portfolio must be an efficient portfolio

Similarly, if in Fig. 7.12, the efficient portfolio H is chosen, then we can create another portfolio organized by H and an asset g:

$$\frac{R_{0H} - E\left[\tilde{R}_H\right]}{0 - \sigma_H} = \frac{E\left[\tilde{R}_H\right] - R_{0H}}{\sigma_H}. \tag{7.19'}$$

and $E\left[\tilde{R}_g\right] = R_{0H} + \left(E\left[\tilde{R}_H\right] - R_{0H}\right) \cdot \beta_{gH}$, where $\beta_{gH} = \dfrac{Cov\left(\tilde{R}_g, \tilde{R}_H\right)}{\sigma_H^2}$. (7.20')

$E\left[\tilde{R}_{P'}\right] = a' \cdot E\left[\tilde{R}_1\right] + (1 - a') \cdot E\left[\tilde{R}_2\right] = R_{0H} + \left(E\left[\tilde{R}_H\right] - R_{0H}\right) \cdot \beta_{P'H} = R_{0H}$

where $\beta_{P'H} = 0 = a' \cdot \beta_{1H} + (1 - a') \cdot \beta_{2H}$,

and hence, $a' = \beta_{2H}/(\beta_{2H} - \beta_{1H}), 1 - a' = -\beta_{1H}/(\beta_{2H} - \beta_{1H})$. (7.21')

A question remains: In Fig. 7.12, is the market portfolio an efficient portfolio? The answer is yes. For example, if all n uncertain assets must be owned by one person, and this person prefers high expected rate of return and low variance of rate of return, then what this person owns is the market portfolio: $\tilde{R}_M = \sum_{i=1}^{n} \tilde{X}_i / \sum_{i=1}^{n} V_i = \sum_{i=1}^{n} [(\tilde{X}_i/V_i)(V_i/\sum_{i=1}^{n} V_i)] = \sum_{i=1}^{n} w_i \cdot \tilde{R}_i$. If as shown in Fig. 7.13, the market portfolio M is not an efficient portfolio, then because M is inferior to P, this person will move to P and P may not contain all n uncertain assets. Thus, Eq.'s (7.20) or (7.20') can be rewritten as:

$$E[\tilde{R}_i] = R_{ZM} + (E[\tilde{R}_M] - R_{ZM}) \cdot \frac{Cov(\tilde{R}_i, \tilde{R}_M)}{\sigma_M^2} \tag{7.22}$$

where R_{ZM} is equal to the expected rate of return of the zero-beta portfolio Z which has $Cov(\tilde{R}_Z, \tilde{R}_M) = 0$ or $\beta_{ZM} = Cov(\tilde{R}_Z, \tilde{R}_M)/\sigma_M^2 = 0$.

An Empirical Example of the Market Model

In practice, the market model suggested by Jensen (1968) is employed to evaluate the performance of mutual funds.[5] For a particular year,

$$Y_{it} = \widehat{a_i} + \widehat{b_i} X_t, \quad t = 1, 2, \ldots, 12. \tag{7.23}$$

where $Y_{it} = R_{it} - r_{ft}$, $X_t = R_{Mt} - r_{ft}$, $r_{ft} =$ (yearly rediscount rate)/12, R_{it} is the rate of return of the i-th stock at the t-th month, and R_{Mt} is the rate of return of the NYSE (or SSE) composite index at the tth month. The estimate $\widehat{a_i}$ is Jensen's alpha which measures whether the i-th stock outperforms (if $\widehat{a_i}$ is positively significant) or underperforms (if $\widehat{a_i}$ is negatively significant) the market. The estimate $\widehat{b_i}$ is a measurement of the beta of the i-th stock.

Tables 7.1 and 7.2 show the ordinary least squares (OLS) estimates of Jensen's alphas and betas of the ten largest capitalization US and Chinese firms in the NYSE and the SSE during 2018–2020. The US firms seem more volatile than the Chinese firms. This may be due to the price limit in the SSE and the governments' different policies toward their stock markets. Note that the beta in the CAPM is a single number used to measure the risk level of an asset. In Chap. 9, I will propose the p-index (which is constructed by put option) to measure the risk structure of an asset, i.e., the vector of risk levels for delivering different rates of return of an asset.

7.4 Some Alternative Models

In the CAPM, the market portfolio should contain *all* uncertain assets (including human capital) and should be mean–variance efficient. Stock index used in the market model (i.e., Eq. (7.23)) may not be appropriate. Hence, the test of the validity of the CAPM is a joint hypothesis test for the model and the mean–variance efficient market portfolio. Empirical studies show, however, that the returns on stocks with higher betas are systematically less than predicted by the CAPM, while those of stocks with lower betas are systematically higher. To evade the problem that the estimated risk-free interest rate is higher than the actual risk-free interest rate, the two-factor model (i.e., Eq. (7.22)) replaces the risk-free rate in the CAPM with the expected rate of return on a portfolio of stocks with zero beta. Some alternative models for estimating the expected rate of return of asset are as follows.

The Arbitrage Pricing Theory

The following are several theories of Linear Algebra regarding the arbitrage pricing theory (APT).[6]

[5] Jensen, Michael (1968) The performance of mutual funds in the period 1945–1964. *Journal of Finance* 23: 389–416.

[6] E.g., Lang, Serge (1987) *Linear Algebra*. Springer Nature, New York.

Table 7.1 Jensen's alpha and beta of the ten largest capitalization US firms in the NYSE (2018–2020)[a]

	2018		2019		2020	
	Alpha	Beta	Alpha	Beta	Alpha	Beta
Apple Inc. (AAPL)	−0.0106	0.5687	0.0239	1.6591	0.0423	1.1869
	(0.072)	(0.413)	(0.211)	(0.008)	(0.089)	(0.001)
Microsoft (MSFT)	0.0264	1.2694	0.0293	0.7974	0.0106	0.6817
	(0.006)	(0.000)	(0.026)	(0.030)	(0.519)	(0.003)
Exxon Mobil (XOM)	−0.0023	1.5039	−0.0237	1.2618	−0.0296	1.4266
	(0.855)	(0.000)	(0.008)	(0.000)	(0.083)	(0.000)
Amazon (AMZN)	0.0427	2.0204	−0.0026	1.4695	0.0455	0.7789
	(0.121)	(0.007)	(0.831)	(0.001)	(0.126)	(0.018)
JPMorgan Chase (JPM)	0.0014	1.0942	0.0103	1.0397	−0.0052	1.1991
	(0.894)	(0.001)	(0.465)	(0.022)	(0.622)	(0.000)
Johnson & Johnson (JNJ)	0.0051	0.9597	−0.0076	0.9768	−0.0047	0.6275
	(0.667)	(0.006)	(0.396)	(0.002)	(0.738)	(0.002)
Berkshire (BRKB)	0.0126	0.9922	−0.0093	0.8853	−0.0050	0.7743
	(0.183)	(0.001)	(0.421)	(0.017)	(0.673)	(0.000)
Meta (META)	−0.0181	0.6052	0.0122	2.2675	0.0168	1.1336
	(0.435)	(0.283)	(0.517)	(0.001)	(0.427)	(0.001)
General Electric (GE)	−0.0574	0.5532	−0.0013	2.6974	0.0084	0.9483
	(0.042)	(0.370)	(0.870)	(0.002)	(0.837)	(0.060)
Wells Fargo (WFC)	−0.0123	1.0166	−0.0012	1.0039	−0.0356	1.2879
	(0.500)	(0.036)	(0.910)	(0.007)	(0.130)	(0.000)
Equally-weighted Portfolio		1.0584		1.4058		1.0045

[a]The numbers in the parentheses are the two-sided p-values

Definition 1 A nonempty subset $S \subseteq \mathbb{R}^n$ is a subspace if S satisfies the following condition:

For any vectors u and v in S and any scalars α and β, we have $\alpha u + \beta v \in S$.

Definition 2 Given a subspace S of $\mathbb{R}^n$, the space of all vectors orthogonal to S is called the orthogonal complement of S.

Theorem *Let A be an $m \times n$ matrix. $S_1 = \{Au : u \in \mathbb{R}^n\}$ and $S_2 = \{y : A^T y = 0, y \in \mathbb{R}^m\}$ are orthogonal complements for each other. $S_3 = \{A^T v : v \in \mathbb{R}^m\}$ and $S_4 = \{z : Az = 0, z \in \mathbb{R}^n\}$ are orthogonal complements for each other.*

Table 7.2 Jensen's alpha and beta of the ten largest capitalization Chinese firms in the SSE (2018–2020)[a]

	2018		2019		2020	
	Alpha	Beta	Alpha	Beta	Alpha	Beta
SANY Heavy Industry	−0.1269	0.0254	0.0400	0.998	0.0476	1.1457
	(0.135)	(0.962)	(0.096)	(0.062)	(0.075)	(0.045)
China Merchants Bank	0.1222	1.7630	0.0170	0.831	0.0087	0.6825
	(0.045)	(0.001)	(0.282)	(0.027)	(0.579)	(0.056)
Hengrui Medicine	-0.0456	0.6637	0.028	0.980	0.0395	0.3029
	(0.696)	(0.395)	(0.324)	(0.120)	(0.221)	(0.641)
Kweichow Moutai	0.1124	1.6952	0.047	0.606	0.0369	1.0671
	(0.203)	(0.011)	(0.074)	(0.267)	(0.017)	(0.017)
LONGi Green Energy	0.0378	1.4360	0.008	1.294	0.1006	2.0032
	(0.841)	(0.264)	(0.832)	(0.038)	(0.046)	(0.054)
Industrial Bank	0.0355	1.1597	0.004	0.622	0.0023	0.7177
	(0.435)	(0.002)	(0.839)	(0.167)	(0.911)	(0.111)
Ping An Insurance	0.0594	1.3544	0.018	0.947	–0.0049	0.8591
	(0.216)	(0.001)	(0.323)	(0.031)	(0.773)	(0.031)
I&C Bank of China	0.0821	1.4648	0.001	0.314	-0.0086	0.2701
	(0.261)	(0.009)	(0.922)	(0.297)	(0.415)	(0.228)
Great Wall Motor	0.0286	1.4006	0.024	0.566	0.1237	1.9767
	(0.753)	(0.037)	(0.388)	(0.355)	(0.104)	(0.200)
China Construction Bank	0.1083	1.6575	0.005	0.341	-0.0074	0.3876
	(0.184)	(0.008)	(0.770)	(0.347)	(0.695)	(0.336)
Equally-weighted Portfolio		1.2620		0.749		0.9413

[a]The numbers in the parentheses are the two-sided p-values

Corollary *Let A be an* $m \times n$ *matrix. The equation* $Ax = b$ *is solvable if and only if* $b^T y = 0$ *whenever* $A^T y = 0$.

Ross (1976) directly applies the above corollary to propose the arbitrage pricing theory (APT)[7]:

Assume that there are n assets, and every asset has K risks. Let b_{ik} be the kth risk of the ith asset, where $k = 1, \ldots, K$ and $i = 1, \ldots, n$. Suppose that a zero-investment portfolio:

$$\sum\nolimits_{i=1}^{n} w_i = 0 \tag{7.24}$$

[7] Ross, Stephen (1976) The arbitrage theory of capital asset pricing. *Journal of Economic Theory* 13: 341-360.

is large enough (i.e., $n > K$) such that all risks b_{ik}'s can be diversified away:

$$\sum_{i=1}^{n} w_i b_{ik} = 0, \quad k = 1, \ldots, K. \tag{7.25}$$

Then, with no arbitrage, the expected rate of return of this portfolio should be equal to zero:

$$\sum_{i=1}^{n} w_i \cdot E\left[\tilde{R}_i\right] = 0. \tag{7.26}$$

In terms of the above corollary, Ross' Eq.'s (7.24)–(7.26) are stated as:

$$\underbrace{\left[E[\tilde{R}_1]E[\tilde{R}_2]\ldots E[\tilde{R}_n]\right]}_{b^T}\underbrace{\begin{bmatrix} w_1 \\ w_2 \\ . \\ . \\ w_n \end{bmatrix}}_{y} = 0$$

$$\text{whenever} \quad \underbrace{\begin{bmatrix} 1 & 1 & .. & 1 \\ b_{11} & b_{21} & .. & b_{n1} \\ b_{12} & b_{22} & .. & b_{n2} \\ . & . & .. & . \\ b_{1K} & b_{2K} & .. & b_{nK} \end{bmatrix}}_{A^T}\underbrace{\begin{bmatrix} w_1 \\ w_2 \\ . \\ . \\ w_n \end{bmatrix}}_{y} = \underbrace{\begin{bmatrix} 0 \\ 0 \\ . \\ . \\ 0 \end{bmatrix}}_{0}$$

if and only of

$$\underbrace{\begin{bmatrix} 1 & b_{11} & b_{12} & . & b_{1K} \\ 1 & b_{21} & b_{22} & . & b_{2K} \\ . & . & . & . & . \\ . & . & . & . & . \\ 1 & b_{n1} & b_{n2} & . & b_{nK} \end{bmatrix}}_{A}\underbrace{\begin{bmatrix} X_0 \\ X_1 \\ X_2 \\ . \\ X_K \end{bmatrix}}_{X} = \underbrace{\begin{bmatrix} E\left[\tilde{R}_1\right] \\ E\left[\tilde{R}_2\right] \\ . \\ . \\ E\left[\tilde{R}_n\right] \end{bmatrix}}_{b} \tag{7.27}$$

or $$E\left[\tilde{R}_i\right] = X_0 + X_1 b_{i1} + X_2 b_{i2} + \ldots + X_k b_{iK}, \quad i = 1, 2, \ldots, n. \tag{7.28}$$

Equation (7.28) is the arbitrage pricing theory (APT). Some may argue that the CAPM (i.e., Eq. (7.13)) is a special case of the APT if in Eq. (7.28), $K = 1$ and b_{i1} is beta. However, this claim is not true. These two models are completely different. The CAPM is a behavioral model under the mean–variance framework, i.e., it assumes that investors prefer high expected rate of return and low variance of rate of return. The APT, on the other hand, assumes that investors can diversify away (minimize) *all* kinds of risk but do not know what they are. This is the problem with the APT: *You cannot minimize (or optimize) something that you do not know.* Also, the vector $(X_0, X_1, \ldots, X_K)$ in Eq. (7.27) may not be unique unless the $K + 1$ column vectors of matrix A are linearly independent.

The Three-Factor Model

Fama and French's (1993) three-factor model is:

$$E\left[\tilde{R}_i\right] - r_f = \beta_{iM} \cdot \left(E\left[\tilde{R}_M\right] - r_f\right) + \beta_{iS} \cdot E\left[\tilde{r}_{SMB}\right] + \beta_{iH} \cdot E\left[\tilde{r}_{HML}\right]. \quad (7.29)$$

The excess rate of return $(E\left[\tilde{R}_i\right] - r_f)$ is explained by three factors: (i) the excess return on the market portfolio $(E\left[\tilde{R}_M\right] - r_f)$; (ii) the difference between the return on a portfolio of small firm stocks and the return on a portfolio of large firm stocks $(E[\tilde{r}_{SMB}])$; and (iii) the difference between the return on a portfolio of high-book-to-market stocks and the return on a portfolio of low-book-to-market stocks $(E[\tilde{r}_{HML}])$.[8] The impact of firm's size, i.e., $E[\tilde{r}_{SMB}]$, may include large firm's economies of scale and better network, and small firm's agility, flexibility and less bureaucracy. The influence of firm's book-to-market ratio, i.e., $E[\tilde{r}_{HML}]$, may include finding undervalued stocks and showing investors' expectations about growth stocks. These two independent variables in Eq. (7.29) indicate that the capital market may not be very efficient, and investors can earn excess profits by finding market anomalies.[9] The model however may be criticized by some as "the exercise amounts to data mining".

Summary and Conclusions

- Expected utility function (or the von Neumann-Morgenstern utility function) assumes that there exists a real-value function which can represent peoples' behavior under uncertainty. It finds that concave utility function means risk-averse, convex utility function, risk-love, and linear utility function, risk-neutral.
- The mean–variance portfolio analysis assumes that investors prefer high expected rate of return and low variance of rate of return. An efficient portfolio is defined as: the maximum expected rate of return for a given variance of rate of return. A minimum variance portfolio is defined as: the minimum variance of rate of return for a given expected rate of return.

[8] Fama, Eugene and Kenneth French (1993) Common risk factors in the returns on stocks and bonds. *Journal of Financial Economics* 33: 3–56.

[9] Fama's weak form efficiency refers to a market where share prices fully and fairly reflect all past information. Semi-strong form efficiency emphasizes that public information is already incorporated in a stock's current price, investors cannot utilize either technical or fundamental analysis to make excess profits. Strong form efficiency claims that all public and non-public information is already completely accounted for in current stock prices, and no type of information can give an investor an advantage in the market.

- The market value of a portfolio is the summation of the market value of the assets it contains, i.e., adding up or reorganizing assets do not create value. This is *financial diversification irrelevancy*.
- Under the framework of the mean–variance portfolio analysis, when the number of assets in a portfolio increases, the individual asset's variance of rate of return will disappear (hence, it is not risk), but the covariances of assets' rates of return will remain (hence, it is accounted as risk).
- The capital asset pricing model (CAPM) assumes: (i) mean–variance framework; (ii) complete agreement or homogeneous expectation; (iii) existence of a risk-free (certain payoff) asset; (iv) no transaction costs. The CAPM is a linear function of beta. Higher beta means higher risk and higher opportunity cost of capital, i.e., higher discount/reinvestment rate, for the asset's future cash flows.
- The two-factor model which is similar to the CAPM does not need the existence of a risk-free asset but needs short-selling.
- The arbitrage pricing theory (APT) assumes that all risks can be diversified away but investors do not know what they are.

Problems

1. Are the assumptions of the capital asset pricing model (CAPM) different from those of the arbitrage theory (APT)?
2. When a petrochemical company acquires a retail company, how to calculate the beta of this acquisition?
3. Explain why the market portfolio of the CAPM and the market portfolio of the two-factor model are efficient portfolios.
4. If an asset pricing model can correctly predict future stock prices, what will the capital market equilibrium be?
5. Explain the differences between the three-factor model and the CAPM?

References

Dempsey, M. (2013). The capital asset pricing model (CAPM): The history of a failed revolutionary idea in finance? *Abacus, 49*, 7–23.

Fernandez, P. (2015). CAPM: An absurd model. *Business Valuation Review, 34*, 4–23.

Lintner, J. (1965). The valuation of risky assets and the selection of risky investments in stock portfolios and capital budgets. *Review of Economics and Statistics, 47*, 3–37.

Markowitz, H. (1952). Portfolio selection. *Journal of Finance, 7*, 77–91.

Sharpe, W. (1964). Capital asset prices: A theory of market equilibrium under conditions of risk. *Journal of Finance, 19*, 425–442.

Capital Structure in a Perfect Market

8

In their famous and influential article in 1958, Modigliani and Miller present two propositions: First, the market value of any firm is independent of its capital structure, and second, the expected rate of return on the equity of the levered firm increases in proportion to the debt-equity ratio. It is now well-accepted in the literature that the Modigliani–Miller first proposition hinges on the assumption that "individuals and corporations can borrow at the same rate" (Modigliani & Miller, 1963, p. 437), and the Modigliani–Miller second proposition holds because the equityholders of the levered firm require "a (risk) premium related to financial risk equal to the debt-to-equity ratio times the spread between the expected rate of return on the firm's total assets and the expected rate of return on the debt" (Modigliani & Miller, 1958, p. 271). In this chapter, Sect. 8.1 shows that the Modigliani–Miller first proposition is an example of financial diversification irrelevancy, which can hold in an economy where there is no capital market for lending and borrowing, and there is no need to assume that individuals and corporations can borrow at the same rate. Section 8.2 discusses some fallacious arguments for the Modigliani–Miller second proposition.

8.1 The Modigliani–Miller First Proposition: Capital Structure Irrelevancy

Imagine in a barter economy, there is a group of primitive people, and two cows (firms) eat the same food (costs) and produce identical quantities and quality of milk (cash inflows). One cow is owned by person A (the sole owner/equityholder). Another cow is "owned" by two persons, B and C. If it is possible, person B can have a certain amount of the milk (the debtholder), and person C takes the rest (the equityholder). Suppose all the people (i.e., the market) think that the cow owned by persons B and C (the levered firm) is more valuable than the cow owned by person A (the unlevered firm), say, persons B and C's cow can exchange for six

K.-P. Chang, *Corporate Finance: A Systematic Approach*, Springer Texts in Business and Economics, https://doi.org/10.1007/978-981-19-9119-6_8

sheep, and person A's cow can exchange for only five sheep. Then persons B and C can sell their cow for six sheep and buy person A's cow with five sheep. Now, persons B and C own a cow that produces the same quantities and quality of milk and one more sheep. Of course, in equilibrium, the market value of the two cows must be the same (i.e., person A will increase the price of his cow until the prices of the two cows are equal).[1] This simple tale shows that the market value of the firm is independent of its capital structure (i.e., the Modigliani–Miller first proposition), and there is no need to assume that individuals and corporations can borrow at the same rate.[2]

The above proof implicitly assumes that the two cows (firms) operate in a perfect market, i.e., a frictionless world (i.e., a world with zero transaction cost: perfect information, no taxes, no bankruptcy costs, and no agency costs). Suppose in a frictionless world two firms generate exactly the same perpetual stream of cash flow, $\tilde{X}$, and differ only in their capital structure. If the market value of the levered firm, V_L, is greater than that of the unlevered firm, V_U, then the investors of the levered firm can simply sell their firm for V_L and buy the unlevered firm with V_U (hence, there is no need to short sell). The investors of the levered firm thus obtain net profits: $\Delta V \equiv V_L - V_U > 0$ and the same cash flow $\tilde{X}$ as before. In equilibrium, V_L must be equal to V_U. Conversely, if $V_U > V_L$, we can use the same argument to reach the conclusion that in equilibrium $V_U = V_L$.

The Modigliani–Miller first proposition is simple and straightforward. Imagine that you own both equity and debt of a firm, e.g., debt on the left hand and equity on the right hand. If the maximum certain amount of the firm's cash flow $\tilde{X}$ paid to your left hand increases, then the market value of the debt must increase, and the market value of the equity will decrease (because the rest of $\tilde{X}$ paid to your right hand becomes smaller). However, you still get the same whole cash flow $\tilde{X}$ no matter how debt and equity change, and the market value of the firm

---

[1] A middleman (person D) can also do the arbitrage and get one sheep: Find a person (E) who is willing to pay six sheep for B and C's cow, and buy A's cow with five sheep for B and C, and then do the exchanges among A, B & C, and E simultaneously.

[2] Modigliani and Miller (1958) use the following method to prove their first proposition. Consider two firms generate the same perpetual stream of cash flow, $\tilde{X}$, in each year and differ only in their capital structure. The market value of the unlevered firm is V_U. The market value of the levered firm is $V_L \equiv S_L + B$, where S_L is the market value of equity, and B is the market value of riskless debt. A strategy an investor can take is to buy 15% of the shares of the levered firm. That is, he invests $0.15S_L$ in the beginning and at the end of each year obtains payoffs $0.15(\tilde{X} - Interest)$. Another strategy is to buy 15% of the shares of the unlevered firm, and also borrow $0.15B$ from a bank on his own account on the same terms as the firm. That is, the investor invests $0.15(V_U - B)$ in the beginning and at the end of each year obtains payoffs $0.15(\tilde{X} - Interest)$. Since both the strategies produce exactly the same results: $0.15(\tilde{X} - Interest)$, the initial costs of the two strategies must be the same, i.e., $0.15S_L = 0.15(V_U - B)$ or $V_U = V_L \equiv S_L + B$. This kind of proof hinges on the assumption that individuals and corporations can borrow at the same rate.

will not change. This shows that Modigliani–Miller's capital structure irrelevancy proposition is also an example of financial diversification irrelevancy.[3]

8.2 The Modigliani–Miller Second Proposition: Debt/Equity Ratio, Return, and Risk to Equityholder

The Modigliani–Miller first proposition holds for any firm in any market structure (e.g., monopoly or perfect competition), and the equityholders' and debtholders' attitudes toward risk is irrelevant. The cash flow of the levered firm belongs to and is distributed to the debtholders and equityholders. That is,

$$\tilde{X} \equiv \tilde{X}_B + \tilde{X}_S$$

or

$$E(\tilde{X}) \equiv E(\tilde{X}_B) + E(\tilde{X}_S) \tag{8.1}$$

where $\tilde{X}_B$ is the cash flow for debtholders, and$\tilde{X}_S$, the cash flow for equityholders. Note that Eq. (8.1) is equality by definition. Denote $V_L \equiv S_L + B, E(\tilde{X}) \equiv E(\tilde{r}_{WACC})(S_L + B)$, $E\left(\tilde{X}_B\right) \equiv E(\tilde{r}_B) \cdot B$ and $E\left(\tilde{X}_S\right) \equiv E(\tilde{r}_S) \cdot S_L$, where S_L is the market value of the equity; B, the market value of the debt; $E(\tilde{r}_{WACC})$, the weighted average cost of capital (WACC) on the levered firm's assets; $E(\tilde{r}_B)$, the expected rate of return on the debt; and$E(\tilde{r}_S)$, the expected rate of return on the equity. Equation (8.1) can be rewritten as:

$$E(\tilde{r}_{WACC})(S_L + B) \equiv E(\tilde{r}_B) \cdot B + E(\tilde{r}_S) \cdot S_L, \tag{8.2}$$

or

$$E(\tilde{r}_S) = E(\tilde{r}_{WACC}) + (B/S_L)[E(\tilde{r}_{WACC}) - E(\tilde{r}_B)]. \tag{8.3}$$

The expected cash flow of the firm $E(\tilde{X})$ is assumed to be independent of the debt-equity ratio (B/S_L). From the Modigliani–Miller first proposition, we know that the levered firm's value V_L is independent of the debt-equity ratio. Hence, $E(\tilde{r}_{WACC})$ must be independent of the firm's debt-equity ratio. Modigliani Miller (1958) derive their second proposition from Eq. (8.3): As long as $E(\tilde{r}_{WACC})$ is greater than $E(\tilde{r}_B)$, ***increasing the firm's debt-equity ratio increases its the cost of equity***. This indicates that the existence of the Modigliani–Miller second proposition needs two basic assumptions: (i) the existence of the Modigliani–Miller first proposition; and (ii) $E(\tilde{r}_{WACC}) > E(\tilde{r}_B)$.

[3] In Chap. 9, I will show that the Modigliani–Miller capital structure irrelevancy proposition is a corollary of the put-call parity.

Table 8.1 Outcomes under alternative capital structures

	No debt			With debt		
	Recession	Expected	Expansion	Recession	Expected	Expansion
Rate of return on assets	5%	15%	25%	5%	15%	25%
Earnings before interest	$400	$1,200	$2,000	$400	$1,200	$2,000
Interest	0	0	0	$400	$400	$400
Earnings after interest	$400	$1,200	$2,000	0	$800	$1,600
Rate of return on equity	5%	15%	25%	0%	20%	40%

Some fallacious arguments for the Modigliani–Miller second proposition

In the finance literature, there are three fallacious arguments for the Modigliani–Miller second proposition:

(i) Increasing debt means higher financial risk, and hence, higher expected rate of return on equity.

The following example can be used to illustrate this argument. A totally equity-financed firm's assets are \$8,000. The firm is considering issuing riskless debt to buy half of the equity, i.e., \$4,000. The annual risk-free interest rate is 10%. There are two states of nature: economic expansion and recession, and each state of nature has probability 0.5. The outcomes under alternative capital structures are shown in Table 8.1.

From Eq. (8.3), the expected rate of return on the equity after introducing debt can be calculated as: $20\% = 15\% + \left(\frac{\$4,000}{\$4,000}\right)(15\% - 10\%)$. That is, increasing debt makes the expected rate of return on the equity increase from 15% to 20%. Based on this kind of analysis, it is argued in the corporate finance literature that "the use of debt rather than equity funds to finance a given venture may well increase the expected return to the owners, but only at the cost of increased dispersion of the outcomes" (Modigliani & Miller, 1958, p. 262); "any gains from using more of what might seem to be cheaper debt capital would thus be offset by correspondingly higher cost of the now riskier equity capital" (Miller, 1988, p. 100).[4]

[4] Equation (8.3) can be written as:

$$\tilde{r}_S = \tilde{r}_{WACC} + \left(\frac{B}{S_L}\right)(\tilde{r}_{WACC} - \tilde{r}_B) = \left(1 + \frac{B}{S_L}\right) \cdot \tilde{r}_{WACC} - \left(\frac{B}{S_L}\right) \cdot \tilde{r}_B,$$

where $\tilde{r}_{WACC} = \tilde{X} / (S_L + B)$. Suppose debt is riskless, i.e., $\tilde{r}_B \equiv r$. Then the variance of the rate of return on equity is:

$$Var(\tilde{r}_S) = \left(1 + \frac{B}{S_L}\right)^2 \cdot Var(\tilde{r}_{WACC}).$$

Unfortunately, these claims are not true. As shown in Chap. 7, even in the risk-averse mean–variance world, for any perfectly diversified portfolio it is the covariance and not the variance (or the dispersion) of rate of return termed as the measure for risk. The increase in the variance of rate of return on equity has little impact on the increase of cost of equity.[5]

(ii) From the capital asset pricing model (CAPM), it is found that higher debt means higher beta of equity and, hence, higher expected rate of return on equity.

Suppose the CAPM holds. The expected rates of return on debt and equity can be written as:

$$E\left[\tilde{r}_S\right] = R_f + \left(E\left[\tilde{R}_M\right] - R_f\right) \cdot \beta_S \tag{8.4}$$

$$E\left[\tilde{r}_B\right] = R_f + \left(E\left[\tilde{R}_M\right] - R_f\right) \cdot \beta_B \tag{8.5}$$

Multiply both sides of Eq. (8.4) by S_L, and multiply both sides of Eq. (8.5) by B, and then add them up:

$$\begin{aligned} E\left[\tilde{r}_{WACC}\right] \cdot (S_L + B) &\equiv E\left[\tilde{r}_S\right] \cdot S_L + E\left[\tilde{r}_B\right] \cdot B \\ &= R_f(S_L + B) + \left(E\left[\tilde{R}_M\right] - R_f\right) \cdot (\beta_S S_L + \beta_B B), \end{aligned}$$

or

$$E\left[\tilde{r}_{WACC}\right] = R_f + \left(E\left[\tilde{R}_M\right] - R_f\right) \cdot \left(\beta_S \frac{S_L}{S_L + B} + \beta_B \frac{B}{S_L + B}\right). \tag{8.6}$$

Let

$$\beta_{WACC} = \beta_S \cdot \frac{S_L}{S_L + B} + \beta_B \cdot \frac{B}{S_L + B},$$

then

$$\beta_S = \beta_{WACC} + \left(\frac{B}{S_L}\right) \cdot (\beta_{WACC} - \beta_B). \tag{8.7}$$

Hamada (1969) and others argue that when the Modigliani–Miller first proposition holds, the changes in debt-equity ratio (B/S_L) will not affect

Since the Modigliani–Miller first proposition holds, changes in the debt-equity ratio (B/S_L) will not affect the firm's value ($V_U = V_L = S_L + B$), and the probability density function of $\tilde{r}_{WACC}$ (and $Var(\tilde{r}_{WACC})$) do not change. Thus, when the debt-equity ratio increases, the variance of the rate of return on equity will also increase.

[5] Proposition 9.2 (Capital Structure Irrelevancy Proposition II) of Chapter 9 refutes the Modigliani–Miller second proposition.

the value of $E[\tilde{r}_{WACC}]$ (where $E[\tilde{r}_{WACC}] \equiv E[\tilde{X}]/(S_L + B)$) or the value of β_{WACC} (from Eq. (8.6)). If the debt is riskless (i.e., $\beta_B = 0$), then from Eq. (8.7), it is found that increasing debt-equity ratio (B/S_L) will increase the beta of equity (β_S), and hence, the expected rate of return on equity $E[\tilde{r}_S]$ of Eq. (8.4) will increase.

The above proof is a tautology. If we want to conclude from Eq. (8.7) that increasing debt-equity ratio (B/S_L) increases the beta of equity (β_S), we will have to assume that β_{WACC} is greater than β_B. But assuming that β_{WACC} is greater than β_B is equivalent to assuming that $E[\tilde{r}_{WACC}]$ of Eq. (8.6) is greater than $E[\tilde{r}_B]$ of Eq. (8.5). From Eq. (8.3), we already know that if the Modigliani–Miller first proposition holds and if $E[\tilde{r}_{WACC}]$ is greater than $E[\tilde{r}_B]$, increasing debt-equity ratio will increase the cost of equity, and whether the CAPM or any other asset pricing models hold is irrelevant.

(iii) "Stockholders do receive more earnings per dollar invested, but they also bear more risk, because they have given lenders first claim on the firm's assets and operating income" (Myers, 1984, p. 94).

This is incorrect since, as shown in the story of Robin Hood in Chap. 2, debtholders' so-called first claim will not affect equityholders' wealth (or welfare). For example, in Table 8.1, if the firm asks equityholders to withdraw \$4,000 from the firm and replaces that part of equity with debt, the equityholders can (with 10% riskless rate of return) invest this \$4,000 into the money market and/or to buy the bonds issued by the firm (if they cannot do this, there will be no change in the capital structure). The equityholders can still obtain the same stream of the cash flow and 15% expected rate of return as they do in the totally equity-financed case. We can also think in this way: Even before changing the firm's capital structure, half of the equityholders' investment (i.e., \$4,000) is already paid 20% expected rate of return, and the other half (\$4,000), 10% certain rate of return. It is not the so-called first claim of the debtholders that makes the equityholders have 20% expected rate of return on \$4,000 equity.

The False Proof of the Modigliani–Miller Second Proposition

Note that the example (or the similar ones) in Table 8.1 has been widely used in explaining why increasing debt-equity ratio will increase the expected rate of return on equity. But this example (i.e., Table 8.1) is wrong. To see this let us rewrite Table 8.1's continuous-time example as a one-period binomial example:

It shows that Table 8.1 assumes all the five variables: risk-free interest rate $r =$ 10%; current spot price $S_0 = \$8,000$; future possible prices: $S_0u = \$10,000$ and $S_0d = \$8,400$; and their respective probabilities: $\pi = 0.5$ and $1 - \pi = 0.5$. This is erroneous because an asset's current price (e.g., $S_0 = \$8,000$) is determined by people's expectation of the asset's future possible payoffs and their probabilities, i.e., in Fig. 8.1, among the five variables: π, S_0, S_0u, S_0d, and r, only four of them can be freely assumed (i.e., the degree of freedom is only four, not five).

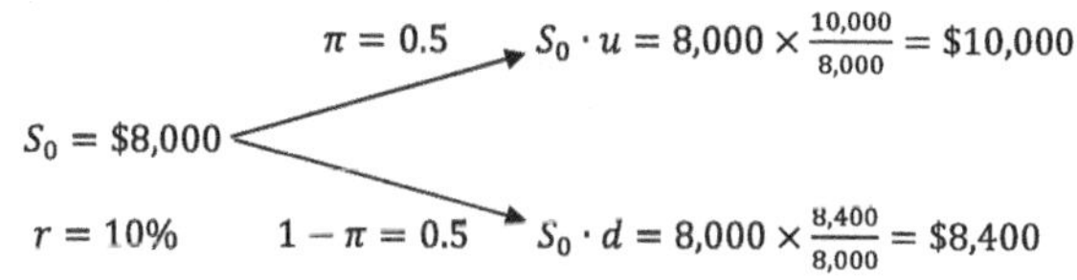

Fig. 8.1 An erroneous binomial model

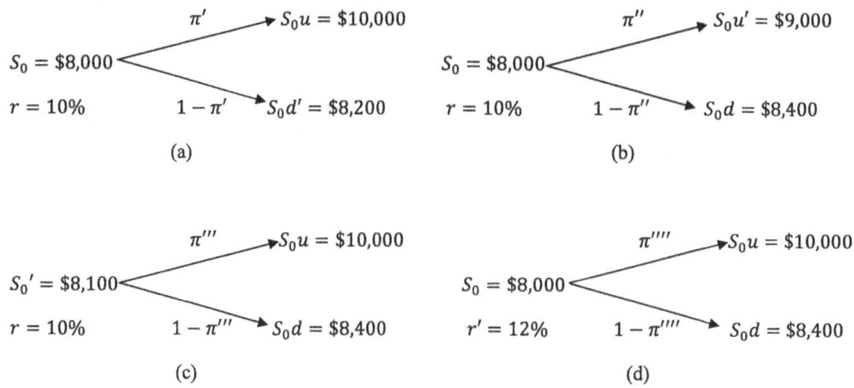

Fig. 8.2 Changes of probabilities

Suppose that in Fig. 8.1, except π, one of the four variables: r, S_0, S_0u, S_0d changes:

Then, in Fig. 8.2,

Case (a): π' must be greater than π of Fig. 8.1. This is because when S_0u and r remain the same, and $S_0d = \$8,400$ decreases to $S_0d' = \$8,200$, the current asset price S_0 can remain the same only when investors (the market) believe the probability of the up move S_0u is higher than before.

Case (b): π'' must be greater than π of Fig. 8.1 because when S_0d and r remain the same, and $S_0u = \$10,000$ decreases to $S_0u' = \$9,000$, the current asset price S_0 can remain the same only when investors (the market) believe the probability of the up move S_0u' is higher than before.

Case (c): π''' must be greater than π of Fig. 8.1 because whenS_0u, S_0d, and r remain the same, the current asset price S_0 can increases from $\$8,000$ to $\$8,100$ only when investors (the market) believe the probability of the up move S_0u is higher than before.

Case (d): π'''' must be greater than π of Fig. 8.1. This is because when S_0u and S_0d remain the same, and r increases from 10 to 12%, the current asset price S_0 can remain the same only when investors (the market) believe the probability of the up move S_0u is higher than before.

These results show that we cannot freely give any real number to *all* the five variables: π, r, S_0, S_0u, S_0d in Fig. 8.1, i.e., the degree of freedom is four, not five. In Chap. 9, I will use the Gordan Theory and Fig. 8.2 to prove that

Fig. 8.1 (Table 8.1) is erroneous, and the Modigliani–Miller second proposition is incorrect.

Summary and Conclusions

- The Modigliani–Miller first proposition (the market value of the firm is independent of the firm's capital structure) is an example of financial diversification irrelevancy, which can hold in an economy where there is no capital market for lending and borrowing, and there is no need to assume that individuals and corporations can borrow at the same rate. Also, the Modigliani–Miller first proposition holds regardless of investors' attitudes toward risk.
- Neither financial risk (which is termed as the additional risk placed on the equityholders when debt financing is used) nor the CAPM's beta nor the so-called first claim of debtholders can explain the Modigliani–Miller second proposition (increasing the firm's debt-equity ratio increases its the cost of equity).

Problems

1. Can you give an example of first claim and residual claim in a corporation?
2. The Modigliani–Miller first proposition is about the irrelevancy of using equity or debt to finance a firm. Can this irrelevancy proposition also hold in the case of using equity, senior and junior debts, or convertible bond to finance a firm?
3. Some scholars argue that under certainty, in a perfect market, production decision is independent of financing decision. True or false?
4. In 'a tale of two cows', what assumptions do we need?
5. In Sect. 2.4 of Chap. 2, we have shown that under certainty, the Modigliani–Miller second proposition does not hold. Under uncertainty, can the Modigliani–Miller second proposition hold?

References

Chang, K.-P. (2015). *The ownership of the firm, corporate finance, and derivatives: Some critical thinking*. Springer Nature.

Chang, K.-P. (2016). The Modigliani-Miller second proposition is dead; long live the second proposition. *Ekonomicko-manažerské Spektrum, 10*, 24–31. http://ssrn.com/abstract=2762158.

Hamada, R. S. (1969). Portfolio analysis, market equilibrium and corporation finance. *Journal of Finance, 24*, 13–31.

Miller, M. (1988). The Modigliani-Miller propositions: After thirty years. *Journal of Economic Perspectives, 2*, 99–120.

Modigliani, F., & Miller, M. (1963). Corporate income taxes and the cost of capital: A correction. *American Economic Review, 53*, 433–443.

Modigliani, F., & Miller, M. (1958). The cost of capital, corporation finance and the theory of investment. *American Economics Review, 48*, 261–297.

Myers, S. (1984). The search for optimal capital structure. *Midland Corporate Finance Journal, 1*, 6-16; also in Stern, J. M., & Chew, D.H. Jr. (Ed.) (1986). *The revolution in corporate finance* (pp. 91-99). Basil Blackwell.

Derivatives and Corporate Finance

9

This chapter discusses how forward and futures contracts and options are related to corporate finance. Section 9.1 shows that spot and forward prices in the forward contract contain the same information about investors' expectations. Section 9.2 introduces model-free and binomial option Greeks and their implications for corporate finance. A new capital structure irrelevancy proposition is introduced in Sect. 9.3. Section 9.4 shows the net present value (NPV) analysis under uncertainty. Section 9.5 suggests the p-index for analyzing risk structures of call option (equity), put option, debt, equity, and asset (firm).

9.1 Forward and Futures Contracts: Expectation Matters

Futures contracts and forward contracts are obligations to buy or sell an asset at a specific price at a specified date in the future. A forward contract is a private and customizable agreement that settles at the end of the contract. A futures contract has standardized terms and is traded on an exchange, where prices are settled on a daily basis until the end of the contract. The following is an example of forward contract.

Suppose that with no default, a buyer (i.e., with a long position) enters into a 6-month forward contract with a seller (i.e., with a short position) on a non-dividend-paying IBM stock when the stock's current spot price is: $S_0 = \$100$ and the simple risk-free interest rate is 10% per annum. What will the forward price of this IBM stock (F) be?

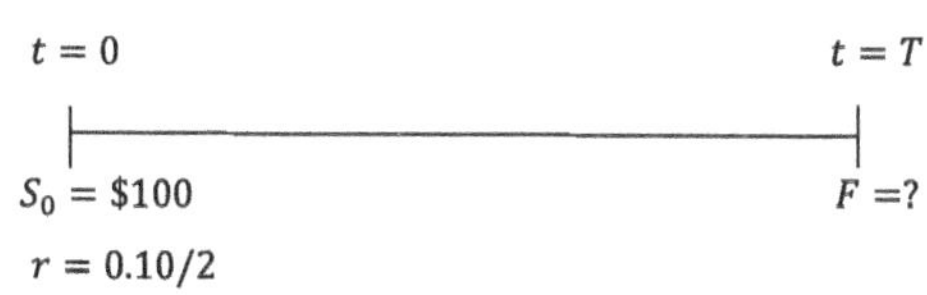

K.-P. Chang, *Corporate Finance: A Systematic Approach*, Springer Texts in Business and Economics, https://doi.org/10.1007/978-981-19-9119-6_9

The seller of course wants the forward price as high as possible, and the lowest price (the opportunity cost) she asks is: $105 = 100(1 + 10\%/2)$. That is, from the point view of the seller, the forward price (F) should be: $F \geq \$100(1 + 5\%)$. However, the forward price of the IBM stock cannot be more than \$105. This is because if at $t = 0$, the seller wants a higher forward price, say, $F = \$106$, the buyer can just take \$100 out of her bank account to buy one share of IBM stock from the spot market and keeps the IBM stock for six months. With no default, take \$100 from your saving account to buy an IBM stock now ($t = 0$) is equivalent to take \$105 out from your saving account to buy an IBM stock after six months ($t = T$). Thus, we have:

$$F = (1 + r)S_0 \tag{9.1}$$

Both the spot price (S_0) and the forward price (F) are not random variables. The spot price is determined by people's expectations about the asset's future possible prices and their probabilities. Just like a deposit in a bank, once the spot price (the deposit at $t = 0$) and the risk-free interest rate are determined, the forward price (the bank's payment at $t = T$) will be determined. Thus, the spot price and the forward price should contain exactly the same information about the market's expectations of the asset's future possible prices and their probabilities, i.e., expectation matters. It is probably meaningless to say that one of them is a leading indicator of the other.

The forward contract example can be used to explain that there is no such thing as the seniority between debt and equity. Assume that at $t = 0$, investor A invests \$200 and investor B invests \$200 to buy a mountain, and at $t = 1$, the mountain will be sold. In this case, the two investors are like two equityholders and at $t = 1$ each one will receive 50% of market value of the mountain. Now, suppose that investor B, with investor A's consent, wants to receive a fixed payment, say, \$250, at $t = 1$. Then, *de jure*, according to the corporate law, investor B is like a debtholder who has the first claim over investor A, the equityholder. The equityholder is thus termed as the residual claimant who bears so-called 'residual risk'.[1]

There are two ways to show that the claim of debt's being senior to equity is de facto not true[2]:

(i) Equity and debt of the firm are like long position (i.e., buyer) and short position (i.e., seller) of a forward contract. At $t = 0$, the equityholder pays \$200 to become the buyer of the forward contract, and the debtholder pays \$200 to become the seller of the forward contract. At $t = 1$, the

[1] E.g., Fama and Jensen (1983, p. 328) argue that "the residual risk—the risk of the difference between stochastic inflows of resources and promised payments to agents—is borne by those who contract for the rights to net cash flows. We call these agents the residual claimants or residual risk bearers".

[2] See also the Robin Hood story in Chap. 2.

debtholder will have a stock from the firm and be obligated to sell it to the equityholder for: $Min[\$250, \text{the market value of the firm}]$, and the equityholder will have the market value of the firm and be obligated to pay: $Min[\$250, \text{the market value of the firm}]$ to buy the stock. In this forward contract, the debtholder is willing to sacrifice the chance of obtaining more than \$250 at the good time in order to avoid the possibility of getting less than \$250 at the bad time. The equityholder, on the other hand, is willing to take the chance (the risk) of getting less than \$250 at the bad time in order to have the opportunity of obtaining more than \$250 at the good time. Just as in any forward contract where there is no first claim and no party is going to compensate another party for bearing any sort of risk, debtholder will not compensate equityholder to have the so-called first claim or seniority.

(ii) There is a "two-step contract" (rather than "seniority") between the equityholder and the debtholder. At $t = 1$, first, split the value of the mountain equally between the equityholder and debtholder; and second, if the debtholder's 50% share is more than \$250 (the upper bound), she will give out any additional money to the equityholder; and if the debtholder's 50% share is less than \$250, the equityholder will use her 50% share to compensate the debtholder until the equityholder's share becomes zero, or the debtholder gets \$250.

9.2 Put-Call Parity, Option Greeks, and Corporate Finance

Unlike forward and futures contracts, options are rights and not obligations. Options also have a limited life time (e.g., from $t = 0$ to $t = T$). A call option gives the holder the right to buy the underlying asset for the strike (exercised) price K by the date T. A put option gives the holder the right to sell the underlying asset for the price K by the date T. The owners of American call or put options can exercise the options any time between $t = 0$ and $t = T$. The owners of European call or put options can exercise the options only at $t = T$ and obtain payoffs: $Max[S_T - K, 0]$ for a European call option, and $Max[K - S_T, 0]$ for a European put option, where S_T is the price of the underlying asset.

At $t = 0$, the price of a European call option is nonnegative: $c \geq 0$, and $c > 0$ if and only if people believe that at $t = T$, it is possible (i.e., there is a positive probability) to have $Max[S_T - K, 0] > 0$. Similarly, at $t = 0$, the price of a European put option is $p \geq 0$, and $p > 0$ if and only if people believe that at $t = T$, it is possible to have $Max[K - S_T, 0] > 0$. If $K = 0$, all options do not exist. At $t = 0$, the price of an asset (again, a right and not an obligation) is: $S_0 \geq 0$. Notice that $S_0 = 0$ if and only if people believe $S_t = 0,\ \forall t > 0$. Since $S_t = 0,\ \forall t > 0$, is not a random variable, all options do not exist.

It can be shown that an American call option on a non-dividend paying stock will never be exercised prior to expiration, and hence, an American call option on a non-dividend paying stock must have the same value as its European counterpart. For example, suppose that in the beginning ($t = 0$), you bought a 3-month American call option with the strike price $K = \$102$ on a non-dividend-paying IBM stock. Suppose now, after one month ($t = 1$), the IBM stock's price becomes: $S_1 = \$105$, and would you exercise the American call to gain \$3 (= 105 − 102)?

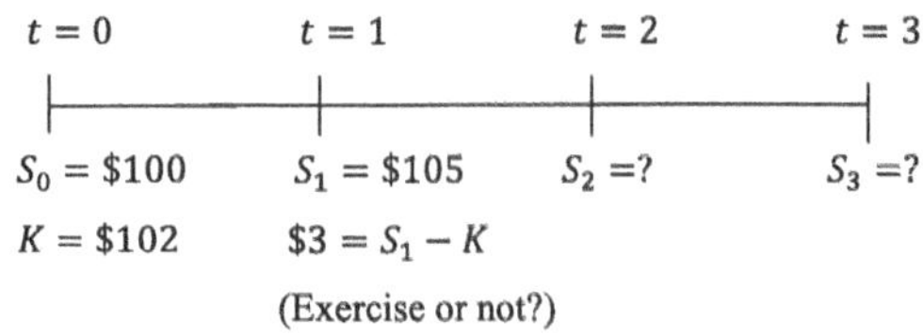

The answer is definitely no. This is because at $t = 1$:

(i) If you exercise or sell the American call to the market, it means that you don't believe the IBM stock price will be more than \$105 in the next two months, i.e., between $t = 1$ and $t = 3$.
(ii) If you sell this American call to the market, then its market price must be greater than \$3. If not, i.e., the market price of the American call is less or equal to \$3, then it means that no one, including you, believes that the IBM stock price will be more than \$105 in the next two months. If no one believes the IBM stock price will be more than \$105 in the next two months, then the current stock price S_1 cannot be \$105, i.e., S_1 must be less than \$105.[3]

In summary, even if on the day before $t = S_3$, the market price of the stock is higher than the strike price $K = \$102$, it is better to sell the American call to gain more than to exercise it.

Put-Call Parity

Suppose that one European call option and one European put option are related to the same one-unit underlying asset, and have the same expiration date T and the same strike price K. Consider two portfolios at $t = 0$:

Portfolio A: one European call option c with strike price K, and cash $\frac{K}{1+r}$ deposited in a bank;
Portfolio B: one European put option p with strike price K, and one unit of the underlying asset S_0.

[3] This is an example of 'expectation matters', i.e., *our expectations for the future will determine our current behavior.*

On the expiration date $t = T$, both portfolios give exactly the same payoff: $Max[S_T, K]$. Thus, the costs of the two portfolios at $t = 0$ must be the same, i.e., the put-call parity:

$$c + \frac{K}{1+r} = S_0 + p \tag{9.2}$$

where r is the simple risk-free interest rate. Note that when $r = 0$, the two portfolios at $t = 0$ are:

Portfolio A: one European call option c with strike price K, and cash K deposited in a bank;
Portfolio B: one European put option p with strike price K, and one unit of the underlying asset S_0.

and at $t = T$, their payoffs are still the same: $Max[S_T, K]$, i.e., the put-call parity:

$$c + K = S_0 + p. \tag{9.3}$$

Capital Structure of the Firm
Rearrange Eq. (9.2): At $t = 0$

$$S_0 = c + \left(\frac{K}{1+r} - p\right), \tag{9.4}$$

where S_0 can be interpreted as the market value of the levered firm; c as the equity of the firm, $\left(\frac{K}{1+r} - p\right)$ as the risky debt of the firm; and p as the insurance to insure the promised payment K to debtholders. This shows that at $t = 0$, the risky debt is equivalent to a portfolio organized by:

(a) deposit $\frac{K}{1+r}$ in a bank; and (b) issue and sell the put option (insurance) p to the market.

At $t = T$,

(i) if $S_T < K$, the equityholders gain: $0 = Max[S_T - K, 0]$, the debtholders gain: $S_T = Min[K, S_T] = K - Max[K - S_T, 0]$, and the owner of the put p obtains: $K - S_T = Max[K - S_T, 0] > 0$;
(ii) if $S_T = K$, the equityholders gain: $0 = Max[S_T - K, 0]$, the debtholders gain: $K = S_T = Min[K, S_T] = K - Max[K - S_T, 0]$, and the owner of the put p obtains: $0 = Max[K - S_T, 0]$.
(iii) if $S_T > K$, the equityholders will be happy to have the market value of the firm S_T and pay K to the debtholders, i.e., the equityholders gain: $S_T - K = Max[S_T - K, 0] > 0$, the debtholders gain: $K = Min[K, S_T] = K - Max[K - S_T, 0]$, and the owner of the put p obtains: $0 = Max[K - S_T, 0]$.

In the case of riskless debt, i.e., the insurance $p = 0$, Eq. (9.4) becomes:

$$S_0 = c + \frac{K}{1+r}, \tag{9.5}$$

where c is the equity, and $\frac{K}{1+r}$ is the riskless debt. At $t = T$, the equityholders gain: $S_T - K$, and the debtholders gain: K.

Partially differentiate both sides of Eq. (9.4) with respect to K:

$$0 = \frac{\partial S_0}{\partial K} = \frac{\partial c}{\partial K} + \frac{\partial}{\partial K}\left(\frac{K}{1+r} - p\right). \tag{9.6}$$

That is, when the payment to the debtholders K increases, the market value of the firm S_0 still remains unchanged, the equity c must decrease: $\frac{\partial c}{\partial K} < 0$, and the debt $\left(\frac{K}{1+r} - p\right)$ must increase: $\frac{\partial}{\partial K}\left(\frac{K}{1+r} - p\right) = \frac{1}{1+r} - \frac{\partial p}{\partial K} > 0$. This implies the following proposition[4]:

Proposition 9.1

(Capital Structure Irrelevancy Proposition I)

The Modigliani–Miller first proposition (the market value of the firm is independent of the firm's capital structure) is an example of financial diversification irrelevancy and is a corollary of the put-call parity.

From the put-call parity Eq. (9.2), we can have: $c = p$ if and only if $S_0 = \frac{K}{1+r}$. However, it is meaningless to say that $c = p = 0$ implies $S_0 = \frac{K}{1+r}$. This is because $c = 0$ implies $S_T \le K$ and $p = 0$ implies $K \le S_T$, i.e., $S_T = K$ is not a random variable, and hence, all options do not exist. Also, in terms of firm's capital structure, $p = 0$ means the promised payment K is riskless (i.e., a riskless debt) and $c = 0$ implies $S_T \le K$, and hence, the asset S_0 must be a default-less fixed-income asset: $S_0 = \frac{K}{1+r}$, as Eq. (9.1)'s relationship between the spot price and the forward price. Therefore, for any uncertain asset we must have:

$$c = p > 0 \text{ if and only if } S_0 = \frac{K}{1+r}. \tag{9.7}$$

Property 9.1 For a leveraged firm, the lower bound for the risky debt is: $K \ge S_0(1+r)$, i.e., the upper bound for the riskless debt is: $K < S_0(1+r)$. If $r = 0$, the lower bound for the risky debt is: $K \ge S_0$, i.e., the upper bound for the riskless debt is: $K < S_0$.

[4] Strictly speaking, the Modigliani–Miller first proposition is: In a complete market with no transaction costs and no arbitrage, the market value of the firm is independent of its capital structure.

From the put-call parity Eq. (9.2), $c = S_0 + p - \frac{K}{1+r}$, and if $p = 0$, i.e., the debt is riskless, we have: $c = S_0 - \frac{K}{1+r} \geq 0$. However, from Eq. (9.7) we know that we cannot have: $c = p = 0$ if and only if $S_0 = \frac{K}{1+r}$. Hence, when the debt is riskless (i.e., $p = 0$), we must have: $c = S_0 - \frac{K}{1+r} > 0$ or $K < S_0(1+r)$. Also, it is easy to see that the promised payment $K = S_0(1+r)$ cannot be riskless. For example, let $K = \$1,100$, $r = 10\%$ and $S_0 = \$1,000$. If at $t = 0$, people believe that $K = \$1,100$ is riskless, then the same people must believe $S_T \geq \$1,100$ at $t = T$. But this will contradict the assumption of $S_0 = \$1,000$, because if people believe $S_T \geq \$1,100$ at $t = T$, its current price S_0 must be greater than \$1,000, i.e., $S_0 > \$1,000$.

Property 9.2 Define the time value of European call option as: $TV^c = c - Max[S_0 - K, 0]$. From Eq. (9.3), where $r = 0$, we have: $c + K = S_0 + p$ and $c = S_0 + p - K \geq Max[S_0 - K, 0]$. Since from the put-call parity, $c = S_0 + p - \frac{K}{1+r} \geq Max[S_0 - \frac{K}{1+r}, 0]$, we have: $TV^c \geq 0$ if $r \geq 0$, and $TV^c > 0$ if $c > 0$, $p > 0$ and $r \geq 0$. This indicates that American call option on a non-dividend-paying stock will never be exercised before the expiration date.

Property 9.3 Define the time value of European put option as: $TV^p = p - Max[K - S_0, 0]$. From Eq. (9.3), where $r = 0$, we have: $c + K = S_0 + p$, we have: $TV^p \geq 0$, and if $K \leq S_0$, $TV^p = p \geq 0$. From Eq. (9.2), where $r > 0$, if $K > S_0$ and $c \geq \frac{rK}{1+r}$, then $TV^p \geq 0$. This is because: $\frac{K}{1+r} + c \geq \frac{rK}{1+r} + \frac{K}{1+r} = K$, and hence, $S_0 + p = \frac{K}{1+r} + c \geq K$ or $TV^p = p - (K - S_0) \geq 0$. This indicates that under:

(i) $r = 0$; or (ii) $K \leq S_0$; or (iii) $r > 0$, $K > S_0$ and $c \geq \frac{rK}{1+r}$,

American put option on a non-dividend-paying stock will never be exercised before the expiration date.

Property 9.4 The changes of the strike price K can affect the time value of European options. From Eq. (9.6), we have: $\frac{\partial c}{\partial K} + \frac{1}{1+r} = \frac{\partial p}{\partial K}$, where $\frac{-1}{1+r} < \frac{\partial c}{\partial K} < 0$ and $\frac{1}{1+r} > \frac{\partial p}{\partial K} > 0$. For $K < S_0$, $\frac{\partial TV^c}{\partial K} = \frac{\partial}{\partial K}(c - S_0 + K) = \frac{\partial c}{\partial K} + 1 > 0$; and $\frac{\partial TV^p}{\partial K} = \frac{\partial p}{\partial K} > 0$. For $K > S_0$, $\frac{\partial TV^c}{\partial K} = \frac{\partial c}{\partial K} < 0$; and $\frac{\partial TV^p}{\partial K} = \frac{\partial}{\partial K}(p - K + S_0) = \frac{\partial p}{\partial K} - 1 < 0$. That is, when $K = S_0$, both TV^c and TV^p will be the highest. Also, in terms of firm's financial policy, when the promised payment K is approaching the market value of the firm S_0, both the owner of the equity c and the owner of the insurance p will be more reluctant to liquidate the firm.

Options as Financial Strips and Financial Diversification Irrelevancy

Options are named as derivatives since they are 'derived' from some underlying asset. As Treasury Strips in Chap. 3 (i.e., a coupon bond's interest payments have been removed to form separate zero-coupon bonds), another name for options may be financial strips which shows financial diversification irrelevancy.

Property 9.5 Suppose that in the put-call parity: $c + \frac{K}{1+r} = S_0 + p$, the promised payment K is divided equally into three portions, i.e., $K = 3 \times \frac{K}{3}$, for three debtholders: $D_i = \frac{K}{3(1+r)} - p_i, i = 1, 2,$ and 3, where $D_1 = D_2$ are senior debts, and D_3 is a junior debt. Then put-call parity can be rewritten as:

$$E + \frac{K}{3(1+r)} + \frac{K}{3(1+r)} + \frac{K}{3(1+r)} = S_0 + p_1 + p_2 + p_3$$

or

$$S_0 = E + \left[\frac{K}{3(1+r)} - p_1\right] + \left[\frac{K}{3(1+r)} - p_2\right] + \left[\frac{K}{3(1+r)} - p_3\right], \quad (9.8)$$

where the market value of the firm S_0 does not change (i.e., financial diversification irrelevancy), and $E = c$ is the equity. At $t = T$, the payment paid to the firm is separated to the equity, the debts and the insurances:

for E: $Max[S_T - K, 0]$; for $D_1 = D_2$: $\frac{1}{2}Min\left[\frac{2}{3}K, S_T\right]$, for D_3: $Min\left\{Max\left[S_T - \frac{2}{3}K, 0\right], \frac{1}{3}K\right\}$,
for $p_1 = p_2$: $\frac{1}{2}Max\left[\frac{2}{3}K - S_T, 0\right]$; and for p_3: $Max\left\{\frac{1}{3}K - Max[S_T - \frac{2}{3}K, 0], 0\right\}$.

Table 9.1 shows that the first claim between senior and junior debts does not affect the non-fixed income asset (i.e., the equity). Also, because of the seniority (first claim) of D_1 and D_2 where in every scenario the future payoff of D_1 or D_2 is no less than that of D_3 and$p_1 = p_2 < p_3$, the present value of the senior debt is greater than that of the junior debt, i.e.,$D_1 = D_2 > D_3$. Thus, at the good time, i.e.,$S_T \geq K$, the maximum rate of return of the junior debt is greater than that of the senior debt. However, this does not mean that higher risk (i.e.,$p_3 > p_1 = p_2$) means higher expected rate of return, or that the expected rate of return of the junior debt is greater than that of the senior debt even though all the debts have the same promised payment$\frac{1}{3}K$.

Property 9.6 Suppose that in Eq. (9.8), the senior debt D_1 is changed into a convertible bond CB which at $t = T$ may be converted to another equity. Then, the

Table 9.1 The extended put-call parity with senior and junior debts

$t = 0$	E	D_1	D_2	D_3	p_1	p_2	p_3
$t = T$							
$S_T < \frac{2}{3}K$	0	$\frac{1}{2}S_T$	$\frac{1}{2}S_T$	0	$\frac{1}{3}K - \frac{1}{2}S_T$	$\frac{1}{3}K - \frac{1}{2}S_T$	$\frac{1}{3}K$
$\frac{2}{3}K \leq S_T < K$	0	$\frac{1}{3}K$	$\frac{1}{3}K$	$S_T - \frac{2}{3}K$	0	0	$K - S_T$
$S_T \geq K$	$S_T - K$	$\frac{1}{3}K$	$\frac{1}{3}K$	$\frac{1}{3}K$	0	0	0

put-call parity can be rewritten as:

$$E + CB + \frac{K}{3(1+r)} + \frac{K}{3(1+r)} = S_0 + p_2 + p_3$$

or

$$S_0 = E + CB + \left[\frac{K}{3(1+r)} - p_2\right] + \left[\frac{K}{3(1+r)} - p_3\right], \quad (9.9)$$

where the market value of the firm S_0 does not change (i.e., financial diversification irrelevancy), $CB = D_1 + p'$, and p' is a put option (insurance). At $t = T$, the payoffs to the equity, the convertible bond, the debts, and the insurances are:

for E: $Max\{Min[\frac{1}{2}Max(S_T - \frac{2}{3}K, 0), S_T - K], 0\}$; for D_2: $\frac{1}{2}Min[\frac{2}{3}K, S_T]$; for p_2: $\frac{1}{2}Max[\frac{2}{3}K - S_T, 0]$; for D_3: $Min\{Max[S_T - \frac{2}{3}K, 0], \frac{1}{3}K\}$; for p_3: $Max\{\frac{1}{3}K - Max[S_T - \frac{2}{3}K, 0], 0\}$; for CB: $Max\{\frac{1}{2}Max[S_T - \frac{2}{3}K, 0], \frac{1}{2}Min[\frac{2}{3}K, S_T]\}$; and for p': $\frac{1}{2}Max[S_T - \frac{4}{3}K, 0]$.

Table 9.2 shows that when the senior debt D_1 is transformed into a convertible bondCB, other debts D_2 and D_3 as well as p_2 and p_3 will not be affected though the original equity E is worse. Thus, at $t = 0$, $E < CB$ and $CB > D_2 > D_3$. At the good time, i.e., $S_T > \frac{4}{3}K$, the maximum rate of return of the equity is greater than that of the convertible bond, and the maximum rate of return of the convertible bond is greater than that of the senior bond. But it does not mean that the expected rate of return of the equity is greater than that of the convertible bond, or the expected rate of return of the convertible bond is greater than that of the senior bond.

Table 9.2 The extended put-call parity with equity, convertible bond and senior and junior debts

$t = 0$	E	CB	D_2	D_3	p'	p_2	p_3
$t = T$							
$S_T < \frac{2}{3}K$	0	$\frac{1}{2}S_T$	$\frac{1}{2}S_T$	0	0	$\frac{1}{3}K - \frac{1}{2}S_T$	$\frac{1}{3}K$
$\frac{2}{3}K \le S_T < K$	0	$\frac{1}{3}K$	$\frac{1}{3}K$	$S_T - \frac{2}{3}K$	0	0	$K - S_T$
$\frac{4}{3}K \ge S_T \ge K$	$S_T - K$	$\frac{1}{3}K$	$\frac{1}{3}K$	$\frac{1}{3}K$	0	0	0
$S_T > \frac{4}{3}K$	$\frac{1}{2}(S_T - \frac{2}{3}K)$	$\frac{1}{2}(S_T - \frac{2}{3}K)$	$\frac{1}{3}K$	$\frac{1}{3}K$	$\frac{1}{2}S_T - \frac{2}{3}K$	0	0

Upper and Lower Bounds for Options Prices
From the put-call parity Eq. (9.2), we have: $p = \frac{K}{1+r} - S_0 + c \geq \frac{K}{1+r} - S_0$, and hence, the lower bound for the European put option is: $p \geq Max\left[\frac{K}{1+r} - S_0, 0\right]$. Also, because the market value of risky debt must be non-negative, i.e., $\frac{K}{1+r} - p \geq 0$, we have: $p \leq \frac{K}{1+r}$. However, it is impossible to have: $p = \frac{K}{1+r}$. This is because at $t = 0$ people will use $\frac{K}{1+r}$ to buy a default-less zero-coupon bond which gives K with certainty at $t = T$ rather than use $\frac{K}{1+r}$ to buy an insurance p which may give at most K at $t = T$. That is, *an asset cannot sell for more than or equal to the present value of a sure payment of its maximum pay-off*. Also, $K > 0$ if and only if the risky debt $\left(\frac{K}{1+r} - p\right) > 0$, and if $K = 0$, then no options can exist and the debt $\left(\frac{K}{1+r} - p\right)$ does not exist. Thus, at $t = 0$, the upper and lower bounds for the European put option are:

$$\frac{K}{1+r} > p \geq Max\left[\frac{K}{1+r} - S_0, 0\right]. \tag{9.10}$$

For the American put option P, its price at $t = 0$ cannot be greater than K, i.e., $P \leq K$. But it is nonsense to have $P = K$ because at $t = 0$, people will not use K to buy an insurance P which later on may give at most K. Thus, at $t = 0$, the upper and the lower bounds for the American put option are[5]:

$$K > P \geq Max[K - S_0, 0]. \tag{9.11}$$

From Eq. (9.2), we also have: $c = S_0 - \frac{K}{1+r} + p \geq S_0 - \frac{K}{1+r}$, and hence, the lower bound for European call option is: $c \geq Max\left[S_0 - \frac{K}{1+r}, 0\right]$. The European call option c cannot be greater than the underlying asset S_0. At $t = T$, the best scenario for the holder of c is payoff S_T where $K = 0$. But $K = 0$ means that all options do not exist. Hence, we must have $c < S_0$. The upper and lower bounds for the European call option at $t = 0$ are:

$$S_0 > c \geq Max\left[S_0 - \frac{K}{1+r}, 0\right]. \tag{9.12}$$

[5] The literature of derivatives (e.g., Hull (2018, p. 269) and Merton (1973b, p. 183)) incorrectly states the upper and lower bounds of the put options as: $\frac{K}{1+r} \geq p \geq Max\left[\frac{K}{1+r} - S_0, 0\right]$ and $K \geq P \geq Max[K - S_0, 0]$. Hull (2018, p. 270) and Merton (1973b, p. 183) erroneously argue that "the maximum pay-off to a European put is the exercise price, K, which occurs if the underlying asset price S_0 is zero". This argument is wrong because $S_0 = 0$ if and only if people believe $S_t = 0, \forall t > 0$. Since $S_t = 0, \forall t > 0$, is not a random variable, all options do not exist.

The upper and lower bounds for the American call option C at $t = 0$ are:

$$S_0 > C \geq Max\left[S_0 - \frac{K}{1+r}, 0\right]. \tag{9.13}$$

When the insurances p and P decrease (i.e., debts become less risky), c and C approach their lower bounds as in Eq. (9.5).

Model-Free Greeks

The put-call parity in Eq. (9.2) shows the interconnection between call and put options. Thus, the Greeks of call and put options must be determined simultaneously. For example, we have:

$$\frac{\partial c}{\partial x} = \frac{\partial p}{\partial x} \text{ for any } x \notin \{S_0, r, K\}. \tag{9.14}$$

Case 1. Either $c = 0$ or $p = 0$.

(i) With $p = 0$, $\frac{\partial p}{\partial S} = 0$ and $\frac{\partial c}{\partial S} = 1 > 0$, where $\frac{\partial c}{\partial S} = 1 + \frac{\partial p}{\partial S}$, indicates that with riskless debt, maximizing the firm's market value is equivalent to maximizing the equityholders' wealth. $\frac{\partial p}{\partial r} = 0$ and $\frac{\partial c}{\partial r} = \frac{K}{(1+r)^2} > 0$ (and $\frac{\partial}{\partial r}\left(\frac{K}{1+r}\right) = \frac{-K}{(1+r)^2} < 0$), where $\frac{\partial c}{\partial r} - \frac{K}{(1+r)^2} = \frac{\partial p}{\partial r}$, indicates that with riskless debt and constant S_0, higher interest rate transfers the debtholders' wealth to the equityholders. $\frac{\partial p}{\partial K} = 0$ and $\frac{\partial c}{\partial K} = \frac{-1}{1+r} < 0$ (and $1 > \frac{\partial}{\partial K}\left(\frac{K}{1+r}\right) = \frac{1}{1+r} > 0$), where $\frac{\partial c}{\partial K} - \frac{1}{1+r} = \frac{\partial p}{\partial K}$, indicates that with riskless debt and constant S_0, higher promised payment K results in higher leveraged firm.

(ii) With $c = 0$, this implies that the debtholder is also the equity holder, i.e., at $t = T$, the debtholder obtains $Min[S_T, K]$ and the equityholder obtains $Max[S_0 - K, 0]$, and $Min[S_T, K] + Max[S_T - K, 0] = S_T$, where S_T is also the payoff of the totally equity-financed firm. $\frac{\partial c}{\partial S} = 0$ and $\frac{\partial p}{\partial S} = -1 < 0$; $\frac{\partial c}{\partial r} = 0$ and $\frac{\partial p}{\partial r} = \frac{-K}{(1+r)^2} < 0$; $\frac{\partial c}{\partial K} = 0$ and $1 > \frac{\partial p}{\partial K} = \frac{1}{1+r} > 0$.

Case 2. $c > 0$ and $p > 0$.

About $\frac{\partial c}{\partial S}$ and $\frac{\partial p}{\partial S}$:

(i) It is impossible to have: $\frac{\partial c}{\partial S} \leq 0$ and $\frac{\partial p}{\partial S} \geq 0$ because from Eq. (9.2), we have: $\frac{\partial c}{\partial S} = 1 + \frac{\partial p}{\partial S}$. This indicates that increasing the market value of the firm cannot lead to: lower (or no change in) equity and lower (or no change in) debt.

(ii) $\frac{\partial c}{\partial S} > 0$ and $\frac{\partial p}{\partial S} < 0$ (where $0 < \frac{\partial c}{\partial S} < 1$ and $-1 < \frac{\partial p}{\partial S} < 0$). This indicates that increasing the firm's market value benefits both the equityholders and the debtholders (by reducing the risk level of debt), and **maximizing the market value of the firm is not equivalent to maximizing the equityholders' wealth**.

Both the Black–Scholes-Merton and the binomial option pricing models have this property (see the following section).

(iii) $\frac{\partial c}{\partial S} = 0$ and $\frac{\partial p}{\partial S} = -1 < 0$. This indicates that increasing the firm's market value only benefits the debtholders, and the equiltyholders get no benefit.

(iv) $\frac{\partial p}{\partial S} = 0$ and $\frac{\partial c}{\partial S} = 1 > 0$. This indicates that increasing the firm's market value only benefits the equiltyholders, and the debtholders get no benefit, i.e., maximizing the firm's market value is equivalent to maximizing the equityholders' wealth.

(v) $\frac{\partial c}{\partial S} > 0$ and $\frac{\partial p}{\partial S} > 0$ (where $\frac{\partial c}{\partial S} > 1$, and $\frac{\partial p}{\partial S} > 0$ leads to $\frac{\partial c}{\partial S} > 0$). This indicates that increasing the firm's market value not only benefits the equiltyholders but transfers parts of the debtholders' wealth to the equiltyholders by increasing p, the risk level of debt.

(vi) $\frac{\partial c}{\partial S} < 0$ and $\frac{\partial p}{\partial S} < 0$ (where $\frac{\partial p}{\partial S} < -1$, and $\frac{\partial c}{\partial S} < 0$ leads to $\frac{\partial p}{\partial S} < 0$). This indicates that increasing the firm's market value not only benefits the debtholders but transfers parts of the equiltyholders' wealth to the debtholders by reducing p, the risk level of debt.

About $\frac{\partial c}{\partial r}$ and $\frac{\partial p}{\partial r}$:

(i) It is impossible to have: $\frac{\partial c}{\partial r} \leq 0$ and $\frac{\partial p}{\partial r} \geq 0$ because from Eq. (9.2), we have: $\frac{\partial c}{\partial r} - \frac{K}{(1+r)^2} = \frac{\partial p}{\partial r}$. This indicates that with higher risk-free interest rate, keeping the same market value of the firm cannot lead to: lower (or no change in) equity and higher (or no change in) insurance p.

(ii) $\frac{\partial c}{\partial r} > 0$ and $\frac{\partial p}{\partial r} < 0$ (where $0 < \frac{\partial c}{\partial r} < \frac{K}{(1+r)^2}$ and $\frac{-K}{(1+r)^2} < \frac{\partial p}{\partial r} < 0$). This indicates that with higher risk-free interest rate, keeping the same market value of the firm leads to higher equity (and hence, lower debt) and lower insurance. Both the Black–Scholes-Merton and the binomial option pricing models have this property (see the following section).

(iii) $\frac{\partial c}{\partial r} = 0$ and $\frac{\partial p}{\partial r} = -\frac{K}{(1+r)^2} < 0$ (or $\frac{\partial}{\partial r}\left(\frac{K}{1+r} - p\right) = 0$). This indicates that with higher risk-free interest rate, keeping the same market value of the firm leads to the same equity (hence, the same debt), and reduce the risk level of debt.

(iv) $\frac{\partial p}{\partial r} = 0$ and $\frac{\partial c}{\partial r} = \frac{K}{(1+r)^2} > 0$. This indicates that with higher risk-free interest rate, keeping the same market value of the firm leads to higher equity (and hence, lower debt) and the same insurance.

(v) $\frac{\partial c}{\partial r} > 0$ and $\frac{\partial p}{\partial r} > 0$ (where $\frac{\partial c}{\partial r} > \frac{K}{(1+r)^2}$, and $\frac{\partial p}{\partial r} > 0$ leads to $\frac{\partial c}{\partial r} > 0$). This indicates that with higher risk-free interest rate, keeping the same market value of the firm leads to higher equity (and hence, lower debt) and higher insurance.

(vi) $\frac{\partial c}{\partial r} < 0$ and $\frac{\partial p}{\partial r} < 0$ (where $\frac{\partial p}{\partial r} < -\frac{K}{(1+r)^2}$, and $\frac{\partial c}{\partial r} < 0$ leads to $\frac{\partial p}{\partial r} < 0$). This indicates that with higher risk-free interest rate, keeping the same market value of the firm leads to lower equity (and hence, higher debt) and lower insurance.

Table 9.3 Current and future possible prices of the firm, equity, insurance, riskless debt and risky debt (four states of nature)

$t = 0$		S_0	c	p	$\frac{K}{1+r}$	$\frac{K}{1+r} - p$
$t = T$	Probabilities					
State 1	π_1	10,000	4,000	0	6,000	6,000
State 2	π_2	8,000	2,000	0	6,000	6,000
State 3	π_3	4,000	0	2,000	6,000	4,000
State 4	π_4	3,000	0	3,000	6,000	3,000

About $\frac{\partial c}{\partial K}$ and $\frac{\partial p}{\partial K}$:

Because at $t = T$, the payoff of c is $Max[S_T - K, 0]$, and the payoff of p is $Max[K - S_T, 0]$, we must have: $\frac{\partial c}{\partial K} < 0$ and $\frac{\partial p}{\partial K} > 0$. Also, from Eq. (9.2), we have: $\frac{\partial c}{\partial K} + \frac{1}{1+r} = \frac{\partial p}{\partial K}$, and hence, $\frac{-1}{1+r} < \frac{\partial c}{\partial K} < 0$ and $\frac{1}{1+r} > \frac{\partial p}{\partial K} > 0$. This indicates that higher promised payment K leads to lower equity (and hence, higher debt, i.e., $\frac{\partial}{\partial K}\left(\frac{K}{1+r} - p\right) > 0$) and higher insurance.

An Example

Assume a four states of nature world with probabilities: $\pi_1, \pi_2, \pi_3, \pi_4 > 0$, and $\sum_{i=1}^{4} \pi_i = 1$. At $t = 0$, the firm (the underlying asset) with current price S_0 has four possible market prices (\$10,000, \$8,000, \$4,000, \$3,000, respectively) at $t = T$. With the promised payment (the exercise price) $K = \$6,000$, at $t = T$, the possible prices of the equity (the call) c, the insurance (the put) p, and the risky debt $\left(\frac{K}{1+r} - p\right)$ are shown in Table 9.3.

Note that in option Greeks, changes in the current price S_0 (or r changes but S_0 remains constant) cannot happen without a cause. These may be caused by changes in probabilities π_i, in future possible payoffs, or in both. Suppose that the probabilities change. The Greeks of call and put options are as the follows:

About $\frac{\partial c}{\partial S}$ and $\frac{\partial p}{\partial S}$:

(i) $\frac{\partial c}{\partial S} > 0$ and $\frac{\partial p}{\partial S} < 0$. That S_0 increases (decreases), c increases (decreases) and p decreases (increases) may be caused by: π_2 becomes $\pi_2' = \pi_2 + (-)\varepsilon$, π_3 becomes $\pi_3' = \pi_3 - (+)\varepsilon$, and π_1 and π_4 remain the same, where ε is a very small positive number. This is the case when the market value of the firm S_0 increases (decreases), the equity c increases (decreases), and debt $\left(\frac{K}{1+r} - p\right)$ increases (decreases) because the insurance p decreases (increases).

(ii) $\frac{\partial c}{\partial S} = 0$ and $\frac{\partial p}{\partial S} = -1 < 0$. That S_0 increases (decreases), c remains constant and p decreases (increases) may be caused by: π_3 becomes $\pi_3' = \pi_3 + (-)\varepsilon$, π_4 becomes $\pi_4' = \pi_4 - (+)\varepsilon$, and π_1 and π_2 remain the same, where ε is a very small positive number. This is the case when the market value of the firm S_0 increases (decreases), the equity c remains constant, and the debt $\left(\frac{K}{1+r} - p\right)$ increases (decreases) because the insurance p decreases (increases).

(iii) $\frac{\partial p}{\partial S} = 0$ and $\frac{\partial c}{\partial S} = 1 > 0$. That S_0 increases (decreases), p remains constant and c increases (decreases) may be caused by: π_1 becomes $\pi_1' = \pi_1 + (-)\varepsilon$, $\pi_2' = \pi_2 - (+)\varepsilon$, and π_3 and π_4 remain the same, where ε is a very small positive number. This is the case when the market value of the firm S_0 increases (decreases), the equity c increases (decreases), and the debt $\left(\frac{K}{1+r} - p\right)$ remains the same because the insurance p does not change.

(iv) $\frac{\partial c}{\partial S} > 0$ and $\frac{\partial p}{\partial S} > 0$. That S_0 increases (decreases), c increases (decreases) and p increases (decreases) may be caused by: π_1 becomes $\pi_1' = \pi_1 + (-)\varepsilon$, π_2 becomes $\pi_2' = \pi_2 - (+)\varepsilon$, π_3 becomes $\pi_3' = \pi_3 - (+)\varepsilon$, and $\pi_4' = \pi_4 + (-)\varepsilon$ where ε is a very small positive number. This is the case when the market value of the firm S_0 increases (decreases), the equity c increases (decreases), and the debt $\left(\frac{K}{1+r} - p\right)$ decreases (increases) because the insurance p increases (decreases).

(v) $\frac{\partial c}{\partial S} < 0$ and $\frac{\partial p}{\partial S} < 0$. That S_0 increases (decreases), c decreases (increases) and p decreases (increases) may be caused by: π_1 becomes $\pi_1' = \pi_1 - (+)\varepsilon$, π_2 becomes $\pi_2' = \pi_2 + (-)\varepsilon$, π_3 becomes $\pi_3' = \pi_3 + (-)\frac{\pi_4}{2}$, and π_4 becomes $\pi_4' = \pi_4 - (+)\frac{\pi_4}{2}$, where ε is a very small positive number. This is the case when the market value of the firm S_0 increases (decreases), the equity c decreases (increases), and the debt $\left(\frac{K}{1+r} - p\right)$ increases (decreases) because the insurance p decreases (increases).

About $\frac{\partial c}{\partial r}$ and $\frac{\partial p}{\partial r}$:

(i) $\frac{\partial c}{\partial r} > 0$ and $\frac{\partial p}{\partial r} < 0$ (where $0 < \frac{\partial c}{\partial r} < \frac{K}{(1+r)^2}$ and $\frac{-K}{(1+r)^2} < \frac{\partial p}{\partial r} < 0$). That r increases (decreases) but S_0 remains constant, c increases (decreases), and both $\left(\frac{K}{1+r} - p\right)$ and p decrease (increase) may be caused by: π_1 becomes $\pi_1' = \pi_1 + (-)\delta$, $\pi_2' = \pi_2 - (+)\delta$, and π_3 and π_4 remain the same, where δ is a very small positive number. In this case, because π_3 and π_4 do not change, for the risky debt: $\frac{\partial}{\partial r}\left(\frac{K}{1+r} - p\right) < 0$ and for the insurance: $\frac{\partial p}{\partial r} < 0$.

(ii) $\frac{\partial c}{\partial r} = 0$ and $\frac{\partial p}{\partial r} = -\frac{K}{(1+r)^2} < 0$. That r increases (decreases) but S_0 remains constant, both c and $\left(\frac{K}{1+r} - p\right)$ remain constant, and p decreases (increases) may be caused by: π_1 becomes $\pi_1' = \pi_1 + (-)\frac{\delta}{2}$, π_2 becomes $\pi_2' = \pi_2 - (+)\frac{\delta}{2}$, π_3 becomes $\pi_3' = \pi_3 + (-)\omega$, and π_4 becomes $\pi_4' = \pi_4 - (+)\omega$, where δ and ω are very small positive numbers. In this case, for the risky debt: $\frac{\partial}{\partial r}\left(\frac{K}{1+r} - p\right) = 0$ and for the insurance: $\frac{\partial p}{\partial r} < 0$.

(iii) $\frac{\partial p}{\partial r} = 0$ and $\frac{\partial c}{\partial r} = \frac{K}{(1+r)^2} > 0$. That r increases (decreases) but S_0 remains constant, c increases (decreases), and p remains constant may be caused by: π_1 becomes $\pi_1' = \pi_1 + (-)2\delta$, π_2 becomes $\pi_2' = \pi_2 - (+)2\delta$, π_3 becomes

$\pi_3' = \pi_3 - (+)\frac{\omega}{2}$, and π_4 becomes $\pi_4' = \pi_4 + (-)\frac{\omega}{2}$, where δ and ω are very small positive numbers. Also, $\frac{\partial c}{\partial r} > 0$ implies $\frac{\partial}{\partial r}\left(\frac{K}{1+r} - p\right) < 0$.

(iv) $\frac{\partial c}{\partial r} > 0$ and $\frac{\partial p}{\partial r} > 0$ (where $\frac{\partial c}{\partial r} > \frac{K}{(1+r)^2}$, and $\frac{\partial p}{\partial r} > 0$ leads to $\frac{\partial c}{\partial r} > 0$). That r increases (decreases) but S_0 remains constant, c increases (decreases), and p increases (decreases) may be caused by: π_1 becomes $\pi_1' = \pi_1 + (-)3\delta$, π_2 becomes $\pi_2' = \pi_2 - (+)3\delta$, π_3 becomes $\pi_3' = \pi_3 - (+)\omega$, and π_4 becomes $\pi_4' = \pi_4 + (-)\omega$, where δ and ω are very small positive numbers. In this case, because S_0 remains constant, $\frac{\partial p}{\partial r} > 0$ implies that for the risky debt: $\frac{\partial}{\partial r}\left(\frac{K}{1+r} - p\right) < 0$, and hence, for the equity: $\frac{\partial c}{\partial r} > 0$.

(v) $\frac{\partial c}{\partial r} < 0$ and $\frac{\partial p}{\partial r} < 0$ (where $\frac{\partial p}{\partial r} < -\frac{K}{(1+r)^2}$, and $\frac{\partial c}{\partial r} < 0$ leads to $\frac{\partial p}{\partial r} < 0$). That r increases (decreases) but S_0 remains constant, c decreases (increases), and p decreases (increases) may be caused by: π_3 becomes $\pi_3' = \pi_3 + (-)\delta$, π_4 becomes $\pi_4' = \pi_4 - (+)\delta$, and π_1 and π_2 remain the same, where δ is a very small positive number. In this case, because π_1 and π_2 do not change, for the equity: $\frac{\partial c}{\partial r} < 0$, and because S_0 remains constant, for the risky debt: $\frac{\partial}{\partial r}\left(\frac{K}{1+r} - p\right) > 0$, and for the insurance: $\frac{\partial p}{\partial r} < 0$.

9.3 The Binomial Option Pricing Model and Corporate Finance

The binomial option pricing model may be presented as the follows. Consider 3-month European call and put options on a non-dividend-paying stock (or a firm or a piece of land) with strike price $K = \$8,900$.

From Fig. 9.1 and Table 9.4, the option Greeks can be easily derived:

(i) $\frac{\partial c}{\partial S} > 0$ and $\frac{\partial p}{\partial S} < 0$. When r, S_0u and S_0d remain constant, S_0 cannot increase (decrease) unless π increases (decreases), i.e., $\frac{\partial \pi}{\partial S} > 0$. Therefore, higher (lower) π leads to higher (lower) c and lower (higher) p.

(ii) $\frac{\partial c}{\partial r} > 0$ and $\frac{\partial p}{\partial r} < 0$. For any asset, an increase (decrease) in r can decrease (increase) its present value. But when r increases (decreases) and S_0u and S_0d

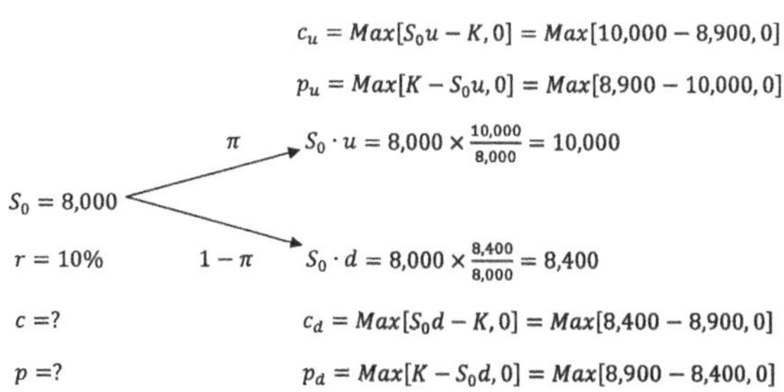

Fig. 9.1 A binomial option pricing model

Table 9.4 Current and future possible prices of the firm, equity, insurance, riskless debt and risky debt (two states of natures)

$t-0$		$S_0 = 8,000$	c	p	$\frac{K}{1+r} = \frac{8,900}{1+0.1}$	$\frac{K}{1+r} - p = \frac{8,900}{1+0.1} - p$
$t = T$	Probabilities					
State 1	π	10, 000	1, 100	0	8, 900	8, 900
State 2	$1-\pi$	8, 400	0	500	8, 900	8, 400

remain constant, constant S_0 cannot happen unless π increases (decreases), i.e., $\frac{\partial \pi}{\partial r} > 0$. Therefore, an increase (decrease) in π leads to lower (higher) p, i.e., $\frac{\partial p}{\partial r} < 0$. Also,

Case (1). Suppose r increases (decreases), but π and $(1-\pi)$ remain the same (and hence, S_0 decreases (increases)). Then, because r increases (decreases), the riskless debt $\frac{K}{1+r}$ will decrease (increase) more than the insurance p, i.e., $\frac{\partial}{\partial r}\left(\frac{K}{1+r} - p\right) = \frac{\partial}{\partial r}\left(\frac{K}{1+r}\right) - \frac{\partial p}{\partial r} < 0$.
Case (2). In the binomial option pricing model, when r increases (decreases), andS_0, S_0u and S_0d remain constant, an increase (decrease) in π implies that the riskless debt $\frac{K}{1+r}$ will decrease (increase) further more than the insurance p, i.e.,$\frac{\partial}{\partial r}\left(\frac{K}{1+r} - p\right) = \frac{\partial}{\partial r}\left(\frac{K}{1+r}\right) - \frac{\partial p}{\partial r} < 0$, and hence, the equity c must increase (decrease), i.e.,$\frac{\partial c}{\partial r} > 0$.

(iii) $\frac{\partial c}{\partial u} = \frac{\partial p}{\partial u} > 0$. When u increases (decreases) to u', i.e., $S_0u' > (<) S_0u$, and r and S_0d remain constant, constant S_0 cannot happen unless π decreases (increases), i.e.,$\frac{\partial \pi}{\partial u} < 0$. Hence, higher (lower) $1-\pi$ leads to higher (lower) p. Because in Eq. (9.14), $\frac{\partial c}{\partial x} = \frac{\partial p}{\partial x}$ for any $x \notin \{S_0, r, K\}$, we must have:$\frac{\partial c}{\partial u} = \frac{\partial p}{\partial u} > 0$.
(iv) $\frac{\partial c}{\partial d} = \frac{\partial p}{\partial d} < 0$. When d decreases (increases) to d', i.e., $S_0d' < (>) S_0d$, and r and S_0u remain constant, constant S_0 cannot happen unless π increases (decreases), i.e.,$\frac{\partial \pi}{\partial d} < 0$. Hence, higher (lower) π leads to higher (lower) c. Because $\frac{\partial c}{\partial x} = \frac{\partial p}{\partial x}$ for any $x \notin \{S_0, r, K\}$, we must have:$\frac{\partial c}{\partial d} = \frac{\partial p}{\partial d} < 0$.

For a more rigorous proof for the option Greeks, we need the following theory introduced by Chang (2015, p. 41).[6]

---

[6] The Gordan theory is a corollary of Farkas theory:

Let $\boldsymbol{A}$ be a $m \times n$ matrix and $\boldsymbol{c} \in R^n$ be a vector. Then, exactly one of the following systems has a solution:

System 1: $\boldsymbol{Ax} \geq 0$ and $\boldsymbol{c}^t\boldsymbol{x} < 0$ for some $\boldsymbol{x} \in R^n$;

System 2: $\boldsymbol{A}^t\boldsymbol{y} = \boldsymbol{c}$ and $\boldsymbol{y} \geq 0$ for some $\boldsymbol{y} \in R^m$.

The Farkas theory is a corollary of Separating Hyperplane Theory:

Gordan Theorem (the Arbitrage Theorem)
Let $\boldsymbol{A}$ be an $m \times n$ matrix. Then, exactly one of the following systems has a solution:

System 1: $\boldsymbol{Ax} > \boldsymbol{0}$ for some $\boldsymbol{x} \in R^n$

System 2: $\boldsymbol{A}^t \boldsymbol{p} = \boldsymbol{0}$ for some $\boldsymbol{p} \in R^m$, $\boldsymbol{p} \geq \boldsymbol{0}$, $\boldsymbol{e}^t \boldsymbol{p} = 1$ where $\boldsymbol{e} = \begin{bmatrix} 1 \\ 1 \\ \cdot \\ \cdot \\ 1 \end{bmatrix}$

In System 2 of the Gordan Theorem (the Arbitrage Theorem), the vector $\boldsymbol{p}$ is a probability measure, and p_i, $i = 1, \ldots, m$, can be interpreted as the current price of one dollar received at the end of period if state i occurs. If System 2 holds (i.e., no arbitrage) and the matrix $\boldsymbol{A}$ has rank $m - 1$ (i.e., the matrix has $m - 1$ independent rows), the probability measure $\boldsymbol{p}$ will be unique.[7] The existence of a unique vector $\boldsymbol{p}$ means **the complete market**, i.e., any future payoff (a vector) of a new asset can be replicated by the assets in the complete market. Also, if System 2 does not hold, then investors can always do an arbitrage to make excess profits (see the example in Appendix of this chapter).

Thus, in terms of Fig. 9.1, System 2 of the Arbitrage Theorem is:

$$\underbrace{\begin{bmatrix} 1.10 - 1(1+0.10) & 1.10 - 1(1+0.10) \\ 10,000 - 8,000(1+0.10) & 8,400 - 8,000(1+0.10) \\ 1,100 - 250(1+0.10) & 0 - 250(1+0.10) \\ 0 - \frac{3,750}{11}(1+0.1) & 500 - \frac{3,750}{11}(1+0.1) \end{bmatrix}}_{\boldsymbol{A}^t} \underbrace{\begin{bmatrix} 1/4 \\ 3/4 \end{bmatrix} = \begin{bmatrix} 0 \\ 0 \\ 0 \\ 0 \end{bmatrix}}_{\boldsymbol{p} = \boldsymbol{0}}$$

or

$$\begin{cases} \text{Money market}: \ 1 = \frac{1}{1+r}[\pi(1+r) + (1-\pi)(1+r)] = \frac{1}{1+0.1}\left[\frac{1}{4}(1.10) + \frac{3}{4}(1.10)\right] \\ \text{The firm}: S_0 = 8,000 = \frac{1}{1+r}[\pi \cdot S_0 u + (1-\pi) \cdot S_0 d] = \frac{1}{1+0.1}\left[\frac{1}{4}(10,000) + \frac{3}{4}(8,400)\right] \\ \text{Call option}: c = 250 = \frac{1}{1+r}[\pi \cdot (S_0 u - K) + (1-\pi) \cdot 0] = \frac{1}{1+0.1}\left[\frac{1}{4}(1,100) + \frac{3}{4}(0)\right] \\ \text{Put option}: p = \frac{3,750}{11} = \frac{1}{1+r}[\pi \cdot 0 + (1-\pi) \cdot (K - S_0 d)] = \frac{1}{1+0.1}\left[\frac{1}{4}(0) + \frac{3}{4}(500)\right] \end{cases} \tag{9.15}$$

where $\pi = 1/4$ is calculated from the second equation of Eq. (9.15): $S_0 = 8,000 = \frac{1}{1+0.1}[\pi(10,000) + (1-\pi)(8,400)]$, and c and p can be derived by substituting $\pi = 1/4$ into the third and fourth equations.

Let S be a nonempty, closed convex set in R^n and $\boldsymbol{y} \notin S$. Then, there exists a nonzero vector $z \in R^n$ and a scalar α such that $\boldsymbol{z}^t \boldsymbol{y} < \alpha$ and $\boldsymbol{z}^t \boldsymbol{x} \geq \alpha$ for each $\boldsymbol{x} \in S$.

[7] $\boldsymbol{A}^t \boldsymbol{p} = 0$ And $\boldsymbol{p}$ is a non-zero vector imply the rank of $\boldsymbol{A}^t$, $R(\boldsymbol{A}^t)$, is less than m. Unique solution for $(p_1, \ldots, p_m)$ and $\sum_{i=1}^m p_i = 1$ imply $R(\boldsymbol{A}^t) = m - 1$.

Note that from Eq. (9.15): $S_0 = \frac{1}{1+r}[\pi \cdot S_0u + (1-\pi) \cdot S_0d]$, we know that $\pi = \frac{(1+r)-d}{u-d} > 0$ and $1-\pi = \frac{u-(1+r)}{u-d} > 0$, and hence,[8]

$$\frac{\partial \pi}{\partial r} = \frac{1}{u-d} > 0, \frac{\partial \pi}{\partial u} = \frac{d-(1+r)}{(u-d)^2} < 0 \text{ and } \frac{\partial \pi}{\partial d} = \frac{(1+r)-u}{(u-d)^2} < 0. \quad (9.16)$$

From Eq. (9.15), the option Greeks under the binomial option pricing model are:

(i) $1 > \frac{\partial c}{\partial S} > 0$ and $-1 < \frac{\partial p}{\partial S} < 0$; and $\frac{\partial^2 c}{\partial S^2} = \frac{\partial^2 p}{\partial S^2} = 0$. Let $S_0' = \frac{1}{1+r}\left[\pi' \cdot S_0u + \left(1-\pi'\right) \cdot S_0d\right]$ and $S_0 = \frac{1}{1+r}[\pi \cdot S_0u + (1-\pi) \cdot S_0d]$. We have: $\frac{\pi'-\pi}{S_0'-S_0} = \frac{1+r}{S_0u-S_0d} > 0$, i.e., $\frac{\partial \pi}{\partial S} = \frac{1+r}{S_0u-S_0d} > 0$ and $\frac{\partial^2 \pi}{\partial S^2} = 0$. For the call option, $c' = \frac{1}{1+r}\left[\pi' \cdot (S_0u - K)\right]$ and $c = \frac{1}{1+r}[\pi \cdot (S_0u - K)]$, and hence, $1 > \frac{c'-c}{S_0'-S_0} = \frac{S_0u-K}{S_0u-S_0d} > 0$, i.e., $1 > \frac{\partial c}{\partial S} = \frac{S_0u-K}{S_0u-S_0d} > 0$ and $\frac{\partial^2 c}{\partial S^2} = 0$. For the put option, $p' = \frac{1}{1+r}\left[\left(1-\pi'\right) \cdot (K - S_0d)\right]$ and $p = \frac{1}{1+r}[(1-\pi) \cdot (K - S_0d)]$, and hence, $-1 < \frac{p'-p}{S_0'-S_0} = \frac{-(K-S_0d)}{S_0u-S_0d} < 0$, i.e., $-1 < \frac{\partial p}{\partial S} = \frac{-(K-S_0d)}{S_0u-S_0d} < 0$ and $\frac{\partial^2 p}{\partial S^2} = 0$. Both the binomial and the Black–Scholes-Merton option pricing models have[9]: $1 > \frac{\partial c}{\partial S} > 0$ and $-1 < \frac{\partial p}{\partial S} < 0$ (and hence, $\frac{\partial}{\partial S}\left(\frac{K}{1+r} - p\right) = -\frac{\partial p}{\partial S} > 0$), which indicate both models implicitly assume that maximizing the market value of the firm is not equivalent to maximizing the equityholders' wealth and that increasing (decreasing) the market value of the firm can decrease (increase) the risk level of the debt. Also, $\frac{\partial^2 c}{\partial S^2} = \frac{\partial^2 p}{\partial S^2} = 0$ of the binomial option pricing model indicates that the model implicitly assumes that further increasing (decreasing) in the market value of the firm affects neither the speed of increasing (decreasing) in the equity nor the speed of decreasing (increasing) in the risk level of the debt. The Black–Scholes-Merton option pricing model, on the other hand, has $\frac{\partial^2 c}{\partial S^2} = \frac{\partial^2 p}{\partial S^2} > 0$ which indicates the model implicitly assumes that further increasing (decreasing) the market value of the firm will: (1) increase (decrease) the speed of increasing (decreasing) in the equity though bounded by $1 > \frac{\partial c}{\partial S} > 0$; and (2) decrease (increase) the speed of decreasing (increasing) in the risk level of the debt though bounded by $-1 < \frac{\partial p}{\partial S} < 0$.

[8] Chang (2017) has shown that because an asset's current price (e.g., $S_0 = \$8,000$) is determined by people's expectation of the asset's future possible payoffs and their probabilities, the probabilities of the Gordan theory derived from S_0 (e.g., π and $1-\pi$ in Eq. (9.15)) are the actual world (not the risk-neutral world) probabilities.

[9] The Black–Scholes-Merton option pricing model is: $c = S_0 \cdot N(d_1) - K \cdot e^{-rT} \cdot N(d_2)$; $p = Ke^{-rT} \cdot [1 - N(d_2)] - S_0[1 - N(d_1)]$,

where $d_1 = \frac{ln(\frac{S_0}{K})+(r+\frac{\sigma^2}{2})T}{\sigma\sqrt{T}}$, $d_2 = d_1 - \sigma\sqrt{T}$.

(ii) $\frac{K}{(1+r)^2} > \frac{\partial c}{\partial r} > 0$ and $\frac{-K}{(1+r)^2} < \frac{\partial p}{\partial r} < 0$; and $\frac{\partial^2 c}{\partial r^2} < 0$ and $\frac{\partial^2 p}{\partial r^2} > 0$. $\frac{\partial c}{\partial r} = \frac{\partial}{\partial r}\left[\frac{\pi \cdot (S_0 u - K)}{1+r}\right] = \frac{d \cdot (S_0 u - K)}{(1+r)^2 (u-d)} > 0$, and $\frac{\partial^2 c}{\partial r^2} = \frac{-2d(S_0 u - K)}{(1+r)^3 (u-d)} < 0$. $\frac{\partial p}{\partial r} = \frac{\partial}{\partial r}\left[\frac{(1-\pi)(K - S_0 d)}{1+r}\right] = \frac{-u \cdot (K - S_0 d)}{(1+r)^2 (u-d)} < 0$, and $\frac{\partial^2 p}{\partial r^2} = \frac{2u(K - S_0 d)}{(1+r)^3 (u-d)} > 0$. Both the binomial and the Black–Scholes Merton option pricing models have: $\frac{\partial c}{\partial r} > 0$ and $\frac{\partial p}{\partial r} < 0$, which indicates both models implicitly assume that increasing (decreasing) in r can increase (decrease) the equity c and decrease (increase) both the risky debt $\frac{K}{1+r} - p$ and the insurance p, where $0 = \frac{\partial S_0}{\partial r} = \frac{\partial c}{\partial r} + \frac{\partial}{\partial r}\left(\frac{K}{1+r} - p\right)$. Also, both the binomial and the Black–Scholes-Merton option pricing models have: $\frac{\partial^2 c}{\partial r^2} < 0$ and $\frac{\partial^2 p}{\partial r^2} > 0$, which indicate both models implicitly assume that further increasing (decreasing) in r will: (1) decrease (increase) the speed of increasing (decreasing) in the equity though bounded by $0 < \frac{\partial c}{\partial r} < \frac{K}{(1+r)^2}$; and (2) decrease (increase) the speed of decreasing (increasing) in the insurance though bounded by $\frac{-K}{(1+r)^2} < \frac{\partial p}{\partial r} < 0$.

(iii) $\frac{-1}{1+r} < \frac{\partial c}{\partial K} < 0$ and $\frac{1}{1+r} > \frac{\partial p}{\partial K} > 0$; and $\frac{\partial^2 c}{\partial K^2} = \frac{\partial^2 p}{\partial K^2} = 0$. $\frac{\partial c}{\partial K} = \frac{\partial}{\partial K}\left[\frac{\pi \cdot (S_0 u - K)}{1+r}\right] = \frac{-\pi}{1+r} < 0$ and hence, $\frac{\partial^2 c}{\partial K^2} = 0$. $\frac{\partial p}{\partial K} = \frac{\partial}{\partial K}\left[\frac{(1-\pi)(K - S_0 d)}{1+r}\right] = \frac{1-\pi}{1+r} > 0$ and hence, $\frac{\partial^2 p}{\partial K^2} = 0$. This indicates that the binomial model implicitly assumes that further increasing (decreasing) K affects neither the speed of decreasing (increasing) in the equity c nor the speed of increasing (decreasing) in the insurance p. The Black–Scholes-Merton option pricing model, on the other hand, has $\frac{\partial^2 c}{\partial K^2} = \frac{\partial^2 p}{\partial K^2} > 0$,[10] which indicates the model implicitly assumes that further increasing (decreasing) in K will: (1) decrease (increase) the speed of decreasing (increasing) in the equity though bounded by $\frac{-1}{1+r} < \frac{\partial c}{\partial K} < 0$; and (2) increase (decrease) the speed of increasing (decreasing) in the insurance though bounded by $\frac{1}{1+r} > \frac{\partial p}{\partial K} > 0$.

(iv) $\frac{\partial c}{\partial u} = \frac{\partial p}{\partial u} > 0$; and $\frac{\partial^2 c}{\partial u^2} = \frac{\partial^2 p}{\partial u^2} < 0$. As shown in Eq. (9.14), we must have: $\frac{\partial c}{\partial u} = \frac{\partial p}{\partial u}$ and $\frac{\partial c}{\partial d} = \frac{\partial p}{\partial d}$. From Eq. (9.15), $\frac{\partial c}{\partial u} = \frac{\partial}{\partial u}\left[\frac{\pi \cdot (S_0 u - K)}{1+r}\right] = \frac{\partial p}{\partial u} = \frac{\partial}{\partial u}\left[\frac{(1-\pi) \cdot (K - S_0 d)}{1+r}\right] = \frac{(K - S_0 d)(1+r-d)}{(1+r)(u-d)^2} > 0$; and $\frac{\partial^2 c}{\partial u^2} = \frac{\partial^2 p}{\partial u^2} = \frac{-2(K - S_0 d)(1+r-d)}{(1+r)(u-d)^3} < 0$.

---

[10] The Dupire formula.

$\frac{\partial c}{\partial d} = \frac{\partial p}{\partial d} < 0$ and $\frac{\partial^2 c}{\partial d^2} = \frac{\partial^2 p}{\partial d^2} < 0$. $\frac{\partial c}{\partial d} = \frac{\partial}{\partial d}\left[\frac{\pi\cdot(S_0u-K)}{1+r}\right] = \frac{\partial p}{\partial d} = \frac{\partial}{\partial d}\left[\frac{(1-\pi)\cdot(K-S_0d)}{1+r}\right] = \frac{-(S_0u-K)[u-(1+r)]}{(1+r)(u-d)^2} < 0$; and $\frac{\partial^2 c}{\partial d^2} = \frac{\partial^2 p}{\partial d^2} = \frac{-2(S_0u-K)[u-(1+r)]}{(1+r)(u-d)^3} < 0$.[11]

For the binomial option pricing example in Fig. 9.1, there is an alternative way to estimate the call c. At $t = 0$, we can buy n units of the asset S_0 and sell one call to construct a portfolio which gives a certain future payoff at $t = T$, and then use the risk-free interest rate $r = 10\%$ to calculate the present value of the portfolio which (with no arbitrage) must be equal to the initial cost of organizing this portfolio, i.e.,

$$\begin{cases} 10,000(n) - 1,100 = 8,400(n) - 0 \Rightarrow n = \frac{11}{16} \\ \frac{8,400(11/16)}{1+10\%} = 8,000(11/16) - c \Rightarrow c = 250 \end{cases} \tag{9.17}$$

That is, from: $n \cdot S_0u - c_u = n \cdot S_0d - c_d$, we derive: $n = \frac{c_u - c_d}{S_0(u-d)}$, and hence, $\left[S_0d \cdot \frac{c_u-c_d}{S_0(u-d)} - c_d\right]/(1+r) = S_0 \cdot \frac{c_u-c_d}{S_0(u-d)} - c$. The call option c can be derived as: $c = \frac{1}{1+r}[\pi \cdot c_u + (1-\pi)c_d]$, where $\pi = \frac{(1+r)-d}{u-d}$ and, $1 - \pi = \frac{u-(1+r)}{u-d}$.

When using Eq. (9.17) to estimate the call option c, many people claim that the value of an option is independent of the probabilities of the underlying asset price moving up or down. Some even claim: "we get the same option price when the probability of an upward movement is 0.5 as we do when it is 0.9".

These claims are false. In terms of Fig. 9.1, if the probability of upward move (π) is0.9, then S_0 cannot remain as \$8,000, i.e., it must be very close to \$10,000/(1 + 10%). If the probability of upward move (π) is 0.01, then S_0 must be very close to \$8,400/(1 + 10%). From System 2 of the Gordan Theorem, i.e., Eq. (9.15), we know that the current asset price: S_0 is determined by investors' expectations of the asset's future possible prices: S_0u, S_0d and their respective probabilities: π, $1-\pi$; and that $\frac{\partial \pi}{\partial S} > 0$, $\frac{\partial \pi}{\partial r} > 0$, $\frac{\partial \pi}{\partial u} < 0$ and $\frac{\partial \pi}{\partial d} < 0$ (i.e., Eq. (9.16)). Also, in Eq. (9.15), $\frac{\pi}{1-\pi} = \frac{1/4}{3/4} = \frac{1}{3}$ means that at $t = 1$ the value of one dollar of good time is only one-third of the value of one dollar of bad time. This implies that investors (the market) believe that the probability of good time is only one-third of the probability of bad time. In sum, the probabilities (π and $1-\pi$) used in pricing assets are the actual world probabilities, not the so-called unreal *risk-neutral* world probabilities.

[11] Chang (2015, pp. 49-51) has shown that when both u and d change, and let $(S_0u - S_0d)$ be the range, the sign of $\frac{\partial c}{\partial(S_0u-S_0d)} = \frac{\partial p}{\partial(S_0u-S_0d)}$ could be positive or negative. The Black-Scholes-Merton option pricing model, on the other hand, has: $\frac{\partial c}{\partial \sigma} = \frac{\partial p}{\partial \sigma} > 0$, where σ is the volatility. Ross (1993, p. 470) and Chang (2014) have shown that with complete market, no transaction costs and no arbitrage, the Black-Scholes-Merton option pricing model has the restriction: $r = \mu + \frac{1}{2}\sigma^2$.

Capital Structure of the Firm

In Chap. 8, Fig. 8.1 for explaining the Modigliani–Miller Second Proposition is:

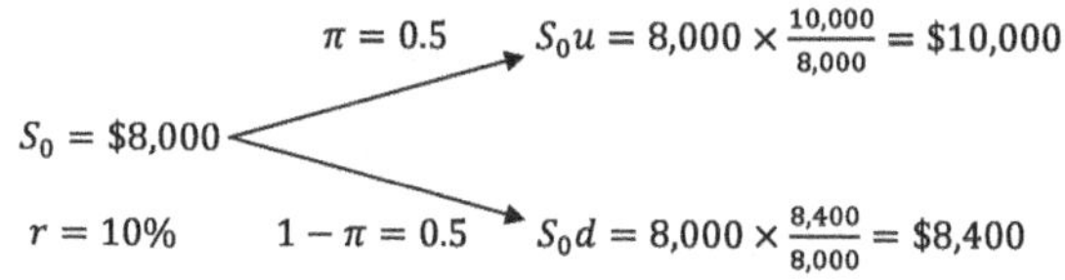

When comparing Fig. 8.1 with Fig. 9.1, it is apparent that Fig. 8.1 (as well as Table 8.1) is wrong: If $S_0 = \$8,000$, $r = 10\%$, $S_0 u = \$10,000$ and $S_0 d = \$8,400$ are defined, then the probabilities cannot be freely given as: $\pi = 0.5, 1 - \pi = 0.5$. In fact, according to the Gordan Theorem, i.e., Eq. (9.15), these probabilities should be calculated as: $\pi = 1/4, 1 - \pi = 3/4$.

Also, in Fig. 9.1 (and Fig. 8.2 in Chapter 8), if except π, one of the four variables: r, S_0, $S_0 u$, $S_0 d$ changes, where $\pi = \frac{1+r-d}{u-d}$:

Case (a): when $S_0 d = 8,400$ decreases to $S_0 d' = 8,200$, $\pi' = \frac{1.1-1.025}{1.25-1.025} = \frac{1}{3} > \pi = \frac{1.1-1.05}{1.25-1.05} = \frac{1}{4}$, and hence, $\frac{\partial \pi}{\partial d} < 0$ leads to $\frac{\partial c}{\partial d} = \frac{\partial p}{\partial d} < 0$.

Case (b): when $S_0 u = 10,000$ decreases to $S_0 u' = 9,000$, $\pi'' = \frac{1.1-1.05}{1.125-1.05} = \frac{2}{3} > \pi = \frac{1}{4}$, and hence, $\frac{\partial \pi}{\partial u} < 0$ leads to $\frac{\partial c}{\partial u} = \frac{\partial p}{\partial u} > 0$.

Case (c): when $S_0 = 8,000$ increases to $S_0' = 8,100$, $\pi''' = \frac{1.1-8,400/8,100}{10,000/8,100-8,400/8,100} = \frac{51}{160} > \pi = \frac{1}{4}$, and hence, $\frac{\partial \pi}{\partial S} > 0$ leads to $\frac{\partial c}{\partial S} > 0$ and $\frac{\partial p}{\partial S} < 0$.

Case (d): when $r = 10\%$ increases to $r' = 12\%$, $\pi'''' = \frac{1.12-1.05}{1.25-1.05} = \frac{7}{20} > \pi = \frac{1}{4}$, and hence, $\frac{\partial \pi}{\partial r} > 0$ leads to $\frac{\partial c}{\partial r} > 0$ and $\frac{\partial p}{\partial r} < 0$.

Note that from Eq. (9.15), we can show the put-call parity:

$$\begin{aligned} S_0 + p &= \frac{1}{1+r}[\pi \cdot S_0 u + (1-p) \cdot S_0 d] + \frac{1}{1+r}[(1-\pi)(K - S_0 d)] \\ &= \frac{1}{1+r}[\pi \cdot (S_0 u - K)] + \frac{K}{1+r} = c + \frac{K}{1+r} \end{aligned} \tag{9.18}$$

and $S_0 = c + \left(\frac{K}{1+r} - p\right)$, where S_0 is the market value of the levered firm, c the equity of the firm, and $\left(\frac{K}{1+r} - p\right)$ the risky debt of the firm. In the case of riskless debt, $p = 0$ and $S_0 = c + \frac{K}{1+r}$, where $\frac{K}{1+r}$ is the riskless debt. At $t = T$, if the equity-holders pay K to the debt holders, then the equity holders can have S_T. Thus,

(i) Under riskless debt (i.e., $K \le S_0 d = \$8,400$) where $d < 1 + r < u$.

At $t = T$, rate of return on equity at good time is: $\frac{S_0 u - K}{c} = \frac{S_0 u - K}{S_0 - \frac{K}{1+r}} = (1+r) \cdot \frac{S_0 u - K}{S_0(1+r) - K}$, and higher K means higher $\frac{S_0 u - K}{c}$.

At $t = T$, rate of return on equity at the bad time is: $\frac{S_0 d - K}{c} = \frac{S_0 d - K}{S_0 - \frac{K}{1+r}} = (1+r) \cdot \frac{S_0 d - K}{S_0(1+r) - K}$, and higher K means lower $\frac{S_0 d - K}{c}$.

		$t = 0$		$t = T$
K	Debt: $\frac{K}{1+r}$	Equity: $c = S_0 - \frac{K}{1+r}$	Rate of return on debt	Rate of return on equity
0	0	8,000	–	good time: $\frac{10,000}{8,000} = 1.25$ bad time: $\frac{8,400}{8,000} = 1.05$
100	90.9090	7,909.0910	1.1	good time: $\frac{9,900}{7,909.0910} = 1.2517$ bad time: $\frac{8,300}{7,909.0910} = 1.0494$
200	181.8182	7,818.1818	1.1	good time: $\frac{9,800}{7,818.1818} = 1.2535$ bad time: $\frac{8200}{7,818.1818} = 1.0488$
8200	7,454.5455	545.4545	1.1	good time: $\frac{1,800}{545.4545} = 3.30$ bad time: $\frac{200}{545.4545} = 0.3667$
8300	7,545.4545	454.5455	1.1	good time: $\frac{1,700}{454.5455} = 3.74$ bad time: $\frac{100}{454.5455} = 0.22$
8400	7,636.3636	363.6364	1.1	good time: $\frac{1,600}{363.6364} = 4.4$ bad time: $\frac{0}{363.6364} = 0$

(ii) Under risky debt (i.e., $K > S_0 d = \$8,400$).

At $t = T$, rate of return on equity at good time is a constant: $\frac{S_0 u - K}{c} = \frac{S_0 u - K}{\frac{1}{1+r}[\pi(S_0 u - K)]} = \frac{1+r}{\pi}$; and rate of return on equity at bad time is zero: $\frac{0}{c} = 0$. That is, changes in the debt-equity ratio (i.e., changes in $\boldsymbol{K}$) have no effect on the rate of return on equity.

At $t = T$, rate of return on debt at good time is: $\frac{K}{S_0 - c} = \frac{K}{\frac{1}{1+r}\left[\pi \cdot S_0 u + (1-\pi) S_0 d\right] - \frac{1}{1+r}\left[\pi(S_0 u - K)\right]} = \frac{1+r}{\pi + (1-\pi)\frac{S_0 d}{K}}$, and higher K means higher $\frac{K}{S_0 - c}$.

At $t = T$, rate of return on debt at the bad time is: $\frac{S_0 d}{S_0 - c} = \frac{S_0 d}{S_0 - \frac{1}{1+r}[\pi(S_0 u - K)]}$, and higher K means lower c and lower $\frac{S_0 d}{S_0 - c}$.

		$t=0$		$t=T$
K	Debt: $S_0 - c$	Equity: $c = \frac{\pi(S_0u-K)}{1+r}$	Rate of return on debt	Rate of return on equity
8,500	7,659.0909	340.9091	good time: $\frac{8,500}{7,659.0909} = 1.1098$ bad time: $\frac{8,400}{7,659.0909} = 1.0967$	good time: 4.4 bad time: 0.0
8,600	7,681.8182	318.1818	good time: $\frac{8,600}{7,681.8181} = 1.1195$ bad time: $\frac{8,400}{7681.8181} = 1.0935$	good time: 4.4 bad time: 0.0
8,700	7,704.5455	295.4545	good time: $\frac{8,700}{7,704.5455} = 1.1292$ bad time: $\frac{8,400}{7,704.5455} = 1.0903$	good time: 4.4 bad time: 0.0
8,800	7,727.2727	272.7273	good time: $\frac{8,800}{7,727.2727} = 1.1388$ bad time: $\frac{8,400}{7,727.2727} = 1.0871$	good time: 4.4 bad time: 0.0
8,900	7,750	250	good time: $\frac{8,900}{7,750} = 1.1484$ bad time: $\frac{8,400}{7,750} = 1.0839$	good time: 4.4 bad time: 0.0
10,000	8,000	0	good time: $\frac{10000}{8000} = 1.25$ bad time: $\frac{8400}{8000} = 1.05$	–

In summary, we now have a new capital structure irrelevancy proposition:

Proposition 9.2

(Capital Structure Irrelevancy Proposition II)

In a complete market with no transaction costs and no arbitrage, with the binomial distribution: (i) under riskless debt, increasing the debt-equity ratio increases the variance of the rate of return on equity and has no effect on the rate of return on debt; and (ii) under risky debt, increasing the debt-equity ratio increases the variance of the rate of return on debt but does not affect the probability density function of the rate of return on equity.

This proposition refutes the Modigliani–Miller second proposition that "the use of debt rather than equity funds to finance a given venture may well increase the expected return to the owners, but only at the cost of increased dispersion of the outcomes" (1958, p. 262); "any gains from using more of what might seem to be cheaper debt capital would thus be offset by correspondingly higher cost of the now riskier equity capital" (Miller, 1988, p. 100).

Also, note that from Eq. (9.8.3) of Chap. 8:

$$E(\tilde{r}_S) = E(\tilde{r}_{WACC}) + (B/S_L)\left[E(\tilde{r}_{WACC}) - E(\tilde{r}_B)\right] \tag{9.8.3}$$

Table 9.5 Future possible cash flows and their probabilities

Probability	Cash flow
0.5	\$2,000
0.5	\$800

where $E(\tilde{r}_S)$ is the expected rate of return on the equity, $E(\tilde{r}_{WACC})$, the weighted average cost of capital (WACC) on the levered firm's assets, $E(\tilde{r}_B)$, the expected rate of return on the debt, B, the debt, and S_L, the equity. From Proposition 9.2, under risky debt, $E(\tilde{r}_S)$ is independent of B/S_L. Since the Modigliani–Miller first proposition holds (i.e., the market value of the firm is independent of B/S_L), $E(\tilde{r}_{WACC})$ is also independent of B/S_L. Thus, in terms of Eq. (9.8.3) we shall have: $E(\tilde{r}_S) = E(\tilde{r}_{WACC}) = E(\tilde{r}_B)$. Also, from Eq. (9.15), since the probabilities are the actual world probabilities, all assets will have the same expected rate of return which is equal to the risk-free interest rate. This result may seem counter-intuitive. But note that Eq. (9.8.3) implicitly assumes: (i) the firm always exists and produces two possible cash flows in each year; (ii) both the debtholders and the equityholders (i.e., investors) can live forever and will never need to use these cash flows for consumption or investment; and (iii) the storage cost of these cash flows is zero. Under these three assumptions, investors will care only about the expected rate of return of asset, and thus, all assets will produce exactly the same expected rate of return which is equal to the risk-free interest rate.[12]

9.4 The NPV Analysis Under Uncertainty

In previous chapters we have derived the discount rate (i.e., the opportunity cost of capital) to discount assets' future cash flows under uncertainty, e.g., the capital asset pricing model (CAPM) uses beta as a risk measure to calculate the project's discount rate. Based on the Gordan Theorem, e.g., Eq. (9.15), investors' attitudes toward risk are incorporated into the probabilities: π and $1 - \pi$. The following example shows how to apply the Gordan (Arbitrage) Theorem to price an uncertain project.

Consider a one-year project with initial investment \$1,000 at $t = 0$. At the end of the project ($t = 1$), two possible cash flows and their respective probabilities are shown in Table 9.5.

If the project's beta (β) is 2.0, one-year risk-free interest rate is 5%, and the expected rate of return of the market portfolio is 13%, then from the CAPM, the discount rate is calculated as:

$$E\left(\tilde{R}\right) = 0.05 + (0.13 - 0.05) \cdot 2.0 = 0.21.$$

[12] Under certainty, the example which uses Eq. (2.4) in Chapter 2 also shows the same result: $r_S = r_{WACC} = r_B$.

In practice, the net present value (NPV) is usually calculated as:

$$NPV = -\$1,000 + \frac{0.5(\$2,000) + 0.5(\$800)}{1 + 0.21} = \$157.02. \tag{9.19}$$

This means that the market value of the project at $t = 0$ is: \$1, 157.02.

However, this kind of calculating NPV is not correct. To see this, let us assume that the owner of the project is going to issue a one-year European call option c on this project with strike price $K = \$900$. This is equivalent to issue both equity and debt to finance the project's initial cost \$1,000, where the promised payment to the debtholder at $t = 1$ is: $K = \$900$. Thus, based on Eq. (9.15), i.e., System 2 of the Gordan Theorem, we have:

$$\begin{cases} \text{Money market}: 1 = \frac{1}{1+r}[\pi(1+r) + (1-\pi)(1+r)] = \frac{1}{1+0.05}\left[\frac{1}{2}(1.05) + \frac{1}{2}(1.05)\right] \\ \text{The project}: S_0 = 1,333.33 = \frac{1}{1+r}[\pi \cdot S_0 u + (1-\pi) \cdot S_0 d] = \frac{1}{1+0.05}\left[\frac{1}{2}(2,000) + \frac{1}{2}(800)\right] \\ \text{Call option}: c = 523.81 = \frac{1}{1+r}[\pi \cdot (S_0 u - K) + (1-\pi) \cdot 0] = \frac{1}{1+0.05}\left[\frac{1}{2}(1,100) + \frac{1}{2}(0)\right] \\ \text{Put option}: p = 47.62 = \frac{1}{1+r}[\pi \cdot 0 + (1-\pi) \cdot (K - S_0 d)] = \frac{1}{1+0.05}\left[\frac{1}{2}(0) + \frac{1}{2}(100)\right] \end{cases} \tag{9.20}$$

Thus, the correct NPV of the project is \$333.33(= \$1, 333.33 − \$1, 000) rather than \$157.02 in Eq. (9.19). Equation (9.20) also shows that $\frac{\pi}{1-\pi} = \frac{0.5}{0.5} = \frac{1}{1}$, i.e., the values of one dollar of the two states are the same.

If the incorrect NPV (i.e., Eq. (9.19)) is used, then Eq. (9.20) becomes:

$$\begin{cases} \text{Money market}: 1 = \frac{1}{1+r}[\pi'(1+r) + (1-\pi')(1+r)] = \frac{1}{1+0.05}[0.3457(1.05) + 0.6543(1.05)] \\ \text{The project}: S_0 = 1,157.02 = \frac{1}{1+r}[\pi' \cdot S_0 u + (1-\pi') \cdot S_0 d] = \frac{1}{1+0.05}[0.3457(2,000) + 0.6543(800)] \\ \text{Call option}: c = 362.16 = \frac{1}{1+r}[\pi' \cdot (S_0 u - K) + (1-\pi') \cdot 0] = \frac{1}{1+0.05}[0.3457(1,100) + 0.6543(0)] \\ \text{Put option}: p = 62.31 = \frac{1}{1+r}[\pi' \cdot 0 + (1-\pi') \cdot (K - S_0 d)] = \frac{1}{1+0.05}[0.3457(0) + 0.6543(100)] \end{cases} \tag{9.21}$$

Equation (9.21) shows that $\frac{\pi'}{1-\pi'} = \frac{0.3457}{0.6543} = \frac{0.5284}{1}$, i.e., the value of one dollar of State 1 is only 52.84% of the value of one dollar of State 2. This contradicts the probabilities in Table 9.5 which says that the values of one dollar of the two states are equal.

9.5 P-Index: The Measure of Risk Structure of Asset

In Chap. 7, beta or variance is termed as the risk level of asset. We can use put option to construct the p-index to measure risk levels (likelihoods) of asset's providing various rates of return, i.e., risk structure of asset.

Risk can be defined as the likelihood that you can deliver your promise. For every asset which provides uncertain payoff at $t = T$, there exists a corresponding put-call parity at $t = 0$: $c + \frac{K}{1+r} = S_0 + p$. At $t = T$, the payoff of the European put option p is $Max[K - S_T, 0]$, and hence, the put option p can be interpreted as the insurance to ensure that the owner of S_0 can have at least K at $t = T$.

Divide p by K and let $K = (1+\delta)S_0$ where $\delta > -1$, we have the p-index for the asset S_0:

$$\frac{p}{K} = \frac{p}{(1+\delta)S_0}. \tag{9.22}$$

The p-index measures the insurance fees for each insured dollar at $t = T$. Higher p-index means higher risk (i.e., less likelihood) for the asset $\mathbf{S_0}$ to deliver at least $\boldsymbol{\delta}$ rate of return. Different δ's mean different p-indexes. Thus, the p-index is a vector which measures the risk structure of asset. Also, because

$$\frac{\partial}{\partial K}\left(\frac{p}{K}\right) = \frac{\partial p/\partial K}{K} - \frac{p}{K^2} = p \cdot \frac{(\partial p/\partial K)(K/p) - 1}{K^2},$$

we have:

$$\frac{\partial}{\partial K}\left(\frac{p}{K}\right) > (<)0 \text{ if and only if } \frac{\partial p/p}{\partial K/K} > (<)1. \tag{9.23}$$

As shown in Eq. (9.10), upper and lower bounds for the put option p is: $Max\left[\frac{K}{1+r} - S_0, 0\right] \le p < \frac{K}{1+r}$. Hence, upper and lower bounds for the p-index is:

$$Max\left[\frac{1}{1+r} - \frac{1}{1+\delta}, 0\right] \le \frac{p}{S_0(1+\delta)} < \frac{1}{1+r}. \tag{9.24}$$

When δ rate of return is very large (i.e., a very large K) that the call option $c = 0$, from the put-call parity the p-index for the asset is: $\frac{p}{(1+\delta)S_0} = \frac{1}{1+r} - \frac{1}{1+\delta}$ where $\delta > r$, and $\frac{\partial}{\partial \delta}\left[\frac{p}{(1+\delta)S_0}\right] = \frac{1}{(1+\delta)^2} > 0$, $\frac{\partial^2}{\partial \delta^2}\left[\frac{p}{(1+\delta)S_0}\right] = \frac{-2}{(1+\delta)^3} < 0$.

The Binomial Case

The binomial option pricing model may be presented as the follows.

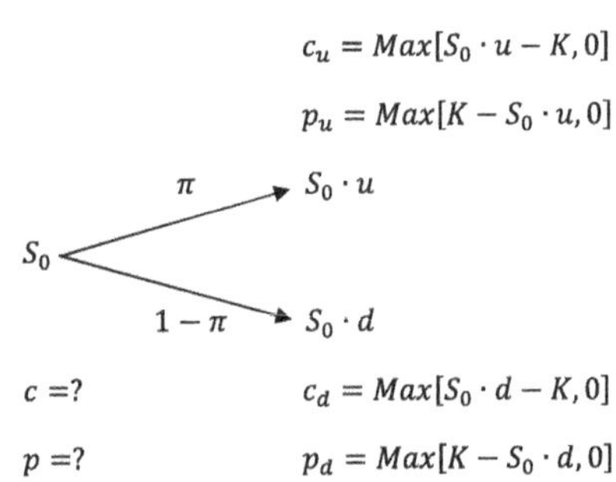

where $u > 1 + r$, $0 < d < 1 + r$, r is the simple risk-free interest rate, and K is the strike price.

From System 2 of Gordan Theorem we have:

$$\begin{cases} \text{Money market}: 1 = \frac{1}{1+r}[\pi(1+r) + (1-\pi)(1+r)] \\ \text{The asset}: S_0 = \frac{1}{1+r}[\pi \cdot S_0 u + (1-\pi) \cdot S_0 d] \\ \text{Call option}: c = \frac{1}{1+r}[\pi \cdot (S_0 u - K) + (1-\pi) \cdot 0] \\ \text{Put option}: p = \frac{1}{1+r}[\pi \cdot 0 + (1-\pi) \cdot (K - S_0 d)] \end{cases}$$

where $S_0 d < K < S_0 u$, $\pi = \frac{(1+r)-d}{u-d}$ and $1 - \pi = \frac{u-(1+r)}{u-d}$. The p-index for the asset S_0 is:

$$\frac{p}{K} = \frac{\frac{1-\pi}{1+r}[S_0(1+\delta) - S_0 d]}{(1+\delta)S_0} = \frac{(1+\delta)-d}{1+\delta} \cdot \frac{1-\pi}{1+r} \tag{9.25}$$

It shows that for any given δ rate of return, lower down move d means higher risk level, i.e., $\frac{\partial}{\partial d}\left[\frac{p}{(1+\delta)S_0}\right] = \frac{-1}{1+\delta} \cdot \frac{1-\pi}{1+r} < 0$, $\frac{\partial^2}{\partial d^2}\left[\frac{p}{(1+\delta)S_0}\right] = 0$; and $\frac{\partial}{\partial \delta}\left[\frac{p}{(1+\delta)S_0}\right] = \frac{d}{(1+\delta)^2} \cdot \frac{1-\pi}{1+r} > 0$, $\frac{\partial^2}{\partial \delta^2}\left[\frac{p}{(1+\delta)S_0}\right] < 0$.[13] Also, assets having $d = 0$ will have exactly the same constant p-index: $\frac{p}{K} = \frac{p}{(1+\delta)S_0} = \frac{1-\pi}{1+r}$, i.e., the same risk.

For any given δ such that $S_0 d < K = (1+\delta)S_0 < S_0 u$, the p-index for the call option c is (where $0 < K_c = c(1+\delta') < S_0 u - (1+\delta)S_0$ and $\delta' > -1$):

$$\frac{p'}{(1+\delta')c} = \frac{\frac{1-\pi}{1+r}\left[c(1+\delta') - 0\right]}{c(1+\delta')} = \frac{1-\pi}{1+r}, \tag{9.26}$$

which is the same as the p-index for any underlying asset having $d = 0$. The p-index for the put option p is (where $0 < K_p = p(1+\delta'') < (1+\delta)S_0 - S_0 d$ and $\delta'' > -1$):

$$\frac{p''}{p(1+\delta'')} = \frac{\frac{\pi}{1+r}[p(1+\delta'') - 0]}{p(1+\delta'')} = \frac{\pi}{1+r}. \tag{9.27}$$

Equation's (9.26) and (9.27) show that since u, d, δ, δ' and δ'' are independent of the p-indexes, all assets' call options have exactly the same constant risk level, and all assets' put options have exactly the same constant risk level. Note that the p-index for the asset S_0 in Eq. (9.25) is always less or equal to the p-index for its

---

[13] In the Black–Scholes-Merton option pricing model, the p-index is:

$\frac{p}{K} = \frac{p}{e^{\delta T} S_0} = e^{-rT} \cdot [1 - N(d_2)] - e^{-\delta T} \cdot [1 - N(d_1)]$, where $d_1 = \frac{\ln(e^{-\delta T}) + \left(r + \frac{\sigma^2}{2}\right)T}{\sigma\sqrt{T}}$ and $d_2 = d_1 - \sigma\sqrt{T}$.

Because $\frac{\partial c}{\partial \sigma} = \frac{\partial p}{\partial \sigma} > 0$, higher σ means higher risk of the asset's providing at least δ rate of return.

call option in Eq. (9.26), i.e., the underlying asset cannot be riskier than its call option. However, comparing Eq. (9.25) with Eq. (9.27), it is found that when both π and d are very small, the underlying asset's p-index can be larger than its put option's p-index, i.e., the underlying asset can be riskier than its put option.

Example 9.1 Let $K = (1+\delta)S_0$ and $S_0 d < (1+\delta)S_0 < S_0 u$.

$$\begin{cases} \text{Money market}: 1 = \frac{1}{1+0.25}\left[\frac{3}{4}\cdot(1+0.25)+\frac{1}{4}\cdot(1+0.25)\right] \\ \text{Asset A}: S_A = 48 = \frac{1}{1+0.25}\left[\frac{3}{4}\cdot(70)+\frac{1}{4}\cdot(30)\right] \\ \text{Asset B}: S_B = 60 = \frac{1}{1+0.25}\left[\frac{3}{4}\cdot(85)+\frac{1}{4}\cdot(45)\right] \\ \text{Call option for Asset A}: c_A = \frac{1}{1+0.25}\left[\frac{3}{4}\cdot\left(48\cdot\left(\frac{70}{48}\right)-48(1+\delta)\right)+\frac{1}{4}\cdot 0\right] \\ \text{Put option for Asset A}: p_A = \frac{1}{1+0.25}\left[\frac{3}{4}\cdot 0+\frac{1}{4}\cdot\left(48(1+\delta)-48\cdot\left(\frac{30}{48}\right)\right)\right] \\ \text{Call option for Asset B}: c_B = \frac{1}{1+0.25}\left[\frac{3}{4}\cdot\left(60\cdot\left(\frac{85}{60}\right)-60(1+\delta)\right)+\frac{1}{4}\cdot 0\right] \\ \text{Put option for Asset B}: p_B = \frac{1}{1+0.25}\left[\frac{3}{4}\cdot 0+\frac{1}{4}\cdot\left(60(1+\delta)-60\cdot\left(\frac{45}{60}\right)\right)\right] \end{cases}$$

		p-index			
		$\delta = -25\%$	$\delta = r = 25\%$	$\delta = 40\%$	$\delta = 500\%$
Asset A	$\frac{p_A}{(1+\delta)S_A}$	0.0333	0.1	0.1107	0.6333
Asset B	$\frac{p_B}{(1+\delta)S_B}$	0.0	0.08	0.0929	0.6333
		With $K = (1+0.25)S_0$, $c_A = c_B = p_A = p_B = 6$			
Call option for Asset A	$\frac{p'_A}{(1+\delta)c_A}$	0.2	0.2	0.2	0.6333
Call option for Asset B	$\frac{p'_B}{(1+\delta)c_B}$	0.2	0.2	0.2	0.6333
Put option for Asset A	$\frac{p''_A}{(1+\delta)p_A}$	0.6	0.6	0.6	0.6333
Put option for Asset B	$\frac{p''_B}{(1+\delta)p_B}$	0.6	0.6	0.6	0.6333

Since Asset A's $d = 0.625$ is less than Asset B's $d = 0.75$, Asset A is riskier than Asset B in providing at least δ rate of return. Call options have the same risk level 0.2. Put options have the same risk level 0.6.

Example 9.2 Let $K = (1+\delta)S_0$ and $S_0 d < (1+\delta)S_0 < S_0 u$.

$$\begin{cases} \text{Money market}: 1 = \frac{1}{1+0.25}\left[\frac{1}{4}\cdot(1+0.25)+\frac{3}{4}\cdot(1+0.25)\right] \\ \text{Asset}: S_0 = 20 = \frac{1}{1+0.25}\left[\frac{1}{4}\cdot(88)+\frac{3}{4}\cdot(4)\right] \\ \text{Call option}: c = \frac{1}{1+0.25}\left[\frac{1}{4}\cdot\left(20\cdot\left(\frac{88}{20}\right)-20(1+\delta)\right)+\frac{3}{4}\cdot 0\right] \\ \text{Put option}: p = \frac{1}{1+0.25}\left[\frac{1}{4}\cdot 0+\frac{3}{4}\cdot\left(20(1+\delta)-20\cdot\left(\frac{4}{20}\right)\right)\right] \end{cases}$$

		p-index			
		$\delta = -25\%$	$\delta = r = 25\%$	$\delta = 40\%$	$\delta = 500\%$
Asset	$\frac{p}{(1+\delta)S_0}$	0.44	0.504	0.5143	0.6333
	With $K = 20(1+0.25), c = p = 12.6.$				
Call option for Asset	$\frac{p'}{(1+\delta)c}$	0.6	0.6	0.6	0.6333
Put option for Asset	$\frac{p''}{(1+\delta)p}$	0.2	0.2	0.2	0.6333

This indicates that an underlying asset can be riskier than its put option.

The Trinomial Case

Example 9.3 Let $K = (1+\delta)S_0$.

$$\begin{cases} \text{Money market}: 1 = \frac{1}{1+0.25}\left[\frac{1}{4}\cdot(1+0.25)+\frac{3}{8}\cdot(1+0.25)+\frac{3}{8}\cdot(1+0.25)\right] \\ \text{Asset A}: S_A = 48 = \frac{1}{1+0.25}\left[\frac{1}{4}\cdot(21)+\frac{3}{8}\cdot(56)+\frac{3}{8}\cdot(90)\right] \\ \text{Asset B}: S_B = 48 = \frac{1}{1+0.25}\left[\frac{1}{4}\cdot(18)+\frac{3}{8}\cdot(70)+\frac{3}{8}\cdot(78)\right] \\ c_A = \frac{1}{1+0.25}\left[\frac{1}{4}\cdot Max(21-48(1+\delta),0)+\frac{3}{8}\cdot Max(56-48(1+\delta),0)+\frac{3}{8}\cdot Max(90-48(1+\delta),0)\right] \\ p_A = \frac{1}{1+0.25}\left[\frac{1}{4}\cdot Max(48(1+\delta)-21,0)+\frac{3}{8}\cdot Max(48(1+\delta)-56,0)+\frac{3}{8}\cdot Max(48(1+\delta)-90,0)\right] \\ c_B = \frac{1}{1+0.25}\left[\frac{1}{4}\cdot Max(18-48(1+\delta),0)+\frac{3}{8}\cdot Max(70-48(1+\delta),0)+\frac{3}{8}\cdot Max(78-48(1+\delta),0)\right] \\ p_B = \frac{1}{1+0.25}\left[\frac{1}{4}\cdot Max(48(1+\delta)-18,0)+\frac{3}{8}\cdot Max(48(1+\delta)-70,0)+\frac{3}{8}\cdot Max(48(1+\delta)-78,0)\right] \end{cases}$$

		p-index			
		$\delta = -50\%$	$\delta = r = 25\%$	$\delta = 50\%$	$\delta = 500\%$
Asset A	$\frac{p_A}{(1+\delta)S_A}$	0.025	0.15	0.2083	0.6333
Asset B	$\frac{p_B}{(1+\delta)S_B}$	0.05	0.14	0.1583	0.6333

When providing at least −50% rate of return, Asset B is riskier than Asset A (i.e., $\frac{p_B}{(1-0.5)S_B} = 0.05 > \frac{p_A}{(1-0.5)S_A} = 0.025$). But when providing at least 25% or 50% rate of return, Asset A is riskier than Asset B. This shows that the ranking of risk levels of assets' providing different rates of returns could reverse.

An Empirical Example of the P-index

In Tables 7.1 and 7.2 in Chap. 7, for the ten largest capitalization US and Chinese firms in the NYSE and the SSE during 2018–2020, we have estimated Jensen's alphas (positive sign means overperformance; negative sign underperformance) and betas (higher β means higher risk). The following Tables 9.6 and 9.7 show the p-indexes for these US and Chinese firms during 2018–2020.

Three steps to estimate the p-index (for example in 2018) are:

Step 1. Use "NYSE (SSE) index in the beginning of 2018: $\widehat{S_{0NY}}$ ($\widehat{S_{0SH}}$); highest NYSE (SSE) index: $S_{0NY}u_{NY}$ ($S_{0SH}u_{SH}$); lowest NYSE (SSE) index:

Table 9.6 P-index of the ten largest capitalization US firms in the NYSE (2018–2020)

		Overvalued (Undervalued)	$\delta = r$	$\delta = 5\%$	$\delta = 10\%$	Alpha	Beta
Apple Inc. (AAPL)	2018	(19.59%)	0.0488	0.0500	0.0518	−0.0106	0.5687
	2019	(2.72%)	0.1173	0.1372	0.1686	0.0239	1.6591
	2020	(42.06%)	0.0478	0.0479	0.0495	0.0423	1.1869
Microsoft (MSFT)	2018	(20.75%)	0.0346	0.0365	0.0395	0.0264	1.2694
	2019	(3.50%)	0.0738	0.0950	0.1284	0.0293	0.7974
	2020	(27.95%)	0.0342	0.0344	0.0365	0.0106	0.6817
Exxon Mobil (XOM)	2018	1.76%	0.0345	0.0365	0.0395	−0.0023	1.5039
	2019	2.65%	0.0309	0.0533	0.0885	−0.0237	1.2618
	2020	5.17%	0.0452	0.0453	0.0470	−0.0296	1.4266
Amazon (AMZN)	2018	(36.33%)	0.0559	0.0567	0.0579	0.0427	2.0204
	2019	(0.65%)	0.0423	0.0643	0.0991	−0.0026	1.4695
	2020	(43.03%)	0.0424	0.0425	0.0443	0.0455	0.7789
JPMorgan Chase (JPM)	2018	(3.73%)	0.0291	0.0313	0.0348	0.0014	1.0942
	2019	(2.23%)	0.0523	0.0741	0.1084	0.0103	1.0397
	2020	5.02%	0.0357	0.0359	0.0380	−0.0052	1.1991
Johnson & Johnson (JNJ)	2018	(0.92%)	0.0251	0.0275	0.0313	0.0051	0.9597
	2019	1.12%	0.0206	0.0433	0.0790	−0.0076	0.9768
	2020	(4.07%)	0.0246	0.0248	0.0274	−0.0047	0.6275
Berkshire (BRKB)	2018	(7.37%)	0.0224	0.0249	0.0289	0.0126	0.9922
	2019	4.98%	0.0230	0.0456	0.0812	−0.0093	0.8853
	2020	1.12%	0.0256	0.0258	0.0283	−0.0050	0.7743
Meta (META)	2018	(8.71%)	0.0576	0.0584	0.0594	−0.0181	0.6052
	2019	(3.56%)	0.0682	0.0896	0.1231	0.0122	2.2675
	2020	(26.90%)	0.0419	0.0421	0.0438	0.0168	1.1336
General Electric (GE)	2018	7.24%	0.0900	0.0892	0.0875	−0.0574	0.5532
	2019	(5.24%)	0.0591	0.0807	0.1147	−0.0013	2.6974
	2020	(3.34%)	0.0469	0.0470	0.0486	0.0084	0.9483
Wells Fargo (WFC)	2018	(0.061%)	0.0448	0.0462	0.0484	−0.0123	1.0166
	2019	6.22%	0.0315	0.0539	0.0891	−0.0012	1.0039
	2020	6.89%	0.0488	0.0489	0.0504	−0.0356	1.2879
Equally-weighted Portfolio	2018	–	0.0443	0.0457	0.0479	–	1.0584
	2019	–	0.0519	0.0737	0.1080	–	1.4058
	2020	–	0.0393	0.0395	0.0414	–	1.0045
NYSE Index	2018	–	0.0273	0.0295	0.0332	–	–

(continued)

Table 9.6 (continued)

	Overvalued (Undervalued)	$\delta = r$	$\delta = 5\%$	$\delta = 10\%$	Alpha	Beta
2019	–	0.0304	0.0528	0.0881	–	–
2020	–	0.0327	0.0329	0.0351	–	–

$S_{0NY}d_{NY}$ ($S_{0SH}d_{SH}$); annual risk-free interest rate: r" to calculate probability: π.

Step 2. Choose ten largest companies in the NYSE (SSE), and for the i-th company, use "probability: π; highest stock price: $S_{0i}u_i$; lowest price: $S_{0i}d_i$; and annual risk-free interest rate: r" to estimate its theoretical stock price in the beginning of 2018: S_{0i}.

Step 3. Use the actual index: $\widehat{S_{0NY}}$ ($\widehat{S_{0SH}}$) to estimate NYSE (SSE) index's p-index. Use the theoretical price: S_{0i} to estimate the i-th company's p-index.

Example Let $K = (1+\delta)S_0$ and $S_0d < (1+\delta)S_0 < S_0u$, where $\delta = r, 5\%, 10\%$.

$$\begin{cases} \text{NYSE index 2018}: \widehat{S_{0NY}} = \frac{1}{1+r}[\pi \cdot S_{0NY}u_{NY} + (1-\pi)\cdot S_{0NY}d_{NY}] \\ \text{i} - \text{th company 2018}: S_{0i} = \frac{1}{1+r}[\pi \cdot S_{0i}u_i + (1-\pi)\cdot S_{0i}d_i] \\ \text{NYSE index 2018 Call option}: c_{NY} = \frac{1}{1+r}[\pi \cdot (S_{0NY}u_{NY} - K) + (1-\pi)\cdot 0] \\ \text{NYSE index 2018 Put option}: p_{NY} = \frac{1}{1+r}[\pi \cdot 0 + (1-\pi)\cdot (K - S_{0NY}d_{NY})] \\ \text{i} - \text{th company 2018 Call option}: c_i = \frac{1}{1+r}[\pi \cdot (S_{0i}u_i - K) + (1-\pi)\cdot 0] \\ \text{i} - \text{th company 2018 Put option}: p_i = \frac{1}{1+r}[\pi \cdot 0 + (1-\pi)\cdot (K - S_{0i}d_i)] \end{cases}$$

Also, from the put-call parity, Eq. (9.3), we have:

$$S_{0i} = c_i + \frac{K_i}{1+r} - p_i, i = 1, \ldots, n.$$

Divide both sides of this equation by S_{0i}:

$$1 = \frac{c_i}{S_{0i}} + \frac{K_i/S_{0i}}{1+r} - \frac{p_i}{S_{0i}}, i = 1, \ldots, n.$$

Let $K_i = S_{0i}(1+\delta)$,

$$1 = \frac{c_i}{S_{0i}} + \frac{1+\delta}{1+r} - \frac{p_i}{S_{0i}}, i = 1, \ldots, n.$$

Table 9.7 P-index of the ten largest capitalization Chinese firms in the SSE (2018–2020)

		Overvalued (Undervalued)	$\delta = r$	$\delta = 5\%$	$\delta = 10\%$	Alpha	Beta
SANY Heavy Industry	2018	(20.43%)	0.0092	0.0100	0.0123	−0.1269	0.0254
	2019	(5.41%)	0.0954	0.1148	0.1496	0.0400	0.9980
	2020	(33.62%)	0.1966	0.2044	0.2147	0.0476	1.1457
China Merchants Bank	2018	(10.62%)	0.0148	0.0155	0.0176	0.1222	1.7630
	2019	(2.39%)	0.0477	0.0683	0.1052	0.0170	0.8310
	2020	(4.12%)	0.1237	0.1340	0.1475	0.0087	0.6825
Hengrui Medicine	2018	(15.62%)	0.0226	0.0232	0.0249	−0.0456	0.6637
	2019	(0.26%)	0.0745	0.0945	0.1302	0.0280	0.9800
	2020	(20.65%)	0.1356	0.1455	0.1585	0.0395	0.3029
Kweichow Moutai	2018	(4.14%)	0.0162	0.0169	0.0189	0.1124	1.6952
	2019	(5.21%)	0.0885	0.1081	0.1432	0.0470	0.6060
	2020	(26.47%)	0.1654	0.1743	0.1859	0.0369	1.0671
LONGi Green Energy	2018	2.73%	0.0378	0.0382	0.0391	0.0378	1.4360
	2019	(2.41%)	0.0636	0.0838	0.1200	0.0080	1.2940
	2020	(59.74%)	0.2830	0.2879	0.2945	0.1006	2.0032
Industrial Bank	2018	(4.45%)	0.0131	0.0139	0.0159	0.0355	1.1597
	2019	(1.03%)	0.0341	0.0551	0.0926	0.0040	0.6220
	2020	(4.40%)	0.1013	0.1123	0.1268	0.0023	0.7177
Ping An Insurance	2018	(1.26%)	0.0144	0.0152	0.0172	0.0594	1.3544
	2019	(3.65%)	0.0556	0.0760	0.1126	0.0180	0.9470
	2020	4.31%	0.0908	0.1021	0.1171	−0.0049	0.8591
I&C Bank of China	2018	(13.03%)	0.0167	0.0174	0.0193	0.0821	1.4648
	2019	1.59%	0.0154	0.0368	0.0751	0.0010	0.3140
	2020	6.95%	0.0529	0.0655	0.0821	−0.0086	0.2701
Great Wall Motor	2018	(3.41%)	0.0327	0.0332	0.0344	0.0286	1.4006
	2019	(5.11%)	0.0806	0.1004	0.1358	0.0240	0.5660
	2020	(64.45%)	0.3057	0.3099	0.3155	0.1237	1.9767
China Construction Bank	2018	(14.82%)	0.0189	0.0189	0.0214	0.1083	1.6575
	2019	0.73%	0.0227	0.0439	0.0819	0.0050	0.3410
	2020	4.31%	0.0603	0.0727	0.0889	−0.0074	0.3876
Equally-weighted Portfolio	2018	–	0.0196	0.0202	0.0221	–	1.2620
	2019	–	0.0578	0.0782	0.1146	–	0.7490
	2020	–	0.1515	0.1609	0.1732	–	0.9413
SSE Index	2018	–	0.0162	0.0169	0.0188	–	–

(continued)

Table 9.7 (continued)

		Overvalued (Undervalued)	$\delta = r$	$\delta = 5\%$	$\delta = 10\%$	Alpha	Beta
	2019	–	0.0291	0.0502	0.0879	–	–
	2020	–	0.0645	0.0768	0.0929	–	–

Invest n dollars to organize an equally-weighted portfolio[14]:

$$n = \sum_{i=1}^{n} \frac{c_i}{S_{0i}} + \frac{n(1+\delta)}{1+r} - \sum_{i=1}^{n} \frac{p_i}{S_{0i}}$$

Thus, the p-index of this equally-weighted portfolio is:

$$\frac{1}{n(1+\delta)} \sum_{i=1}^{n} \frac{p_i}{S_{0i}} = \frac{1}{n} \sum_{i=1}^{n} \frac{p_i}{S_{0i}(1+\delta)}$$

Also, adding up n assets' put-call parities (where $K_i = S_{0i}(1+\delta), i = 1, \ldots, n$):

$$\sum_{i=1}^{n} S_{0i} = \sum_{i=1}^{n} c_i + \frac{(1+\delta)\sum_{i=1}^{n} S_{0i}}{1+r} - \sum_{i=1}^{n} p_i$$

Divide both sides of this equation by $\sum_{i=1}^{n} S_{0i}$:

$$1 = \frac{\sum_{i=1}^{n} c_i}{\sum_{i=1}^{n} S_{0i}} + \frac{(1+\delta)}{1+r} - \frac{\sum_{i=1}^{n} p_i}{\sum_{i=1}^{n} S_{0i}}$$

Thus, the p-index of this value-weighted portfolio is:

$$\frac{1}{(1+\delta)} \cdot \frac{\sum_{i=1}^{n} p_i}{\sum_{i=1}^{n} S_{0i}} = \frac{\sum_{i=1}^{n} p_i}{\sum_{i=1}^{n} S_{0i}(1+\delta)}$$

In Table 9.7, both the p-index of the equally-weighted portfolio of the ten firms in SSE and the p-index of SSE show increasing risk-level during 2018–2020. In Table 9.6, both the p-index of the equally-weighted portfolio of the ten firms in NYSE and the p-index of NYSE index show increasing risk-level in 2019 and decreasing risk-level in 2020. It also shows that the risk-level of SSE index changes more than that of NYSE.

[14] This is financial diversification irrelevancy, i.e., it does not add or decrease value.

Credit Risk

From Eq. (9.4), at $t = 0$, the market value of the risky debt of a levered firm is: $\frac{K}{1+r} - p$. At $t = T$, the maximum value of debt is: K, and hence, the maximum rate of return of the debt (r_D^{max}) is calculated from[15]:

$$\frac{K}{\frac{K}{1+r} - p} = 1 + r_D^{max}$$

or

$$0 = -\left(\frac{K}{1+r} - p\right) + \frac{K}{1 + r_D^{max}}. \tag{9.28}$$

or

$$\frac{1}{1 + r_D^{max}} = \frac{\frac{K}{1+r} - p}{K} = \frac{1}{1+r} - \frac{p}{K} > 0. \tag{9.29}$$

Equation (9.28) shows that the maximum rate of return of the debt: r_D^{max} is the yield to maturity (YTM) or the internal rate of return of the debt. In Eq. (9.29), the p-index of the debt: $\frac{p}{K}$ represents the risk-level for the firm to deliver the promised payment K at $t = T$, i.e., the insurance fees for each insured dollar of K. Also, because $\frac{p}{K}$ cannot be negative, we must have: $r_D^{max} > r$.

Property 9.7 Regarding a firm's (an asset's) debt, for every dollar of the maximum payoff (or the promised payment) of the debt (K) at$t = T$, the debtholder at $t = 0$ needs to pay: $\frac{\frac{K}{1+r} - p}{K} = \frac{1}{1+r} - \frac{p}{K}$, where $\left[1/\left(\frac{1}{1+r} - \frac{p}{K}\right) - 1\right]$ is equal to the yield to maturity (YTM) of debt:r_D^{max}. That is, for corporate debt, higher $\frac{p}{K}$ (i.e., higher risk) means higher YTM of debt. Note that this does not say that higher risk means higher *expected* rate of return.

The credit spread (or yield spread) is defined as the difference in yield between a corporate bond and a government bond at each point of maturity. From Eq. (9.29), we know that higher corporate spread: $(r_D^{max} - r)$ means higher p-index $\left(\frac{p}{K}\right)$, i.e., higher risk. Suppose with the same maturity, the YTM of a Japan's government bond is: 2%, and the YTM of Sony bond is: 4%. The YTM of a US government bond is: 3%, and the YTM of IBM bond is: 5%. The credit spreads of Sony bond and IBM bond are the same: 2% (= 4% − 2% = 5% − 3%). But from Eq. (9.28), we know that Sony bond will have higher p-index (higher risk) than IBM bond:

---

[15] Also, let the maximum value of the debt at $t = T$ be: $K = S_0^D(1 + r_D^{max})$ where S_0^D is the market value of the debt at $t = 0$. Then the debt's call option is: $c = 0$ and the debt's put-call parity is: $0 = \frac{0}{S_0^D(1+r_D^{max})} = \left[\frac{1}{1+r_D^{max}} - \frac{1}{1+r}\right] + \frac{p}{K}$.

(p-index of Sony bond) $0.01885 = \frac{1}{1.02} - \frac{1}{1.04} > \frac{1}{1.03} - \frac{1}{1.05} = 0.01849$ (p-index of IBM bond)

Property 9.8 Higher corporate spread means higher p-index, i.e., higher risk. If two bonds in two different countries have the same credit spreads, the one with lower risk-free interest rate is riskier (i.e., having higher p-index) than the other.

From Eq. (9.23), we know that $\frac{\partial}{\partial K}\left(\frac{p}{K}\right) > 0$ if and only if $\frac{\partial p/p}{\partial K/K} > 1$. I n the binomial case, e.g., Fig. 9.1, the market value of an asset at $t = 0$ is: $S_0 = \frac{1}{1+r}[\pi \cdot S_0u + (1-\pi) \cdot S_0d]$. With the strike price (i.e., the promised payment to debtholders) K and $S_0d < K < S_0u$, we have the following:

$$\begin{aligned} \frac{\partial p/p}{\partial K/K} &= \frac{K}{\frac{1}{1+r}(1-\pi)(K - S_0d)} \cdot \frac{\partial}{\partial K}\left[\frac{1}{1+r}(1-\pi)(K - S_0d)\right] \\ &= \frac{K}{K - S_0d} > 1 \Rightarrow \frac{\partial}{\partial K}\left(\frac{p}{K}\right) > 0 \end{aligned}$$

Property 9.9 Under the binomial option pricing framework, (1) for riskless debt, an increase in K, i.e., more debt, results in higher p-index (i.e., higher risk) for equity and no risk for debt; (2) for risky debt, an increase in K increases debt's risk level but does not affect the risk level of equity.[16]

For example, in Eq. (9.15), let $K_1 = \$1,100$, $K_2 = \$2,200$, $K_3 = \$8,900$, and $K_4 = \$8,944$,

$$\begin{cases} \text{Money market}: 1 = \frac{1}{1+r}[\pi(1+r) + (1-\pi)(1+r)] = \frac{1}{1+0.1}\left[\frac{1}{4}(1.10) + \frac{3}{4}(1.10)\right] \\ \text{The firm}: S_0 = 8,000 = \frac{1}{1+r}[\pi \cdot S_0u + (1-\pi) \cdot S_0d] = \frac{1}{1+0.1}\left[\frac{1}{4}(10,000) + \frac{3}{4}(8,400)\right] \\ \text{Equity 1}: c_1 = 7,000 = \frac{1}{1+r}[\pi \cdot (S_0u - K_1) + (1-\pi) \cdot (S_0d - K_1)] = \frac{1}{1+0.1}\left[\frac{1}{4}(8,900) + \frac{3}{4}(7,300)\right] \\ \text{Riskless Debt 1}: \frac{K_1}{1+r} = 1,000 = \frac{1}{1+r}[\pi \cdot K_1 + (1-\pi) \cdot K_1] = \frac{1}{1+0.1}\left[\frac{1}{4}(1,100) + \frac{3}{4}(1,100)\right] \\ \text{Equity 2}: c_2 = 6,000 = \frac{1}{1+r}[\pi \cdot (S_0u - K_2) + (1-\pi) \cdot (S_0d - K_2)] = \frac{1}{1+0.1}\left[\frac{1}{4}(7,800) + \frac{3}{4}(6,200)\right] \\ \text{Riskless Debt 2}: \frac{K_2}{1+r} = 1,000 = \frac{1}{1+r}[\pi \cdot K_2 + (1-\pi) \cdot K_2] = \frac{1}{1+0.1}\left[\frac{1}{4}(2,200) + \frac{3}{4}(2,200)\right] \\ \text{Equity 3}: c_3 = 250 = \frac{1}{1+r}[\pi \cdot (S_0u - K_3) + (1-\pi) \cdot 0)] = \frac{1}{1+0.1}\left[\frac{1}{4}(1,100) + \frac{3}{4} \cdot 0\right] \\ \text{Risky Debt 3}: \frac{K_3}{1+r} - p_3 = 7,750 = \frac{1}{1+r}[\pi \cdot (K_3 - S_0u) + (1-\pi) \cdot (K_3 - S_0d)] = \frac{1}{1+0.1}\left[\frac{1}{4}(8,900) + \frac{3}{4}(8,400)\right] \\ \text{Equity 4}: c_4 = 240 = \frac{1}{1+r}[\pi \cdot (S_0u - K_4) + (1-\pi) \cdot 0)] = \frac{1}{1+0.1}\left[\frac{1}{4}(1,056) + \frac{3}{4} \cdot 0\right] \\ \text{Risky Debt 4}: \frac{K_4}{1+r} - p_4 = 7,760 = \frac{1}{1+r}[\pi \cdot (K_4 - S_0u) + (1-\pi) \cdot (K_4 - S_0d)] = \frac{1}{1+0.1}\left[\frac{1}{4}(8,944) + \frac{3}{4}(8,400)\right] \end{cases}$$

(i) Riskless debt.
Let the strike price of the put option of the equity c_i be: $V_i = (1 + 0.1125) \cdot c_i$, $i = 1, 2$, where $c_i = S_0 - \frac{K_i}{1+r}$. The p-indexes of the equities are: $\frac{p_1}{V_1} = \frac{\frac{(3/4)}{1.1}[7{,}000(1+0.1125) - 7{,}300]}{7{,}000(1+0.1125)} = 0.0427 < \frac{p_2}{V_2} = \frac{\frac{(3/4)}{1.1}[6{,}000(1+0.1125) - 6{,}200]}{6{,}000(1+0.1125)} = 0.0485$, i.e., when the firm has higher debt: $K_2 > K_1$, the p-index of the

[16] See also Proposition 9.2.

equity c_2's delivering at least 11.25% rate of return is greater than the p-index of the equity c_1's delivering at least 11.25% rate of return. That is, higher promised payment to debtholders makes equity riskier but has no effect on debt's risk level.

(ii) Risky debt.
Let the strike price of the put option of the debt D_j be: $V_j = (1+0.1125)\cdot D_j, j = 3, 4$, where $D_j = \frac{K_j}{1+r} - p_j$. The p-indexes of the debts are: $\frac{p_3}{V_3} = \frac{\frac{(3/4)}{1.1}[7{,}750(1+0.1125)-8{,}400]}{7{,}750(1+0.1125)} = 0.0175 < \frac{p_4}{V_4} = \frac{\frac{(3/4)}{1.1}[7{,}760(1+0.1125)-8{,}400]}{7{,}760(1+0.1125)} = 0.0184$, i.e., when the firm has higher debt: $K_4 > K_3$, the p-index of the higher debt D_4's delivering at least 11.25% rate of return is greater than the p-index of the lower debt D_3's delivering at least 11.25% rate of return. That is, higher promised payment to debtholders makes debt riskier. Because from Eq. (9.26) the p-index of the equity is a constant: $\frac{p_3}{c_3} = \frac{p_4}{c_4} = \frac{1-\pi}{1+r} = 0.6818$, change in the promised payment to debtholders has no effect on equity's risk level.

Property 9.10 Under the binomial option pricing framework, let $S_0d < K = (1+\delta)S_0 < S_0u$, the p-index for the firm is: $\frac{p}{K} = \frac{\frac{1-\pi}{1+r}[S_0(1+\delta)-S_0d]}{(1+\delta)S_0} = \frac{(1+\delta)-d}{1+\delta}\cdot\frac{1-\pi}{1+r}$, and the p-index for the equity of the firm is: $\frac{p'}{(1+\delta')c} = \frac{\frac{1-\pi}{1+r}[c(1+\delta')-0]}{c(1+\delta')} = \frac{1-\pi}{1+r}$.

(i) Capital structure does not affect equity's risk structure.
(ii) Unless $d = 0$, the risk level of the firm must be less than that of the firm's equity. All firms' equities have the same p-index (i.e., the same risk structure): $\frac{1-\pi}{1+r}$, and the same return's probability density function.
(iii) Unless $d = 0$, the risk level of debt must be less than that of equity. Also, the maximum rate of return of equity cannot be less than that of debt.
(iv) When $d > 0$, $S_0 = \frac{1}{1+r}[\pi\cdot S_0u + (1-\pi)\cdot S_0d]$ implies $1 = \frac{1}{1+r}[\pi\cdot u + (1-\pi)\cdot d]$. Since $\left(\frac{\pi}{1+r}\cdot u\right)$ and $\left(\frac{1-\pi}{1+r}\cdot d\right)$ are strictly positive, we must have: $\frac{\pi}{1+r}\cdot u < 1$ or $u < \frac{1+r}{\pi}$; and $\frac{1-\pi}{1+r}\cdot d < 1$ or $d < \frac{1+r}{1-\pi}$. Hence, the maximum rate of return of asset (firm)S_0: $\frac{S_0u}{S_0} = u$ is less than the maximum rate of return of its call (equity) c: $\frac{S_0u-K}{\frac{1}{1+r}[\pi(S_0u-K)]} = \frac{1+r}{\pi}$.

Summary and Conclusions

- In terms of the theory of the firm, it is found that both the Black–Scholes-Merton and the binomial option pricing models implicitly assume that maximizing the market value of the firm is not equivalent to maximizing the equityholders' wealth. The binomial option pricing model implicitly assumes that further increasing (decreasing) the promised payment to debtholders affects neither the speed of decreasing (increasing) in the equity nor the speed of increasing (decreasing) in the insurance. The Black–Scholes-Merton option pricing model, on the other hand, implicitly assumes that further increasing (decreasing) in the promised payment to debtholders will: (1) decrease (increase) the speed of decreasing (increasing) in the equity though bounded by upper and lower bounds; and (2) increase (decrease) the speed of increasing (decreasing) in the insurance though bounded by upper and lower bounds.

- The Modigliani–Miller first proposition is a corollary of the put-call parity and an example of financial diversification irrelevancy. In the binomial option pricing case, (i) under riskless debt, increasing the debt-equity ratio increases the variance of the rate of return on equity and has no effect on the rate of return on debt; and (ii) under risky debt, increasing the debt-equity ratio increases the variance of the rate of return on debt but does not affect the probability density function of the rate of return on equity. These findings refute the Modigliani–Miller second proposition that the expected rate of return on the equity of the levered firm increases in proportion to the debt-equity ratio.
- The risk of an asset (a firm) is defined as the likelihood that the asset (the firm) can deliver at least a specific rate of return. European put option is used to construct the p-index to measure risk levels (likelihoods) of asset's providing various rates of return, i.e., risk structure of asset. In the binomial case with up move and down move, (i) assets having lower down move have higher p-index, i.e., higher risk; (ii) all call options (firms' equities) have the same p-index, i.e., the same risk level, and all put options have the same p-index; and (iii) underlying asset (the firm) may be riskier than its put option and may have the same risk level as its call option (equity).
- Under the binomial option pricing framework, (1) for riskless debt, increase the promised payment to debtholders, i.e., more debt, leads to higher p-index (i.e., higher risk) for equity and no risk for debt; (2) for risky debt, increase the promised payment to debtholders increases debt's risk level but does not affect the risk level of equity.

Appendix: Do Arbitrage When System 2 of the Gordan Theorem Fails

Assume a one-period, two states (good time and bad time) of nature world with no transaction costs (i.e., a perfect market). There are two assets: a money market (Security 1) which provides $1 + 0.25$ dollars at $t = 1$ if one dollar is invested at $t = 0$ (i.e., the risk-free interest rate is $r = 0.25$), and two other securities (Security 2 and Security 3) with current market prices \$4 and \$48, respectively, which at $t = 1$ provide:

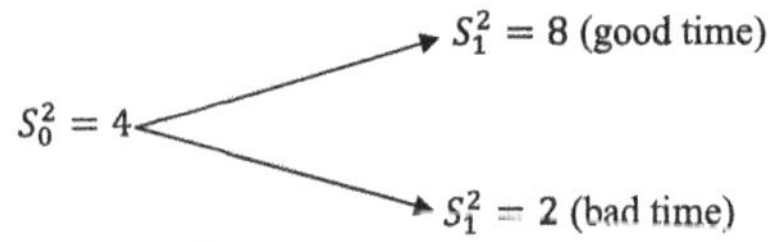

Security 2

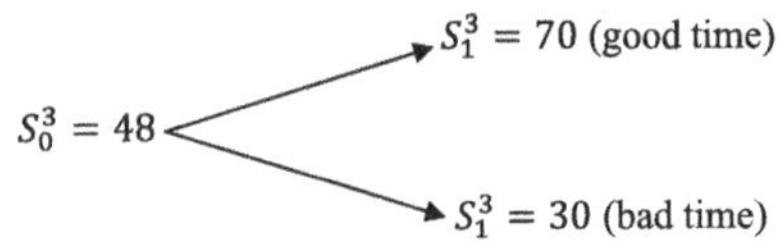

Security 3

That is, at $t = 1$, when Security 2 provides \$8, Security 3 will provide \$70; and when Security 2 provides \$2, Security 3 will provide \$30. In this case, the two securities are not governed by the same probability measure (i.e., System 2 of the Gordan (Arbitrage) Theorem has no solution):

$$\begin{cases} \text{Security 1:} \quad S_0^1 = 1 = \frac{1}{1+0.25}(\pi \times 1.25 + (1-\pi) \times 1.25); \\ \text{Security 2:} \quad S_0^2 = 4 = \frac{1}{1+0.25}\left(\frac{1}{2} \times 8 + \frac{1}{2} \times 2\right); \quad p' = \begin{bmatrix} 1/2 \\ 1/2 \end{bmatrix} \\ \text{Security 3:} \quad S_0^3 = 48 = \frac{1}{1+0.25}\left(\frac{3}{4} \times 70 + \frac{1}{4} \times 30\right); \quad p'' = \begin{bmatrix} 3/4 \\ 1/4 \end{bmatrix} \end{cases}$$

i.e., we cannot find a vector $\boldsymbol{p} = \begin{bmatrix} \pi \\ 1-\pi \end{bmatrix}$, $0 \le \pi \le 1$, such that System 2 holds:

$$\begin{bmatrix} 1.25 - 1(1+0.25) & 1.25 - 1(1+0.25) \\ 8 - 4(1+0.25) & 2 - 4(1+0.25) \\ 70 - 48(1+0.25) & 30 - 48(1+0.25) \end{bmatrix} \begin{bmatrix} \pi \\ 1-\pi \end{bmatrix} \neq \begin{bmatrix} 0 \\ 0 \\ 0 \end{bmatrix}.$$

By System 1 of the Arbitrage Theorem, there must exist an arbitrage opportunity. For example, at$t = 0$, we can short sell one share of Security 3 and buy 5 shares of Security 2 and invest \$28 ($= 48 - 4 \times 5$) in the money market, and at $t = 1$ we can earn excess profits, i.e.,

$$\begin{bmatrix} 1.25 - 1(1+0.25) & 8 - 4(1+0.25) & 70 - 48(1+0.25) \\ 1.25 - 1(1+0.25) & 2 - 4(1+0.25) & 30 - 48(1+0.25) \end{bmatrix} \begin{bmatrix} x \\ 5 \\ -1 \end{bmatrix} \begin{bmatrix} 5 \\ 15 \end{bmatrix} > \begin{bmatrix} 0 \\ 0 \end{bmatrix}.$$

When investors adopt this arbitrage strategy at $t = 0$, the market price of Security 2 will go up and that of Security 3 will go down. In equilibrium (i.e., no arbitrage), the market prices of the two securities at $t = 0$ will adjust to the point that they all are priced by the same probability measure, say, $\boldsymbol{p} = \begin{bmatrix} 2/3 \\ 1/3 \end{bmatrix}$,

$$\begin{cases} \text{Money Market(Security 1):} & S_0^1 = 1 = \frac{1}{1+0.25}\left(\frac{2}{3} \times 1.25 + \frac{1}{3} \times 1.25\right) \\ \text{Security 2:} & S_0^2 = 4.8 = \frac{1}{1+0.25}\left(\frac{2}{3} \times 8 + \frac{1}{3} \times 2\right) \\ \text{Security 3:} & S_0^3 = 45\frac{1}{3} = \frac{1}{1+0.25}\left(\frac{2}{3} \times 70 + \frac{1}{3} \times 30\right) \end{cases}$$

or

$$\underbrace{\begin{bmatrix} 1.25-1(1+0.25) & 1.25-1(1+0.25) \\ 8-4.8(1+0.25) & 2-4.8(1+0.25) \\ 70-45\frac{1}{3}(1+0.25) & 30-45\frac{1}{3}(1+0.25) \end{bmatrix}}_{\boldsymbol{A}^t} \underbrace{\begin{bmatrix} 2/3 \\ 1/3 \end{bmatrix} = \begin{bmatrix} 0 \\ 0 \\ 0 \end{bmatrix}}_{\boldsymbol{p}=\boldsymbol{0}}.$$

Since, in the above equation, the rank of the matrix $\boldsymbol{A}$ is: $1 = m - 1$, the market is complete, and the probability measure $\boldsymbol{p} = \begin{bmatrix} \pi \\ 1-\pi \end{bmatrix} = \begin{bmatrix} 2/3 \\ 1/3 \end{bmatrix}$ must be unique. In this example, $\frac{\pi}{1-\pi} = \frac{2}{1}$ can be termed as the relative price ratio between the two states, i.e., at $t = 1$ the value of one dollar of good time is 200% greater than that of bad time. This implies that investors (the market) believe that the probability of good time is twice as many as that of bad time.

Problems

1. Comment on the following statements[17]:
   (a) Wilmott (2007, p. 77): Assume: "(1) two stocks A and B; (2) both have the same value, same volatility and are denominated in the same currency; (3) both have call options with the same strike and expiration; (4) stock A is doubling in value every year, stock B is halving. Therefore, both call options have the same value. But which will you buy? That one stock is doubling and the other halving is irrelevant. That option prices don't depend on the direction that the stock is going can be difficult to accept initially".
   (b) Ross (1998, p. 701): "Take two stocks that both follow binomial processes and that are not perfectly correlated. Further, suppose that the stocks differ only in that one has a much higher probability of an up jump than does the other. If our analysis is to be believed, then when the stock prices of each are equal the two option values will be equal! How can this be? How can the value of an option on a stock be independent of the probability that the stock will go up?".
2. With zero interest rate, do the arbitrage for the following two assets:

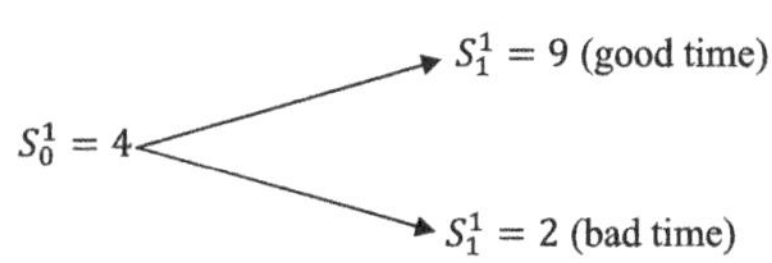

Asset 1

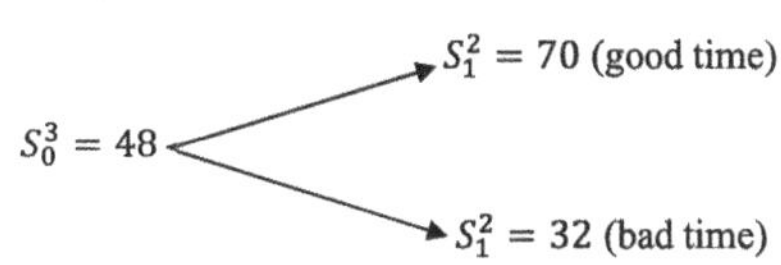

Asset 2

[17] Ross, Stephen (1998) The Mathematics of finance: pricing derivatives. *Quarterly of Applied Mathematics* 56: 695-706. Wilmott, Paul (2007) Paul Wilmott Introduces Quantitative Finance. John Wiley & Sons, West Sussex, England.

3. Explain under what conditions an American put option will not be early exercised. How to use these conditions to determine the best time to liquidate a firm?
4. Explain how to use the p-index to invest in stocks. What are the limitations of the p-index?
5. Explain why the Black–Scholes-Merton option pricing model has: $\frac{\partial c}{\partial \sigma} = \frac{\partial p}{\partial \sigma}$ and the binomial option pricing model has: $\frac{\partial c}{\partial u} = \frac{\partial p}{\partial u}$ and $\frac{\partial c}{\partial d} = \frac{\partial p}{\partial d}$.

References

Black, F., & Scholes, M. (1973). The pricing of options and corporate liabilities. *Journal of Political Economy, 81*, 637–654.

Chang, K.-P. (2014). Some misconceptions in derivative pricing. http://ssrn.com/abstract=2138357.

Chang, K.-P. (2015). *The ownership of the firm, corporate finance, and derivatives: Some critical thinking*. Springer Nature.

Chang, K.-P. (2016). The Modigliani-Miller second proposition is dead; long live the second proposition. *Ekonomicko-manažerské Spektrum, 10*, 24–31. http://ssrn.com/abstract=2762158.

Chang, K.-P. (2017). On using risk-neutral probabilities to price assets. http://ssrn.com/abstract=3114126

Chang, K.-P. (2023). Measuring risk structures of assets: p-index and c-index. http://ssrn.com/abstract=4352457

Chang, K.-P. (2020). On option Greeks and corporate finance. *Journal of Advanced Studies in Finance, 11*, 183–193. https://doi.org/10.14505/jasf.v11.2(22).09

Cox, J., Ross, S., & Rubinstein, M. (1979). Option pricing: A simplified approach. *Journal of Financial Economics, 7*, 229–263.

Fama, Eugene and Michael Jensen. (1983). Agency problems and residual claims. *Journal of Law and Economics, 26*, 327–349.

Hull, J. (2018). *Options, futures, and other derivatives*. Pearson Education Limited.

Merton, R. (1973a). Theory of rational option pricing. *Bell Journal of Economics and Management Science, 4*, 141–183.

Merton, R. (1973b). The relationship between put and call option prices: Comment. *Journal of Finance, 28*, 183–184.

Myers, S. (1984). The search for optimal capital structure. *Midland Corporate Finance Journal, 1*, 6-16; also in Stern, J. M., & Chew, D.H., Jr. (Eds.). (1986). *The revolution in corporate finance* (pp. 91-99). Basil Blackwell

Stoll, H. (1969). The relationship between put and call option prices. *Journal of Finance, 24*, 801–824.

10 Real Options

Among the derivatives mentioned in Chap. 9, forward and futures contracts are obligations, and options are rights. For example, suppose that at $t = 0$, a three-month forward contract's forward price for the IBM stock is $100. Then after three months, at $t = 3$ the buyer (a long position) is obligated to use $100 to buy the stock, and the seller (a short position) is obligated to sell the stock at the price $100. Since both buyer and seller have only obligations and their choice sets have not changed, neither party needs to pay the other party to sign the contract. From the perspective of risk transferring, (a) the buyer is willing to take the risk if at $t = 3$ the stock's price is less than $100 to exchange for a possible benefit if at $t = 3$ the stock's price is more than $100; and (b) the seller is willing to sacrifice the possible benefit if at $t = 3$ the stock's price is more than $100 to avoid the risk if at $t = 3$ the stock's price is less than $100. Because each party has possible gain to compensate for taking risk (i.e., taking possible loss), none will pay the other to sign the contract.

Suppose that at $t = 0$, a three-month European put option contract's strike price for the IBM stock is $100. Then after three months, at $t = 3$ the owner of the put has the right to sell the stock to the issuer of the put at the price $100. Since the issuer of the put has a smaller choice set (i.e., has an obligation to buy the stock for $100) and the owner of the put has a larger choice set (i.e., has a choice to sell the stock to the issuer for $100), the put option is a right and has a price. From the perspective of risk transferring: (a) the owner of the stock can pay a price to buy the put such that at $t = 3$, if the market price of the stock is less than $100, she has the right to sell her stock to the issuer for $100; and (b) the issuer of the put cannot gain any if the stock price is greater than $100 but will lose if the stock price is less than $100. That is, to buy a put is to transfer the risk of the asset's price being less than the strike price to the issuer.

Real options are choices you may have if you adopt some strategies. In many cases, there is no counterparty you can pay to gain some right to do something. Section 10.1 shows how a firm makes decisions on expanding its operations.

K.-P. Chang, *Corporate Finance: A Systematic Approach*, Springer Texts in Business and Economics, https://doi.org/10.1007/978-981-19-9119-6_10

Section 10.2 explains options (choices) to abandon. Section 10.3 is about timing options (choices).

10.1 The Option (Choice) to Expand

Suppose MBI corporation is producing a single product and its market price drops and profit is deteriorating. Each year the firm spends \$5,000,000 operating cost to produce two possible cash flows with probabilities: $\pi = 0.5$ and $1 - \pi = 0.5$, and risk-free interest rate $r = 10\%$.

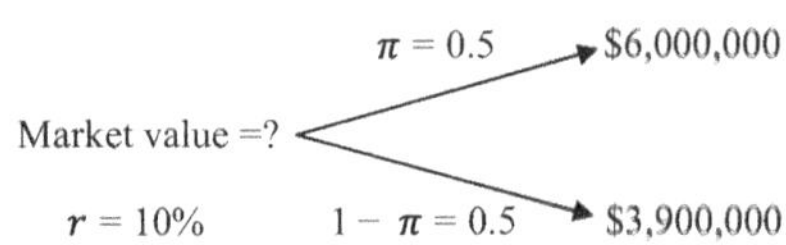

The market value (MV) of the production in each year is: $S_0 = \$4,500,000 = \frac{1}{1+0.1}\left[\frac{1}{2} \cdot (6,000,000) + \frac{1}{2} \cdot (3,900,000)\right]$. The net present value (NPV) of the production in each year is:

$$NPV = -5,000,000 + 4,500,000 = -\$500,000$$

Since the NPV in each year is negative, the finance department suggests that this product be discarded. One strategy to deal with it is to move the production abroad where the production cost is lower. But the management team thinks the current product still has some value unrecognized by the market (e.g., some special production process) which can be integrated into a new product. The R&D and marketing departments report that in each year, the production cost of the new product is \$7,000,000 and its possible cash flows in each year are:

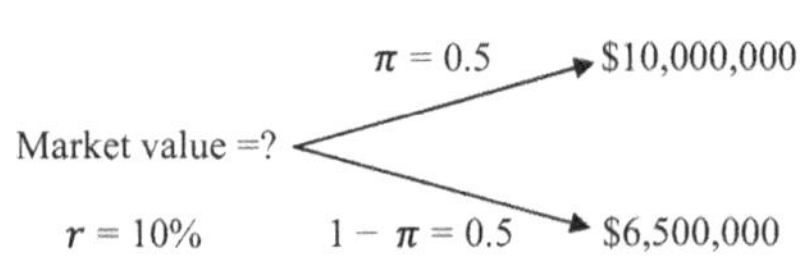

In each year, the NPV of the new product is positive: $NPV = 500,000 = -\$7,000,000 + \frac{1}{1+0.1}\left[\frac{1}{2} \cdot (10,000,000) + \frac{1}{2} \cdot (6,500,000)\right]$. Thus, this project is feasible.

The above is the improvement of the original product which may bring in more profits. Another common strategy is to increase the capacity of an existing product line, e.g., economics of scale. When quantity of output increases, unit price of material used usually decreases. The firm can also sell the product to foreign countries where the price of the product is higher.

10.2 The Option (Choice) to Abandon

Suppose that MBI corporation wants to explore the possibility of producing a new product. The R&D cost is $3,400,000, and it needs 1 year to design and develop the new production line. The probabilities for this R&D are: 0.8 (succeed) and 0.2 (fail). After one year, if it succeeds, in each year the operating cost is $3,000,000 and two possible cash flows are: $6,300, 000 and $2,500,000.

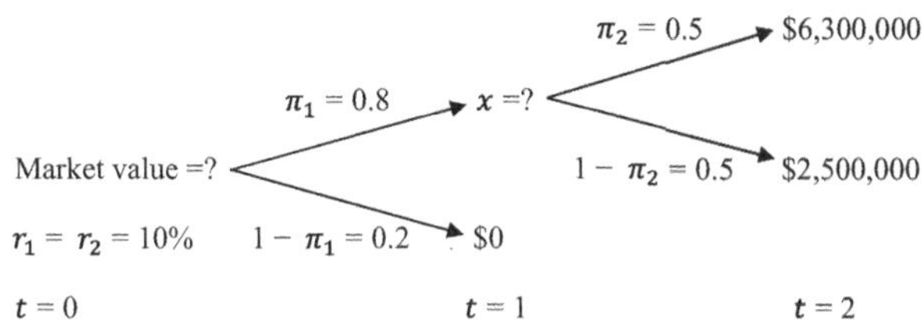

Thus, after one year, if R&D succeeds, the NPV of each year's production activity is: $NPV = \$1,000,000 = -3,000,000 + \frac{1}{1+0.1}\left[\frac{1}{2}\cdot(6,300,000) + \frac{1}{2}\cdot(2,500,000)\right]$. MBI corporation believes that the expected benefits per year: $\$800,000 = 1,000,000(0.8) + 0(0.2)$ can sustain at least ten years, and hence, the expected benefits of the whole project (i.e., R&D plus production) should be greater than the R&D cost $3,400,000.

Suppose that after one-year, the firm finds that the NPV of each year's production activity is negative, the firm will abandon the plan of the production. The firm can also license the patent to other companies to recover some R&D expenditures, or spin off the new business unit as another company and seek new funding.

10.3 Timing Options (Choices)

In the previous case, MBI corporation can delay its production of the new product if the production is not profitable. Companies have patents can also delay their use. But competitors may accelerate R&D process and enter the market. In some cases, during economic recession, firms may expand their capacity to ensure their market shares when the economy expands. That is, even though *option (choice) to delay* is valuable, but timing options is not an easy task.

Summary and Conclusions

- In practice, unit prices of inputs are not fixed. When the firm increases its production (i.e., expansion), the unit prices of inputs will decrease and production costs are lower. Keeping and making improvements on the existing product may be profitable.

- Design and develop new technology (new product) by investing in R&D gives the firm the option/choice to produce or not to produce (i.e., abandon) the new product. The patent on hand can be licensed to others. The firm can also spin off the new business unit.
- Option to wait (delay) is valuable. But it may come at a cost: competitors may enter the market during the waiting period. In some cases, it's difficult to recover lost clients.

Reference

Mun, J. (2002). *Real XE "Real option" options XE "Options" analysis: Tools and techniques for valuing strategic investments and decisions*. Wiley.

Behavioral Finance and Corporate Finance

11

The seminal works by Daniel Kahneman, Amos Tversky and Richard Thaler have inspired many researches in behavioral economics. Behavioral economics and behavioral finance incorporate the concepts and methods in psychology science into traditional economics (finance). It has found consistent and pervasive anomalies in common people's behaviors. These anomalies, such as preference reversals (on the existence of a real-valued utility function), isolation effect (on framing effect), sunk cost fallacy (on the concept of opportunity cost), and endowment effect (on the law of one price), challenge the rational behavior assumption in traditional economics and finance.

This chapter uses the concepts in traditional economics (e.g., choice, relative price, and opportunity cost) to analyze the anomalies found in behavioral economics. The results show that because people do not have choice in the first stage, Kahneman and Tversky's two-stage game is in fact a one stage game, and their findings of preference reversal and isolation effect do not exist. In Thaler's free ticket to game example, there is no sunk cost fallacy involved because comparing with buying a ticket (i.e., prefer game to good meal), not buying a ticket but receiving it as a gift (i.e., prefer good meal to game) will be less likely to drive through a snowstorm to watch the game. Escalation of commitment to a failing course of action does not imply a sunk cost fallacy. A sunk cost fallacy occurs only when people escalate commitment without considering all other alternatives. After people compared different alternatives and made decision, there will be no opportunity cost. Prospect theory is about relative price ratio (or rate of return). People won't care much if a gain or a loss is relative smaller than their monthly income. Loss aversion can be interpreted as effort aversion, i.e., people don't like the idea of making more efforts to earn the same amount of money. These findings show that common people may not be as irrational as behavioral economists have suggested.

In this chapter, Sect. 11.1 discusses preference reversal and isolation effect within the framework of prospect theory. This section also shows the fallacies

K.-P. Chang, *Corporate Finance: A Systematic Approach*, Springer Texts in Business and Economics, https://doi.org/10.1007/978-981-19-9119-6_11

of sunk cost fallacy, applies the concept of opportunity cost, use the concept of relative price ratio (rate of return) to analyze the anomalies. Section 11.2 explains the investment decision and its various biases.

11.1 Behavioral Economics Versus Traditional Economics

Have a Choice versus Have No Choice

Kahneman and Tversky (1979, 1984), Tversky and Kahneman (1981, 1986) and Kahneman (2011) have used the following experiment to show that people often disregard components that alternatives share, and focus on the components that distinguish them:

Example 11.1 Consider the following two-stage game. In the first stage, there is a 75% chance to end the game without winning anything, and a 25% chance to move into the second stage. If you reach the second stage, you have a choice between:

(A) 80% chance to win $4,000 and 20% chance to win nothing;
(B) $3,000 with certainty.

Your choice must be made before the game starts, i.e., before the outcome of the first stage is known.

Kahneman and Tversky (1979, p. 271) argue that "in this game, one has a choice between $0.25 \times 0.80 = 0.20$ chance to win 4,000, and a $0.25 \times 1.0 = 0.25$ chance to win 3,000", and hence, in terms of probabilities and outcomes this two-stage game (i.e., Example 1) is identical to the following game:

Example 11.2 People are asked to choose from:

(A) 20% chance to win $4,000 and 80% chance to win nothing;
(B) 25% chance to win $3,000 and 75% chance to win nothing.

Kahneman et al. find that in Example 11.1, most subjects chose (B), but in Example 11.2, most subjects chose (A). They refer this phenomenon as the *isolation effect*, and claim that "evidently, people ignored the first stage of the game, whose outcomes are shared by both prospects" (p. 271), and "the *reversal of preferences* due to the dependency among events is particular significant because it violates the basic supposition of a decision-theoretical analysis, that choices between prospects are determined solely by the probabilities of final states" (p. 272).

Unfortunately, Kahneman et al.'s experiment is erroneous. Their findings of so-called isolation effect and reversal of preferences do not exist. Note that it is meaningless to consider the first stage of the game and calculate the probabilities: $0.25 \times 0.80 = 0.20$ and $0.25 \times 1.0 = 0.25$ because people have no choice in the first stage. People will only consider: which choice I should take if I enter the second stage (i.e., if I "survive"). People will never consider: what I should do next if I do not survive. The magnitude of the probabilities of the first stage is irrelevant to people's decision-making, i.e., the first stage of Example 11.1 is redundant.

Here is a simple example which shows under what condition people have a choice in the first stage: Suppose that people can choose between: (A) the two-stage game in Example 11.1; and (B) $500 with certainty. In this case, the magnitude of the probabilities of the first stage of the two-stage game will matter. For example, when the chance to enter the second stage decreases (e.g., the probability of entering the second stage drops from 0.25 to 0.05), people will be more likely to choose $500 instead of the two-stage game.

Thus, in Example 11.1 we can just ignore the first stage, and Example 11.1 should be written as:

Example 11.3 You have a choice between:

(A) 80% chance to win $4,000 and 20% chance to win nothing;
(B) $3,000 with certainty.

Example 11.3 (i.e., Example 11.1) and Example 11.2 are two different games. It is not surprising to see that the results from these two games are different.

The following is another example. Suppose you apply for a job in a firm, and you have a 0.25 chance to succeed. Once you succeed in entering the firm, you have a choice for your salary between: (A) $4,000 with a probability of 0.80 and $0 with a probability of 0.20; (B) $3,000 for sure. Note that in this game, you only care which salary structure you should choose if you "survive", i.e., if you are hired by the firm. The probability of 0.25, set by the firm, is irrelevant to your making choice.[1]

Fallacies of the Sunk Cost Fallacy

Thaler (2018) uses the following example to explain the sunk cost fallacy in people's behavior[2]:

Example 11.4 My friend Jeffrey and I were given two tickets to a professional basketball game in Buffalo, normally a 75 min drive from Rochester. On the day

[1] Tversky and Kahneman's (1986, p. S268-S269) medical treatment of tumor experiment (Case 3) is exactly the same as Example 11.1 except that the subjects are not required to make a choice before the game starts. Tversky et al. argue that people made mistakes by not using the probabilities: $0.25 \times 0.80 = 0.20$ and $0.25 \times 1.0 = 0.25$ and claim that it is 'pseudocertainty effect'. This is wrong since the probability 0.25 of the testing result that the tumor is treatable in the first stage is not up to the subjects to decide. If the tumor is not treatable, i.e., the subject cannot survive, it will be meaningless to ask which choice (treatment) the subject will choose in the second stage.

[2] See also Thaler (1980).

of the game there was a snowstorm and we sensibly decided to skip the game. But Jeffrey, who is not an economist, remarked, "If we had paid full price for those tickets we would have gone!".

Thaler argues that "as an observation about human behavior he was right, but according to economic theory sunk costs do not matter. Why is going to the game more attractive if we have higher sunk costs?" (p. 1266). However, Thaler's arguments are not correct. People have limited budget (income). Suppose that a basketball game ticket price is $40. A good meal for a person also costs $40. The cost (disutility) of driving through the blizzard of each person is: c(driving to game). There are two possible scenarios in their consumption bundles:

Case 1 Instead of purchasing a ticket, the person purchases a good meal and receives a free ticket.
Case 2 Instead of spending $40 on a good meal, the person purchases a ticket.

In Case 1, the person could afford a basketball game ticket but did not purchase it. This implies that the utility of a basketball game (under not purchase) is less than the utility of a good meal, i.e., $u^{not\_purchase}$(basketball game) < u(good meal). In Case 2, the person purchased a basketball game ticket and did not purchase a good meal. This implies that the utility of a basketball game (under purchase) is greater than the utility of a good meal, i.e., $u^{purchase}$(basketball game) > u(good meal). Since $u^{not\_purchase}$(basketball game) < u(good meal) < $u^{purchase}$(basketball game), we have:

$$u^{not\_purchase}(\text{basketball game}) - c(\text{driving to game})$$
$$< u^{purchase}(\text{basketball game}) - c(\text{driving to game})$$

It implies that [$u^{not\_purchase}$(basketball game) − c(driving to game)] is more likely to be negative than [$u^{purchase}$(basketball game) − c(driving to game)]. That is, comparing with buying a ticket, not buying a ticket but receiving it as a gift will be less likely to drive through a snowstorm to watch the game. In this example, the so-called sunk cost plays no role at all (i.e., they still have the choice to go or not to go to the game). Jeffrey acts more like an economist.

Arkes and Blumer's (1985) experiment of theater ticket prices finds that after randomly assigning season tickets to theater goers, those paying more for their tickets attended significantly more plays within the first half of the season. They claim that this is because "these groups have different sunk costs" (p. 128), i.e., "I have spent so much money and I will use it more frequently". But spend less money on the season ticket also means that you have more extra money and time to do other activities which can produce utilities to compensate the loss of less theater going.[3] Ashraf et al. (2010) employ a disinfectant product use experiment in Zambia to show that higher prices can increase use by a screening effect (targeting distribution to high-use households) but not by sunk cost effect (stimulating use psychologically). Just, and Wansink's (2011) experiment of an all-you-can-eat pizza restaurant finds that "a 50% discount on the price of the meal led customers to consume 27.9% less pizza (2.95 versus 4.09 pieces). A second analysis indicated that individual taste ratings of this pizza tended to be inversely related to how much is consumed. One possible interpretation of these two findings is that individuals in a flat-rate (or fixed-price) context may consume the amount that enables them to get their money's worth rather than consuming until their marginal utility of consumption is 0" (p. 193). But note that people have limited budget (income). Higher price for disinfectant product means that you need to reduce your consumption of other goods in your consumption bundle (i.e., reduce utilities), which implies that you will increase the use of the product to gain more utilities to compensate the loss of the utilities. Lower price at the all-you-can-eat pizza restaurant means that you have more extra money to do other activities (e.g., go swimming) or buy other goods (e.g., an ice cream cone), which can bring utilities to compensate the loss of the utilities by consuming less pizza.

Arkes and Blumer (1985, p. 124) define the sunk cost effect as "a greater tendency to continue an endeavor once an investment in money, effort, or time has been made. The prior investment, which is motivating the present decision to continue, does so despite the fact that it objectively should not influence the decision". Thaler (1980, p. 47) defines the sunk cost effect as "paying for the right to use a good or service will increase the rate at which the good will be utilized, *ceteris paribus*". However, increasing use of a good or escalation of commitment to a failing course of action does not constitute a sunk cost effect (fallacy). A sunk cost fallacy occurs only when you make a choice without considering all other alternatives. For example, having the thinking: "My investment in this stock already lost 50,000 dollars. If I sell the stock now, I will never have the chance to recover my loss" without thinking about whether it is better to move the money from the stock to other alternatives.[4] Brockner et al. (1979) use the example of waiting for a bus to show a sunk cost situation: after a very long wait, people still decide not to take a cab, thereby nullifying all the time they have spent waiting for the bus (time already spent waiting is a sunk cost). Northcraft and Wolf (1984) argue that continued investment in many of them does not necessarily represent an economically irrational behavior (e.g., continued waiting for the bus will increase the

[3] For the second half of the season, Arkes et al. find that all the groups attend about the same number of plays. However, this may be due to that people in the second half of the season had new choices which can produce higher net utilities rather than Arkes et al.'s 'diminishing sunk cost effect'. Gourville and Soman's (1998) experiment of gym memberships and attendance also finds that the price paid for an item has a diminishing effect on consumption behavior as time goes on, and there was a substantial spike in attendance following payment.

[4] See Appendix A for a real story of the sunk cost fallacy.

probability that one's waiting behavior will be rewarded). Note that even if continued waiting for the bus will not increase the probability of the arriving of the bus, continued waiting may still be a rational behavior: As long as people's evaluation about which choice (waiting for the bus or taking a cab) is better does not change after a very long wait, continued waiting is not irrational.

Cost is Opportunity Cost

An opportunity cost is "the evaluation placed on the most highly valued of the rejected alternatives or opportunities" (Buchanan, 2008). Buchanan (1969, p. 43) emphasizes that "cost is based on anticipations; it is necessarily a forward-looking or ex-ante concept".[5] Thirlby (1946) argues that "cost occurs only when decisions are made, that is, in planning stages" (p. 259). Thirlby clarifies the distinction between decision, budget, and accounting levels of calculation (Buchanan, 1969, p. 32):

(1) Cost is relevant to decision, and it must reflect the value of foregone alternatives.
(2) A budget reflects the prospective or anticipated revenue and outlay sides of a decision that *has been made.* It is erroneous to consider such prospective outlays as appear in a budget as costs. The budget must, however, also be distinguished from the account, which measures realized revenues and outlays that result from a particular course of action.

In summary, opportunity cost is *ex-ante*, implying that you still have the opportunity to make a choice.

Shafir and Thaler (1998) and Thaler (1999, p. 191) have used an experiment of futures market of wine to examine people's perceptions about opportunity cost:

Example 11.5 Suppose you bought a case of good Bordeaux in the futures market for $20 a bottle. The wine now sells at auction for about $75. You have decided to drink a bottle. Which of the following best captures your feeling of the cost to you of drinking the bottle? (The percentage of people choosing each option is shown in brackets.)

Answers: (1) $0 [30%]; (2) $20 [18%]; (3) $20 plus interest [7%]; (4) $75 [20%]; (5) −$55 [25%].

Thaler et al. argue that the correct answer according to economic theory is $75, since the opportunity cost of drinking the wine is selling it at that price (many economists who completed the survey also agreed). But in this example, since a choice has already been made to drink the bottle, opportunity cost does not exist.

[5] Buchanan (1969, p. 28) introduces Ronald Coase's definition of opportunity cost as: "Any profit opportunity that is within the realm of possibility but which is rejected becomes a cost of undertaking the preferred course of action".

Thaler et al. also asked the subjects how it would feel if they had dropped and broken the bottle. A majority said they felt that dropping the bottle costs them \$75, what they could get for selling it. In this case, again, opportunity cost is irrelevant since people cannot make any choice on a broken bottle of wine.

Ferraro and Taylor (2005) and Frank and Bernanke (2001) provide the following survey of estimating opportunity cost:

Example 11.6 You won a free ticket to see an Eric Clapton concert (which has no resale value). Bob Dylan is performing on the same night and is your next-best alternative activity. Tickets to see Dylan cost \$40. On any given day, you would be willing to pay up to \$50 to see Dylan. Assume there are no other costs of seeing either performer. Based on this information, what is the opportunity cost of seeing Eric Clapton? (The percentage of people choosing each option is shown in brackets.)

Answers: (A) \$0 [25.1%]; (B) \$10 [21.6%]; (C) \$40 [25.6%]; (D) \$50 [27.6%].

Ferraro et al. argue that \$10 is the correct answer because: "When you go to the Clapton concert, you forgo the \$50 of benefits you would have received from going to the Dylan concert. You also forgo the \$40 of costs that you would have incurred by going to the Dylan concert. An avoided benefit is a cost, and an avoided cost is a benefit. Thus, the opportunity cost of seeing Clapton, the value you forgo by not going to the Dylan concert, is \$10—i.e., the net benefit forgone" (p. 3).

However, Ferraro et al.'s arguments are not correct. There are two possible scenarios:

Case 1: You do not have \$40. This implies that you have no choice, i.e., you can only go to the Clapton concert, and hence, opportunity cost does not exist.

Case 2: You have \$40. This means that if you choose to go to the Clapton concert, you can spend that \$40 on other goods which provides utilities: $\mathrm{u}(\$40)$. Thus, the opportunity cost of seeing Clapton is: $\mathrm{u}(\text{Dylan's concert}) - \mathrm{u}(\$40)$, and the opportunity cost of seeing Dylan is: $\mathrm{u}(\text{Clapton's concert}) + \mathrm{u}(\$40)$.

Relative Price Ratio (or Rate of Return) Matters

In traditional economics, suppose that you have initial wealth $\mathrm{w} = \$10,000$. When w increases to \$12,000, *the relative wealth (price) ratio* is: $12,000/10,000 = 1.2/1$, which means you exchange 1 unit of wealth for 1.2 units of wealth or earn 20% rate of return. When \$12,000 increases to \$14,000, $14,000/12,000 = 1.167/1$ means that you exchange 1 unit of wealth for 1.167 units of wealth or earn 16.7% rate of return. This indicates that *a change of wealth* can result in diminishing marginal utility of wealth.[6] Note that if, for example, the initial wealth

[6] Suppose that the increment of wealth is \$200,000 and initial wealth is \$1,000,000. Although the relative wealth ratios show: $1,200,000/1,000,000 = 1.2/1 > 1,400,000/1,200,000 =$

is $w = \$12,000$, the aggravation that people experience in losing $2,000 will be greater than the pleasure associated with gaining $2,000, i.e., losses loom larger than gains. This is because $1.2/1 > 1.167/1$ means: (1) to increase wealth from $12,000 to $14,000 you need to earn just 16.7% rate of return; but (2) once your wealth drops from $12,000 to $10,000, you need to earn 20% rate of return (i.e., you need to make more efforts) to go back to your original position. Loss aversion can thus be interpreted as **effort aversion**, i.e., people don't like the idea of making more efforts to earn the same amount of money ($2,000).[7]

Kahneman and Tversky (1979, p. 278) (and Thaler, 1980) argue that:

Example 11.7 The difference in value between a gain of $100 and a gain of $200 appears to be greater than the difference between a gain of $1,100 and a gain of $1,200. Similarly, the difference between a loss of $100 and a loss of $200 appears greater than the difference between a loss of $1,100 and a loss of $1,200, unless the larger loss is intolerable.[8]

This is *a change of change*. Denote the initial wealth as w. The relative price ratio of increment $200 to increment $100 is: (1) $2/1 = 200/100 = [(w+200) - w]/[(w+100) - w]$; and the relative price ratio of increment $1,200 to increment $1,100 is: (2) $1.091/1 = 1,200/1,100 = [(w+1,200) - w]/[(w+1,100) - w]$. This means: (1) when a gain of $100 becomes a gain of $200, your one unit of gain becomes 2 units of gain, i.e., your rate of return is 100%; (2) when a gain of $1,100 becomes a gain of $1,200, your one unit of gain becomes only 1.091 units of gain, i.e., your rate of return is only 9.1%. For the cases of a loss of $100 and a loss of $200, the relative price ratios are still the same: $(1) 2/1 = -200/-100 = [(w-200) - w]/[(w-100) - w]$; and $(2) 1.091/1 = -1,200/-1,100 = [(w-1,200) - w]/[(w-1,100) - w]$. That is, (1) when a loss of $100 becomes a loss of $200, your one unit of loss becomes 2 units of loss, i.e., your rate of return is -100%; (2) when a loss of $1,100 becomes a loss of $1,200, your one unit of loss becomes 1.091 units of loss, i.e., your rate of return is -9.1%. These results show that people feel happier when gaining $100 becomes gaining $200 than when gaining $1,100 becomes $1,200. People feel more painful when losing $100 becomes losing $200 than when losing $1,100 becomes losing $1,200. This is the results of changes in rate

1.167/1, people may feel equally happy because relative to people's income, $200,000 is a huge amount of money which can be used to buy many pricy commodities.

[7] This result refutes Kahneman and Tversky's (1979) claim that "… utility theory. In that theory, for example, the same utility is assigned to a wealth of $100,000, regardless of whether it was reached from a prior wealth of $95,000 or $105,000. Consequently, the choice between a total wealth of $100,000 and even chances to own $95,000 or $105,000 should be independent of whether one currently owns the smaller or the larger of these two amounts" (p. 273).

[8] Thaler (1980, p. 50) argues that this is the Weber-Frechner law: the just noticeable difference in any stimulus is proportional to the stimulus. However, this law is an application of relative price ratio in decision-making.

of return (or relative price ratio), not of the so-called (psychological) *diminishing sensitivity* to gains and losses.

Example 11.8 Tversky and Kahneman (1981, p. 459) Imagine that you are about to purchase a jacket for ($125)[$15] and a calculator for ($15)[$125]. The calculator salesman informs you that the calculator you wish to buy is on sale for ($10)[$120] at the other branch of the store, located 20 min drive away. Would you make the trip to the other store?[9]

Thaler (1999) argues that "when two versions of this problem are given (one with the figures in parentheses, the other with the figures in brackets), most people say that they will travel to save the $5 when the item costs $15 but not when it costs $125. If people were using a minimal account frame they would be just asking themselves whether they are willing to drive 20 min to save $5, and would give the same answer in either version" (p. 186). However, Tversky et al.'s and Thaler's arguments are not correct because their minimal account frame ignores the relative price information. That is, the question is not "Are you willing to drive 20 min to save $5?", but "Are you willing to drive 20 min to save $5 so that you don't need to:

Case 1. Pay $1.5(=15/10)$ times the price (and let the seller earn 50% more rate of return from you)? or.

Case 2. Pay $1.042(=125/120)$ times the price (and let the seller earn 4.2% more rate of return from you)?".

While considering relative price ratios, most people will choose Case 1. Choose Case 2 will make you look dumb.

Zhang and Sussman (2018, p. 10) (and Sussman & Shafir, 2012) argue that "all else equal, a person's view of her personal wealth should be driven by her net worth—the difference between her assets and debts. Holding constant her overall worth, the level of assets and debt should not matter". They find:

Example 11.9 Financial profiles with higher levels of assets and debt are viewed as wealthier when overall net worth is negative (e.g., $50,000 in assets and $100,000 in debt is preferred to $20,000 in assets and $70,000 in debt) while profiles with lower levels of assets and debt are viewed as wealthier when overall net worth is positive (e.g., $70,000 in assets and $20,000 in debt is preferred to $100,000 in assets and $50,000 in debt).

This is another example of relative price ratio where people pay attention not only to net worth:

[9] See also Thaler (1980, p. 50).

Case 1. Negative net wealth: $\text{asset/debt} = 50,000/100,000 = 0.5/1 > 20,000/70,000 = 0.286/1$.

This means that for \$50,000 in assets and \$100,000 in debt, if default, every one dollar of debt can get 0.5 dollars back; and for \$20,000 in assets and \$70,000 in debt, if default, every one dollar of debt can only get 0.286 dollars back. Thus, higher levels of assets and debt are viewed as wealthier.

Case 2. Positive net wealth:$\text{asset/debt} = 100,000/50,000 = 2/1 < 70,000/20,000 = 3.5/1$.

This means that for \$100,000 in assets and \$50,000 in debt, every one dollar of debt is covered (protected) by 2 dollars; and for \$70,000 in assets and \$20,000 in debt, every one dollar of debt is covered (protected) by 3.5 dollars. Thus, lower levels of assets and debt are viewed as wealthier.

It is interesting to note that the above results also hold for the results of using the current ratio analysis in Chap. 4: (1) when current assets are less than current liabilities, higher levels of current assets and current liabilities are viewed higher liquidity; and (2) when current assets are larger than current liabilities, lower levels of current assets and current liabilities are viewed higher liquidity.

Some Applications

Prospect Theory

Kahneman and Tversky's (1979, p. 268) prospect theory argues that people show risk aversion in the domain of gains and risk seeking in the domain of losses. Kahneman et al. use the following two experiments to prove their arguments:

Example 11.10 People are asked to choose from:

(A) 80% chance to win \$4,000 and 20% chance to win nothing; or
(B) gain \$3,000 for sure.

Example 11.11 People are asked to choose from:

(A) 80% chance to lose \$4,000 and 20% chance to lose nothing; or
(B) lose \$3,000 for sure.

Kahneman et al. find that in Example 11.10, most subjects (80%) chose (B), but in Example 11.11, most subjects (92%) chose (A). They argue that with the same reference point, a person will show risk aversion in the domain of gains (i.e., in Example 11.10) and risk seeking in the domain of losses (i.e., in Example 11.11), and hence, "the value function for changes of wealth is normally concave above the reference point and often convex below it" (p. 278).

However, it may not be: "people will show risk aversion in the domain of gains". In Example 11.10, two points regarding the increment $(\$1000 = \$4,000 - \$3,000)$ of increment ($3,000) should be noted:

(1) The difference between a gain of $0 and a gain of $3,000 is greater than the difference between a gain of $3,000 and a gain of $4,000. This is because $3,000/1 > 4,000/3,000 = 1.333/1$ implies that 33.3% rate of return of $3,000 becoming $4,000 is much smaller than 300,000% rate of return of $1 becoming $3,000.
(2) People have a 80% chance to increase the increment from $3,000 to $4,000 but also have a 20% chance to lose the original increment $3,000. 3,000 dollars is a large amount of money which may afford a couple a four-day tour of Paris.[10]

Based on these two points, people will be very reluctant to choose the risky choice (A).

For Example 11.11, another two points should be noted:

(1) The difference between a loss of $0 and a loss of $3,000 is greater than the difference between a loss of $3,000 and a loss of $4,000 because $3,000/1 > 4,000/3,000 = 1.333/1$ implies that 33.3% rate of return of $3,000 loss becoming $4,000 loss is much smaller than 300,000% rate of return of $1 loss becoming $3,000 loss.
(2) People have a 20% chance to win back the original loss $3,000 but also have a 80% chance to increase the loss from $3,000 to $4,000. Losing $3,000 in your budget (income) could be very painful because you have to determine which commodities you should sacrifice.

Based on the above two points, people will be more willing to choose the risky choice (A).

The following experiment is used to examine whether a small amount (relative to people's budget) of gain and loss affects people's decisions[11]:

Example 11.12 People are asked to choose from:

(A) 80% chance to win CNY4,000 and 20% chance to win nothing [21%];
(B) gain CNY3,000 for sure [67%].
(C) indifferent between (A) and (B) [12%].

---

[10] In Kahneman et al. (1979), 3,000 is the median net monthly income for a family in Israel currency (p. 264).

[11] This experiment was done at Xi'an Jiao Tong University in 2018. The number of the subjects (most are undergraduates) is 158. CNY3,000 is about the median monthly income of a new college graduate. CNY3 is the price of a lottery. The author wishes to thank Professor Qin, Botao for his help in designing this experiment.

Example 11.13 People are asked to choose from:

(A) 80% chance to lose CNY4,000 and 20% chance to lose nothing [61%];
(B) lose CNY3,000 for sure [26%].
(C) (C) indifferent between (A) and (B) [13%.]

Example 11.14 People are asked to choose from:

(A) 80% chance to win CNY4 and 20% chance to win nothing [58%];
(B) gain CNY3 for sure [28%].
(C) indifferent between (A) and (B) [14%].

Example 11.15 People are asked to choose from:

(A) 80% chance to lose CNY4 and 20% chance to lose nothing; [55%]
(B) lose CNY3 for sure. [23%]
(C) indifferent between (A) and (B).[22%]

It shows that when the amount of the outcomes is big (i.e., Examples 11.12 and 11.13), the results are similar to Kahneman and Tversky (1979) (i.e., Examples 11.10 and 11.11). But when the amount of the outcomes is very small (i.e., Examples 11.14 and 11.15), most subjects chose the risky choice (A). This indicates that with small outcomes (which equals the price of a lottery), people will take the games as an entertainment (play for fun) because these outcomes (gains or losses) will not affect people's consumption levels.[12]

Note that if the gain and loss of a game are small relative to people's budgets, people usually will not be interested in it. Friedman and Savage (1948, p. 279) argue that "an individual who buys fire insurance on a house he owns … is choosing certainty in preference to uncertainty", and "an individual who buys a lottery ticket … is choosing uncertainty in preference to certainty". Their arguments are not accurate. An individual could possibly buy both fire insurance and lottery ticket because the insurance premium and lottery ticket price are small relative to her budget. Also, buying a lottery ticket can provide her a chance/choice (even if it is very small) to become a millionaire, and buying a fire insurance can give her a chance/choice to avoid the possibility of losing a big fortune which will affect her consumption levels.

Kahneman and Tversky's (1979, p. 281) experiment of buying lotteries and insurance finds that people prefer a 0.1% chance of $5,000 to a certain gain of $5,

[12] Thaler and Johnson's (1990) experiment find that a large majority of subjects prefer temporal separation of gains to have them occur together. They also find that most subjects prefer temporal separation of losses to have them occur together. I think this may due to the fact that large sum of loss could seriously affect people's consumption levels (life style). People will prefer to amortize the loss to separate periods (as companies always do to avoid a big drop in their stock prices).

but also prefer a certain loss of \$5 to a 0.1% chance of losing \$5,000. Tversky and Kahneman (1992) propose the probability weighting function to explain this result. The weighting function overweights low objective probabilities and underweights high objective probabilities. In addition to use a specific function to consider overweighting and underweighting, we can also use the Gordan (Arbitrage) theory in Chap. 9 to estimate these probabilities. The probabilities (π and $1-\pi$) of the following equation of the Gordan theory are the actual world subjective probabilities:

$$S_{ce} = \frac{1}{1+r}[\pi \cdot S_1 + (1-\pi) \cdot S_2],$$

where S_{ce} is the certainty equivalent, S_1 is the value at state 1, S_2 is the value at state 2, and r is the risk-free interest rate. In Gonzalez and Wu's study (1999), subjects state an average certainty equivalent of \$10 for a 0.05 chance of \$100, and \$63 for a 0.9 chance of \$100. In the above equation where the risk-free interest is 0, we can estimate: $10 = \pi \times 100 + (1-\pi) \times 0$ and $\pi = 0.10$, $63 = \pi' \times 100 + \left(1-\pi'\right) \times 0$ and $\pi' = 0.63$. That is, people's subjective probabilities overweight low objective probabilities and underweights high objective probabilities.

Endowment Effect

Suppose that you just bought a pen for \$10. How much are you willing to sell it for? The answer should be more than \$10. This is because when you decided to use \$10 to buy the pen, you must prefer the pen to \$10, i.e., u(pen) > u(\$10). Hence, when you sell it, you will ask more than 10 dollars, i.e., willing to accept (WTA) is greater than willing to pay (WTP).[13] This result has nothing to do with the psychological aspect of endowment effect, which emphasizes that once you own a thing, you may feel attached to it.

Many experiments have shown that WTA is much greater than WTP. Thaler's (1980) rare fatal disease experiment find that when subjects are told that they had been exposed to a fatal disease and that they now face a 0.1% chance of painless death within two weeks. They must decide how much they would be willing to pay for a vaccine, to be purchased immediately. The same subjects were also asked for the compensation they would demand to participate in a medical experiment in which they face a 0.1% chance of a quick and painless death. The result shows that for most subjects the two prices differed by more than an order of magnitude. Hanemann (1991) argues that large WTA-WTP disparity can also arise from low substitutability between the environmental good and each of the private goods in the individual's utility function. However, large gap between WTA and WTP could be due to that the good you plan to give up (to sell) interconnects with many other goods in your original consumption bundle (e.g., take the risk of a quick death versus a plan to get marry or a trip to Disneyland with your family; no more beautiful scenery outside your house versus entertaining friends in your house).

[13] Microeconomics states that if a good is a normal good and hence a non-Giffen good, then WTA is greater than WTP. When there is no income effect, WTA and WTP are equal.

Kahneman, Knetsch, and Thaler's (1990) experiment is to give half of subjects mugs and another half none, and then ask them at what price they are willing to sell (WTA) and at what price they are willing to buy (WTP). They find that median selling prices are about twice median buying prices. Note that this may be because once a mug is given to a subject, it enters into the subject's consumption bundle and the subject has a plan for it (e.g., put it on a shelf or give it to her mom as a souvenir). When an individual has a high expectation for getting a good (or a job), if she fails, it will greatly disappoint her because she might already have a plan for it. Cohen and Knetsch (1992) find that in tort law judges make the distinction between loss by way of expenditure and failure to make gain, e.g., the plaintiff was able to recover wages paid to employees which were considered "positive outlays" but could not recover lost profits which were merely "negative losses consisting of a mere deprivation of an opportunity to earn an income".

Knetsch and Sinden's (1984) endowment effect experiment find that after subjects were selected at random to receive either $3 or a lottery ticket, of those initially given a lottery ticket 82% chose to keep it, and 62% of those given the $3 would not give it up. Samuelson and Zeckhauser's (1988) experiment assumes: an individual inherited a large sum of money (or a portfolio of cash and securities) from her great-uncle. She is considering different portfolios. Samuelson et al. find that an alternative became significantly more popular when it was designated as the status quo. These results indicate that if people do not have new information or different expectations about the future, they will maintain the status quo (i.e., if it's not broke, don't fix it).

Procrastination

Procrastination is usually defined as "when present costs are unduly salient in comparison with future costs, leading individuals to postpone tasks until tomorrow without foreseeing that when tomorrow comes, the required action will be delayed again." (Arkerlof, 1991, p. 1). However, the reason why people postpone their works, i.e., treasure present more than tomorrow, is that they can have more choices to make a better arrangement for today and tomorrow tasks, although procrastination sometimes could lead to serious losses. For example, the poverty of the elderly may be due to inadequate saving for retirement. But have not saved enough at young age may not be an irrational decision. After all, no one is sure how long she/he can live. Also, even if spend a bit more money in this month, people still have a chance to earn those money back in the future.[14]

Camerer et al. (1997) survey of cab drivers finds that the number of hours that a driver works on a given day is strongly inversely related to his average hourly

[14] Barberis (2013) suggests that "upon receiving a negative income shock, the individual prefers to lower future consumption rather than current consumption. After all, news that future consumption will be lower than expected is less painful than news that current consumption is lower than expected." (p. 188). This indicates that people care more about the current consumption level than the future consumption level because lower consumption now is painful, and if people know that the future consumption may be lower, they still have a chance/choice to work hard to fix it.

wage on that day, i.e., drivers establish a target earnings level per day, and they will tend to quit earlier on good days. This behavior may not be irrational since keep on working for the rest of the day cannot provide windfall gains (i.e., cannot affect drivers' consumption levels too much). Besides, unexpectedly high wages in the morning are not necessarily correlated to the earnings in the afternoon.

Thaler (2018, p. 1265) provides an example of self-control problem: "At a dinner party for fellow economics graduate students I put out a large bowl of cashew nuts to accompany drinks while waiting for dinner to finish cooking. In a short period of time, we devoured half the bowl of nuts. Seeing that our appetites (and waistlines) were in danger I removed the bowl and left it in the kitchen pantry. When I returned everyone thanked me". Again, people may feel that they can start a diet plan the next day (they have choices). Also, they are unsure what the main dish is and how it tastes like. If the main dish and the bowl of cashew nuts are served simultaneously, people will not eat that much cashew.[15]

11.2 Behavioral Finance and Corporate Finance

As discussed in the previous section, effort aversion is defined as: people don't like to make more efforts to earn the same amount of money. Suppose the current wealth is \$10,000. If the wealth increases from \$10,000 to \$12,000, then $12,000/10,000 = 1.2$ means that every original dollar earns 20% rate of return. If the wealth decreases from \$10,000 to \$8,000, then $10,000/8,000 = 1.25$ means that to go back to the original wealth level \$10,000, every dollar needs to earn 25% rate of return. That is, for the same amount of money \$2,000, "25% > 20%" means that people need to make more efforts to go from \$8,000 to \$10,000 than from \$10,000 to \$12,000. Because of effort aversion, i.e., people prefer less cost (effort) and more or the same benefit, people will always turn down gambles where they lose \$2,000 or gain \$2,000, each with 50% probability.[16] Notice that this effort aversion phenomenon is independent of people's attitudes toward risk.

Suppose a person's behavior regarding wealth w can be represented by a real-valued utility function over wealth: $u = u(w)$.[17] Then because of effort aversion,

---

[15] This is not to say that self-control problem, e.g., drug or alcohol addiction, does not exist. DellaVigna, and Malmendier (2006) use a data of three U.S. health club to find that "members who choose a contract with a flat monthly fee of over \$70 attend on average fewer than 4.5 times per month. They pay a price per expected visit of more than \$17, even though they could pay \$10 per visit using a ten-visit pass. On average, these users forego savings of over \$600 during their membership" (p. 716). This shows that people feel they will use the gym more than seven times a month, and hence, choose to pay \$70 a month. However, later on, people may choose other activities which give them higher utilities.

[16] Let the initial wealth be x where $x > \$2000$. Then $(x + \$2,000)/x - x/(x - \$2,000) = -\$4,000,000/[x(x - \$2,000)] < 0$.

[17] The existence of a real-valued utility function requires three assumptions: (i) Completeness: for any two alternatives bundles A and B, at least one of three conditions exists: $A \succsim B$, $B \succsim A$ or $A \sim$

this utility function must be concave, i.e., $u'(w) > 0$ and $u''(w) < 0$, which implies people have diminishing marginal utility of wealth (i.e., when wealth is greater, the same increment of wealth (e.g., $2,000) provides less utilities). Notice that a concave utility function (e.g., $u(w) = \ln w$, $u'(w) = 1/w > 0$, $u''(w) = -1/w^2 < 0$) has nothing to do with people's risk attitude toward risk.

Economists consider expected utility theory as the gold standard for decision making under uncertainty. In expected utility function (or von Neumann-Morgenstern utility function), as shown in Fig. 7.1 of Chap. 7, risk aversion arises if and only if the utility function over wealth is concave. However, because of effort aversion, concave utility function holds for every kind of risk attitude. Appendix B of this chapter shows that under the expected utility framework, risk averse investors also purchase risky assets.

To Invest or Not to Invest

Example 11.16 In Samuelson (1963), Samuelson offered one of his colleagues the following bet: a fifty percent chance to win $200 and a fifty percent chance to lose $100, i.e., (−$100, 0.5; $200, 0.5). . The colleague turned this bet down and said: "I won't bet because I would feel the $100 loss more than $200 gain."[18]

We can use the following calculations of effort aversion (i.e., 'relative price ratios' for wealth) to infer this colleague's wealth (or allowance).

Loss		Gain
Initial wealth: $110	$110/(110-100)-1=10$	$> \ (110+200)/110-1=1.82$
Initial wealth: $180	$180/(180-100)-1=1.25$	$> (180+200)/180-1=1.11$
Initial wealth: $200	$200/(200-100)-1=1.00$	$= \ (200+200)/200-1=1.00$
Initial wealth: $300	$300/(300-100)-1=0.50$	$< \ (300+200)/300-1=0.66$
Initial wealth: $400	$400/(400-100)-1=0.33$	$< \ (400+200)/400-1= 0.50$
Initial wealth: $1,000	$1,000/(1,000-100)-1= 0.11$	$< \ (1,000+200)/1,000-1= 0.2$
Initial wealth: $10,000 1	$0,000/(10,000-100)-1= 0.01$	$< \ (10,000+200)/10,000- 1=0.02$

When the wealth is not greater than $200, the colleague will not bet. When the wealth is larger than $200, the colleague might be willing to bet. But when

B (where $\succsim$ denotes "at least as good as .....", and $\sim$ denotes "indifferent to"); (ii) Transitivity: for any three alternatives A, B and C, if A $\succsim$ B and B $\succsim$ C, then A $\succsim$ C; (iii) Continuous Preference: for any x and z consumption bundles, if $x \succ z$, then for any alternative y which is very close to$x$, we still have$y \succ z$. The first and second assumptions are also called 'rational preference' which are the features of the real number system $\mathbb{R}$.

[18] Samuelson, Paul (1963) Risk and uncertainty: a fallacy of large numbers. *Scientia* 98: 108–13.

the wealth becomes quite large, e.g., more than \$10,000, the colleague might be indifferent because the difference between 2% rate of return and 1% rate of return is not so big.

Example 11.17 Rabin and Thaler (2001) use the expected utility theory to derive the following results[19]:

	If an Expected Utility Maximizer Always Turns Down the 50/50 bet...	Then She Always Turns Down the 50/50 bet...
(1)	lose \$10/gain \$10.10	lose \$1,000/gain \$∞
(2)	lose \$10/gain \$11	lose \$100/gain \$∞
(3)	lose \$100/gain \$101	lose \$10,000/gain \$∞
(4)	lose \$100/gain \$110	lose \$1,000/gain \$∞
(5)	lose \$1,000/gain \$1,100	lose \$10,000/gain \$∞
(6)	lose \$10,000/gain \$11,000	lose \$100,000/gain \$∞

Rabin and Thaler find that if a risk-averse expected utility maximizer will always turn down the 50–50 gamble of losing \$10 or gaining \$11, then she will always turn down any bet with a 50% risk of losing at least \$100, no matter how high the upside gain is.

But in practice, Rabin et al.'s table cannot be true. The reasons are simple:

(i) In the 2000s, losing \$10 is nothing because it won't affect your living standard, and (even with 50% chance to gain) gaining only \$10.10 or \$11 is unattractive and meaningless because, again, it won't affect your living standard. Hence, people will straightforwardly reject the gambles of (\$10.10, 0.50; – \$10, 0.50) and (\$11, 0.50; – \$10, 0.50).
(ii) A wealthy person can afford to lose \$10,000 but won't bet for gaining \$11,000 because \$10,000 can buy many pricy things,[20] and additional \$11,000 won't change her living standard too much.
(iii) Even a beggar would love to use \$10 to bet that he might own the whole wealth on earth. A middle-class family will also use or borrow \$10,000 to gamble that it might own the whole wealth on earth.

In sum, when people make decision under uncertainty, they will consider not only effort aversion (i.e., the relative price ratio about gain or loss) but also how gain or loss affects living standard (i.e., the relative price ratio about wealth).

[19] Rabin, Matthew and Richard Thaler (2001) Anomalies: risk Aversion. *Journal of Economic Perspectives* 15: 219-232.
[20] Also, it won't be easy for a very high-income person to voluntarily pay a tithe.

Another example regarding probabilities is: People prefer ($5000, 0.001; $0, 0.999) to a certain $5, but also prefer a certain loss of $5 to ($0, 0.999; – $5,000, 0.001). Behavioral economists argue that "by overweighting the tail probability of 0.001 sufficiently, cumulative prospect theory can capture both of these choices". However, this may not be due to "overweighting the tail probability", but the fact that buying a $5 lottery can have a chance to win big fortune, and buying a $5 insurance can avoid a possible big loss. They are all about whether gain or loss could seriously affect living standard.

Equity Premium Puzzle

In the past several decades, the US annual real rate of return on stocks has been about 7% but the real rate of return on treasury bill has been less than 1 percent. The question is: why is the equity premium so big? Mehra and Prescott (1985) find that to explain this equity premium puzzle the coefficient of relative risk aversion (from a concave utility function) will be implausibly big.

As discussed above, concave utility function is the result of effort aversion (i.e., relative price ratio or rate of return), which has nothing to do with risk attitudes. The reason why such a big equity premium exists may be the following:

(i) Stock investment is not a small portion of a household's wealth. If it fails, it could lower the living standard of the household.
(ii) Stocks are more volatile than bonds, and annual stock returns are negative much more frequently than annual bond returns are. When stocks suddenly fall, say, 35% in a month, and the household needs money, selling stocks means heavy loss and lower living standard.[21]
(iii) To attract people to participate in the stock market stocks are underpriced. If investors buy and hold for a period of time and have no urgent need to sell stocks, the equity premium can be large.
(iv) The degree of stocks' underpricing may attract some but not many people. This may explain the so-called stock market participation puzzle, i.e., a *significant* fraction of households do not participate in the stock market.

As unemployment, losing a substantial portion of wealth because stocks plummet can seriously affect the living standard of a household. Some may see investors' frequent trading of stocks as an irrational myopic, short term investment strategy.[22] But since the volatility of stocks are quite high and can greatly affect a household's living standard (consumption level), investors will watch stocks more closely and

[21] Some scholars claim that investors may have the so-called narrow framing bias, i.e., investors make investment decisions without considering the context of their entire portfolio. However, using portfolio to diversify cannot create or add value i.e., financial diversification irrelevancy. Also, since stocks and house are the main part of a household's wealth, investors of course will pay much more attention to these two assets.

[22] Benartzi, Shlomo and Richard Thaler (1995) Myopic loss aversion and the equity premium puzzle. *Quarterly Journal of Economics* 110: 73–92.

may trade more frequently though buy and hold for a longer period of time could generate higher real returns.[23]

Disposition Effect

Disposition effect is defined as a tendency to sell winners too early and keep losers too long.[24] Shefrin and Statman (1985) find that investors will hold on to stocks that have lost value (relative to their purchase price) too long and will be eager to sell stocks that have risen in value.[25] Orden (1998) finds that investors held losing stocks a median of 124 days but held winners only 104 days.[26] Investors expected that the losers may bounce back, but in Odean's sample, the unsold losers gave only 5% rate of return in the subsequent year but the winners that were sold later provided 11.6%.

The disposition effect is claimed to be similar as the prospect theory's "risk aversion in the domain of gains and risk seeking in the domain of losses (loss aversion)" (i.e., Examples 11.10 and 11.11). But as shown in the discussions of Examples 11.10 and 11.11 in the previous section, they are the results of relative price ratio (rate of return). For example, suppose a household's stock investment has just

(i) won \$3,000. Then the decision is to sell the stock investment and realize \$3,000 return or to still hold the stock investment and use \$3,000 to exchange for the gamble: (\$4,000, 0.80; \$0, 0.20).

---

[23] Siegel (1992) The Equity premium: stock and bond returns since 1802. *Financial Analysts Journal* 48: 28–38.

[24] There are some other biases which may be related to transaction costs. (1) Herd behavior: people do what others are doing instead of using their own information or making independent decisions. Investors may believe others have already done enough research and imitate their actions. (2) Home bias: individuals and institutions in most countries hold only modest amounts of foreign equity, and tend to strongly favor company stock from their home nation. This may be the result of the extra difficulties associated with investing in foreign equities, such as legal restrictions and additional transaction costs. (3) Overconfidence: people's tendency to overestimate their abilities to make very risky investments. Probably, all start-ups and entrepreneurs have the overconfidence feature to innovate. (4) People rely too much on extrapolation of recent trends. Recent information may signal the beginning of a different path. People will regret if they miss this information/signal. (5) Affect: investors and consumers may feel good about a company that has a good reputation of corporate social responsibility. Good reputation may save the search cost of finding a good investment or product. (6) Equity carve-outs. For example, company A has sold a stake of a subsidiary (company B) to the public and has announced its intention to spin off the remaining shares in company B at some point in the not-too-distant future. However, the market value of A is found lower than the value of the shares of B that it owns. This is an example of limits to arbitrage: the difficulty of short-selling the overpriced carveout shares.

[25] Shefrin, Hersh and Meir Statman (1985) The disposition to sell winners too early and ride losers too long: Theory and evidence. *Journal of Finance* 40: 777–790.

[26] Odean, Terrance (1998) Are investors reluctant to realize their losses? *Journal of Finance* 53: 1775–1798.

Rate of return (or relative price ratio) shows: $3,000/1 > 4,000/3,000 = 1.333/1$ implies that 33.3% rate of return of $3,000 becoming $4,000 is much smaller than 300,000% rate of return of $1 becoming $3,000.

The household has a 80% chance to increase the return from $3,000 to $4,000 but also have a 20% chance to lose the original return $3,000. Since 3,000 dollars is a large amount of money for a family and 300,000 percent gain is greater than 33.3 percent gain, the investor will sell the stock investment and realize $3000 return.

(ii) lost $3,000. Then the decision is to sell the stock investment and suffer $3000 loss or to still hold the stock investment so that $3,000 loss becomes the gamble: ($0, 0.20; – $4,000, 0.80).

Rate of return (or relative price ratio) shows: $3,000/1 > 4,000/3,000 = 1.333/1$ implies that 33.3% rate of return of $3,000 loss becoming $4,000 loss is much smaller than 300,000% rate of return of $1 loss becoming $3,000 loss.

The household has a 20% chance to win back the original loss $3,000 but also have a 80% chance to increase the loss from $3,000 to $4,000. Since losing $3,000 of a household's wealth could affect the household's living standard and 33.3 percent loss is less than 300,000 percent loss, the investor will prefer ($0, 0.20; – $4,000, 0.80) to $3,000 sure loss.

Summary and Conclusions

Behavioral economics and Behavioral finance, incorporating the concepts and methods in psychology science into traditional economics, have found pervasive anomalies in common people's behaviors. This chapter use the concepts in traditional economics (e.g., choice, relative price, and opportunity cost) to analyze these anomalies. The results show that first, because people do not have choice in the first stage, Kahneman and Tversky's two-stage game is in fact a one stage game, and their findings of preference reversal and isolation effect do not exist. Second, in Thaler's free ticket to game example, there is no sunk cost fallacy involved because comparing with buying a ticket (i.e., prefer game to good meal), not buying a ticket but receiving it as a gift (i.e., prefer good meal to game) will be less likely to drive through a snowstorm to watch the game. Also, escalation of commitment to a failing course of action does not imply a sunk cost fallacy. A sunk cost fallacy occurs only when people escalate commitment without considering all other alternatives. Third, people consider opportunity cost when making decision (choice). After people decided to drink a bottle of wine or dropped and broke the bottle, there will be no opportunity cost of the bottle of wine. Fourth, prospect theory is about relative price ratio (or rate of return). People won't care much if a gain or a loss is relative smaller than their monthly income. Loss aversion can be interpreted as effort aversion, i.e., people don't like the idea of making more efforts to earn the same amount of money. Endowment effect can be interpreted as: people's using cash K to buy a thing (e.g., a pen) means the utility of the pen is greater than that of K, and hence, the resell price of the pen must be greater than K. When faced with something we do not want to do, we procrastinate and hope things might change later so that we don't need to do. These findings do not say that people always make rational choices. The findings show that common people may not be as irrational as behavioral economists have suggested (in some situations, common people may act more like a rational economist).

Appendix A: Opportunity Cost in Practice

The following is a true story from Chang (2005). One day a senior student (Jade) came to my office, and told me happily that she just got admitted to a prestigious university to pursue her master degree in finance.

Jade: Professor, I am so happy that I got admitted to X university.

Professor: Congratulations! ... But did you also apply for other disciplines, such as MS or Ph.D. programs in computer science, statistics, or economics?

Jade: No. Why should I? If I pursue these degrees, then my past four-year study of finance would be a waste.

Professor: Apparently, you do not understand the meaning of opportunity cost. Your study of Principles of Economics (Econ101) and Financial Management (Fin101) courses is a waste and futile.

Jade: I don't quite follow you. Could you explain it to me?

Professor: Let me give you an example. A beautiful girl who just enrolls in a university meets a boy. When the boy asks her to go on a date, she agrees. Two weeks later, the boy asks for more dating, and the girl contemplates: "If I stop dating him, then my two weeks of dating (investment) will be a waste." Hence, they continue to date for another two years. After two years, the girl contemplates again: "If I stop dating him, then my previous two years of dating him will be a waste." They continue to date for two more years. After four years, upon graduation, the boy asks the girl to marry him. The girl contemplates: "If I do not marry him, then my four years of dating him will go to waste," and so she marries the boy. You are that girl.

Jade: No, I'm not. I am not that stupid!

Professor: Oh, yes, you are. If you are this discreet with your marriage, then be even more so in choosing your profession.

What matters in Jade's choosing a particular graduate program is: Does it provide positive net present value (NPV, the difference between revenues and costs), and is its NPV the largest one among all the mutually exclusive projects (graduate programs)? Costs in the NPV analysis are opportunity costs, which means that you still have the opportunity to make the choice to spend or not to spend, i.e., opportunity costs are *ex-ante* (Buchanan, 1969). When calculating the NPV of joining a finance graduate program, Jade should consider only how much more costs and time she will spend, and compare them with the revenues (cash flows) she will receive if she finishes the study. Jade's four-year study of finance is already sunk; it is not an opportunity cost, and therefore should not be considered in decision-making.

Appendix B: Expected Utility Theory and Risky Assets

Example A.1 A consumer decides to buy α units of insurance. When there is an event, every unit of insurance bought will pay one dollar. One unit of insurance costs q dollars (where $q < 1$). Suppose the consumer's wealth is w, the probability of event is π, and total loss will be D dollars. The consumer has a strictly concave utility function: $u'(w) > 0$, $u''(w) < 0$, and is using the expected utility function to make decision:

$$\underset{\alpha \geq 0}{Max} \quad U = (1-\pi) \cdot u(w-\alpha q) + \pi \cdot u(w-\alpha q - D + \alpha \cdot 1) \tag{A.1}$$

or

$$\begin{aligned} &\underset{\alpha, s}{Max} \quad U = (1-\pi) \cdot u(w-\alpha q) + \pi \cdot u(w-\alpha q - D + \alpha) \\ &s.t. \quad -\alpha + s^2 = 0 \end{aligned}$$

By the Lagrangian method:

$$\underset{\alpha, \lambda, s}{Max} \quad L = (1-\pi) \cdot u(w-\alpha q) + \pi \cdot u(w-\alpha q - D + \alpha) - \lambda\left[-\alpha + s^2\right] \tag{A.2}$$

Since $u(\cdot)$ is strictly concave, and hence, the expected utility function is also strictly concave. The first-order condition of Eq. (A.2) is both necessary and sufficient conditions:

1st-order condition:

$$\begin{aligned} &\frac{\partial L}{\partial \alpha} = (1-\pi) \cdot u'(w-\alpha q)(-q) + \pi \cdot u'(w - D + \alpha(1-q)) \cdot (1-q) + \lambda \equiv 0 \\ &\frac{\partial L}{\partial \lambda} = -\left[-\alpha + s^2\right] \equiv 0 \\ &\frac{\partial L}{\partial s} = -2\lambda s \equiv 0 \end{aligned}$$

Its Kuhn-Tucker condition is:

$$\begin{cases} \text{(I)} \ \ (1-\pi) \cdot u'\left(w-\alpha^* q\right)(-q) + \pi \cdot u'\left(w - D + \alpha^*(1-q)\right) \cdot (1-q) \leq 0 \\ \text{(II)} \ \ \left[(1-\pi) \cdot u'\left(w-\alpha^* q\right)(-q) + \pi \cdot u'\left(w - D + \alpha^*(1-q)\right) \cdot (1-q)\right] \cdot \alpha^* = 0 \\ \text{(III)} \ \alpha^* \geq 0, \lambda^* \geq 0 \end{cases} \tag{A.3}$$

Assume that the insurance company is risk-neutral (i.e., it treats expected value as certain value) and earns no excess profits:

$$q - [\pi \cdot 1 + (1 - \pi) \cdot 0] = 0 \Rightarrow q = \pi$$

Hence, Eq. (A.3)'s (I) and (II) become:

$$\{(\text{I}) \quad u'\big(w - D + \alpha^*(1 - \pi)\big) - u'\big(w - \alpha^*\pi\big) \leq 0 \tag{A.4a}$$

$$\{(\text{II}) \quad \big[u'\big(w - D + \alpha^*(1 - \pi)\big) - u'\big(w - \alpha^*\pi\big)\big] \cdot \alpha^* = 0 \tag{A.4b}$$

If in Eq. (A.4a), $u'(w - D + \alpha^*(1 - \pi)) - u'(w - \alpha^*\pi) < 0$, then from Eq. (A.4b) we get: $\alpha^* = 0$. But because of $u'(\cdot) > 0$ and $u''(\cdot) < 0$, there will be a contradiction:

$$u'\big(w - D + \alpha^*(1 - \pi)\big) - u'\big(w - \alpha^*\pi\big)\langle 0 \Rightarrow w - D + \alpha^*(1 - \pi)\rangle w - \alpha^*\pi$$
$$\Rightarrow \alpha^* > D.$$

It is impossible to have $\alpha^* > D$. Therefore, from equation (A.4a), we know that $u'(w - D + \alpha^*(1 - \pi)) - u'(w - \alpha^*\pi)$ must be equal to zero. Also, because $u(w)$ is monotonically increasing in w, we have:

$$u'\big(w - D + \alpha^*(1 - \pi)\big) - u'\big(w - \alpha^*\pi\big) = 0 \Rightarrow w - D + \alpha^*(1 - \pi)$$
$$= w - \alpha^*\pi \Rightarrow \alpha^* = D.$$

That is, this consumer will buy 100% insurance. However, to prevent the moral hazard problem (i.e., the insured may handle her asset carelessly), the insurance company may not sell 100% insurance. But according to the endowment effect, the insurance company will sell 100% insurance because the insured feels attached to her asset.

Example A.2 Assume a one-period model, and there are two kinds of assets: one gives certain outcome (one dollar for one dollar), another gives uncertain payoff z where $\int z dF(z) > 1$, $F(z)$ is the cumulative distribution of z. At the beginning of the period, the consumer will allocate her wealth w to the two assets: $w = \alpha + \beta$. At the end of the period, she will get wealth: $\alpha \cdot 1 + \beta \cdot z$. Suppose that her utility function is strictly concave: $u'(w) > 0$ and $u''(w) < 0$, and she makes decision based on the expected utility function:

$$\underset{\alpha,\beta \geq 0}{Max} \quad U = \int u(\alpha + \beta z) dF(z)$$

$$s.t. \quad w = \alpha + \beta \tag{A.5}$$

Substitute $\alpha = w - \beta$ into the objective function:

$$\underset{\beta}{Max} \quad U = \int u(w + \beta(z-1))dF(z)$$

$$s.t. \quad 0 \le \beta \le w\,, \quad \text{or} \quad \begin{cases} \beta \ge 0 \Rightarrow -\beta + s_1^2 = 0 \\ \beta \le w \Rightarrow \beta - w + s_2^2 = 0 \end{cases}$$

By the Lagrangian method:

$$\underset{\substack{\beta, \lambda_1, s_1, \\ \lambda_2, s_2}}{Max} \quad L = \int u(w + \beta(z-1))dF(z) - \lambda_1\left[-\beta + s_1^2\right] - \lambda_2\left[\beta - w + s_2^2\right]$$

1st-order condition:

$$\frac{\partial L}{\partial \beta} = \int u'(w + \beta(z-1))(z-1)dF(z) + \lambda_1 - \lambda_2 \equiv 0$$
$$\frac{\partial L}{\partial \lambda_1} = -\left[-\beta + s_1^2\right] \equiv 0$$
$$\frac{\partial L}{\partial s_1} = -2\lambda_1 s_1 \equiv 0$$
$$\frac{\partial L}{\partial \lambda_2} = -\left[\beta - w + s_2^2\right] \equiv 0$$
$$\frac{\partial L}{\partial s_2} = -2\lambda_2 s_2 \equiv 0$$

Its Kuhn-Tucker condition is:

$$\begin{cases} \text{(I)} \quad \int u'\big(w + \beta^*(z-1)\big)(z-1)dF(z) = \lambda_2^* - \lambda_1^* \\ \text{(II)} \ \lambda_1^* \cdot \beta^* = 0 \\ \text{(III)} \ \lambda_2^* \cdot \left(\beta^* - w\right) = 0 \\ \text{(IV)} \ w \ge \beta^* \ge 0;\ \lambda_1^*, \lambda_2^* \ge 0 \end{cases} \tag{A.6}$$

From the first-order condition and Eq. (A.6):

$$\begin{gathered} \text{If} \quad s_2^* \ne 0 \quad (\text{i.e.,} \quad 0 \le \beta^* < w), \ \text{then } \lambda_2^* = 0 \text{ and} \\ \int u'\big(w + \beta^*(z-1)\big)(z-1)dF(z) = -\lambda_1^* \le 0 \end{gathered} \tag{A.6a}$$

$$\begin{gathered} \text{If} \quad s_1^* \ne 0 \quad (\text{i.e.,} \quad \beta^* > 0), \ \text{then } \lambda_1^* = 0 \text{ and} \\ \int u'\big(w + \beta^*(z-1)\big)(z-1)dF(z) = \lambda_2^* \ge 0 \end{gathered} \tag{A.6b}$$

If in Eq. (A.6a), $\beta^* = 0$, then because $u'(w) > 0$ and $\int(z-1)dF(z) > 0$,

$$\left[\int u'\left(w+\beta^*(z-1)\right)\cdot(z-1)dF(z)\right]_{\beta^*=0} = u'(w)\int(z-1)dF(z) > 0$$

which contradicts Eq. (A.6a). Thus, we must have $0 < \beta^* < w$, i.e., the consumer's investment portfolio must contain some risky assets.

Problems

1. Suppose you're on a game show, and you're given the choice of three doors: Behind one door is \$1,000,000; behind the others, \$0. You choose a door, say No. 1, and the host, who knows what's behind the doors, opens another door, say No. 3, which has \$0. He then says to you, "Do you want to choose door No. 2?"

Questions

(1) How many choices do you have in this game?
(2) If the host opens two other doors, how many choices do you have in this game?
(3) If the host opens no door and asks you to choose again, how many choices do you have in this game?

2. Suppose that an individual is offered a bet: (\$100,000, 0.50; \$50,000, 0.50). Mankiw and Zeldes (1991) argue that a person with a coefficient of relative risk aversion of 30 would be indifferent between this gamble and a certain consumption of \$51,209. Give your comments on this claim.[27]
3. Some researchers claim that most common errors among individuals are: under-diversification, holding onto losers, chasing winners, buying stocks that catch their attention, systematically ignoring important information, paying too little attention to fees and trading too much. What do you think?

References

Akerlof, G. (1991). Procrastination and obedience. *American Economic Review, 81*, 1–19.
Arkes, H., & Blumer, C. (1985). The psychology of sunk cost. *Organizational Behavior and Human Decision Processes, 35*, 124–140.
Ashraf, N., Berry, J., & Shapiro, J. (2010). Can higher prices stimulate product use? evidence from a field experiment in Zambia. *American Economic Review, 100*, 2383–2413.
Barberis, N. (2013). Thirty years of prospect theory in economics: A review and assessment. *Journal of Economic Perspectives, 27*, 173–195.

[27] Mankiw, Gregory and Stephen Zeldes (1991), "The consumption of stockholders and nonstockholders," *Journal of Financial Economics* 29: 97–111.

Brockner, J., Shaw, M., & Rubin, J. (1979). Factors affecting withdrawal from an escalating conflict: Quitting before it's too late. *Journal of Experimental Social Psychology, 15*, 492–503.
Buchanan, J. (1969). *Cost and choice: An inquiry in economic theory*. The University of Chicago Press.
Buchanan, J. (2008) Opportunity cost. In *New Palgrave dictionary of economics*, 2nd ed., eds. by S. N. Durlauf, L. E. Blume. Palgrave Macmillan, New York.
Camerer, C., Babcock, L., Loewenstein, G., & Thaler, R. (1997). Labor supply of New York city cabdrivers: One day at a time. *Quarterly Journal of Economics, 112*, 407–441.
Chang, K.-P. (2015). *The ownership of the firm, corporate finance, and derivatives: Some critical thinking*. Springer.
Chang, K.-P. (2005) Prospect theory or a misuse of the concept of opportunity cost? http://ssrn.com/abstract=687704.
Chang, K.-P. (2018) On using risk-neutral probabilities to price assets. http://ssrn.com/abstract=3114126.
Chang, K.-P. (2019) Behavioral economics versus traditional economics: are they very different? http://ssrn.com/abstract=3350088.
Cohen, D., & Knetsch, J. (1992). Judicial choice and disparities between measures of economic values. *Osgoode Hall Law Journal, 30*, 737–770.
Daniel, K., Knetsch, J., & Thaler, R. (1990). Experimental tests of the endowment effect and the Coase theorem. *Journal of Political Economy, 98*, 1325–1348.
DellaVigna, S., & Malmendier, U. (2006). Paying not to go to the gym. *American Economic Review, 96*, 694–719.
Ferraro, P., Laura, T. (2005) Do economists recognize an opportunity cost when they see one? a dismal performance from the dismal science. *The B.E. Journal of Economic Analysis & Policy, 4*, 1–14.
Frank, R., & Bernanke, B. (2001). *Principles of microeconomics*. McGraw-Hill/Irwin.
Friedman, M., & Savage, L. (1948). The utility analysis of choices involving risk. *Journal of Political Economy, 56*, 279–304.
Friedman, D., Pommerenke, K., Lukose, R., Milam, G., & Huberman, B. (2007). Searching for the sunk cost fallacy. *Experimental Economics, 10*, 79–104.
Gourville, J., & Soman, D. (1998). Payment depreciation: The behavioral effects of temporarily separating payments from consumption. *Journal of Consumer Research, 25*, 160–174.
Just, D., & Wansink, B. (2011). The flat-rate pricing paradox: Conflicting effects of all-you-can-eat buffet pricing. *Review of Economics and Statistics, 93*, 193–200.
Kahneman, D. (2011). *Thinking, fast and slow*. Farrar.
Kahneman, D., & Tversky, A. (1979). Prospect theory: An analysis of decision under risk. *Econometrica, 47*, 263–291.
Kahneman, D., & Tversky, A. (1984). Choices, values, and frames. *The American Psychologist, 39*, 341–350.
Knetsch, J., & Sinden, J. A. (1984). Willingness to pay and compensation demanded: Experimental evidence of an unexpected disparity in measures of value. *Quarterly Journal of Economics, 99*, 507–521.
Michael, H. (1991). Willingness to pay and willingness to accept: How much can they differ? *American Economic Review, 81*, 635–647.
Northcraft, G., & Wolf, G. (1984). Dollars, sense, and sunk costs: A life-cycle model of resource allocation decisions. *Academy of Management Review, 9*, 225–234.
Shafir, E., & Thaler, R. (2006). Invest now, drink later, spend never: On the mental accounting of delayed consumption. *Journal of Economic Psychology, 27*, 694–712.
Sussman, A. B., & Shafir, E. (2012). On assets and debt in the psychology of perceived wealth. *Psychological Science, 23*, 101–108.
Thaler, R. (1980). Toward a positive theory of consumer choice. *Journal of Economic Behavior and Organization, 1*, 39–60.
Thaler, R. (2018). From cashews to nudges: The evolution of behavioral economics. *American Economic Review, 108*, 1265–1287.

Thaler, R., & Johnson, E. (1990). Gambling with the house money and trying to break even: The effects of prior outcomes on risky choice. *Management Science, 36*, 643–660.

Thirlby, G. F. (1946). The ruler. *South African Journal of Economics, 14*, 253–276.

Tversky, A., Kahneman, D. (1986). Rational choice and the framing of decisions. Journal of Business, *59*(4), part 2: The behavioral foundations of economic theory, S251–S278.

Tversky, A., & Kahneman, D. (1981). The framing of decisions and the rationality of choice. *Science, 211*, 453–458.

Tversky, A., & Kahneman, D. (1992). Advances in prospect theory: Cumulative representation of uncertainty. *Journal of Risk and Uncertainty, 5*, 297–323.

Zhang, Y., & Sussman, A. (2018). Perspectives on mental accounting: An exploration of budgeting and investing. *Financial Planning Review, 2018*(1), e1011. https://doi.org/10.1002/cfp2.1011

Capital Structure in an Imperfect Market

12

In this chapter, transaction costs are defined as the costs when people cooperate to produce or to trade. Section 12.1 shows the transaction costs if the firm has low debt. The transaction costs with high debt are presented in Sect. 12.2. Section 12.3 discuss the trade-off theory and the pecking order theory for firm's capital structure.

12.1 Transaction Costs with Low Debt

In this section, we will discuss the transaction costs under low debt.

Taxes

From the Robin Hood story of Chap. 2 we know that every resource provider has contributed something and hence, is entitled to have a portion of the pie generated in each robbery. In this example, no government is involved, and there is be no tax. In the modern world, however, government is everywhere, and companies and individuals need to pay taxes. A shown in the income statement in Chap. 4 (e.g., Table 4.2), deduct: cost of sale, sales, general and administration expenses, depreciation, and interest expense from total sales we obtain pretax income (i.e., taxable income). If the firm has lower debt, interest expense will be lower, taxes, higher, and the cash flow distributed to capital providers (e.g., debtholder and equityholder) smaller.

Suppose that the levered firm has riskless debt: B, equity: S_L, annual cash inflow: $\tilde{X}$, and expected annual cash inflow: $E\left[\tilde{X}\right]$. Corporate income tax rate is: τ_C, risk-free interest rate on debt: r_B, and expected rate of return on equity: $E\left[\tilde{r}_S\right]$. The expected annual cash flow: $E\left[\tilde{X}\right]$ is divided into three parts: government obtains corporate income taxes: $\tau_C\left(E\left[\tilde{X}\right] - r_B \cdot B\right)$, the debtholders obtain: $r_B \cdot$

K.-P. Chang, *Corporate Finance: A Systematic Approach*, Springer Texts in Business and Economics, https://doi.org/10.1007/978-981-19-9119-6_12

B, and the equityholders obtain: $(1-\tau_C)\cdot\left(E\left[\tilde{X}\right]-r_B\cdot B\right)$. The sum of the payments to debtholders and equityholders can be written as:

$$(1-\tau_C)\cdot E\left[\tilde{X}\right]+r_B\cdot B\cdot\tau_C\equiv E\left[\tilde{r}_S\right]\cdot S_L+r_B\cdot B \tag{12.1}$$

where $(1-\tau_C)\cdot E\left[\tilde{X}\right]$ can be interpreted as the after-tax annual cashflow paid to the equityholders of the unlevered firm. The certain profit: $(r_B\cdot B\cdot\tau_C)$ is the benefit of debt financing. Define the weighted average cost of capital (WACC) as: $E\left[\tilde{r}_{WACC}\right]$. With corporate income tax rate τ_C, the market value of the unlevered firm is calculated as: $V_U\equiv(1-\tau_C)\cdot E\left[\tilde{X}\right]/E\left[\tilde{r}_{WACC}\right]$, and the market value of the benefit of debt financing is calculated as: $B\cdot\tau_C=(r_B\cdot B\cdot\tau_C)/r_B$. Hence, with corporate income tax rate τ_C, the market value of the levered firm is:

$$V_L=V_U+B\cdot\tau_C \tag{12.2}$$

Equation (12.2) shows that for a given investment (or production plan) which generates annual cash inflow $\tilde{X}$, higher debt implies higher market value of the firm. With $E\left[\tilde{r}_{WACC}\right]\cdot V_U\equiv(1-\tau_C)\cdot E\left[\tilde{X}\right]$ and $V_L\equiv S_L+B$, Eq. (12.1) can be rewritten as:

$$\begin{aligned}(1-\tau_C)\cdot E\left[\tilde{X}\right]+r_B\cdot B\cdot\tau_C&=E\left[\tilde{r}_{WACC}\right]\cdot V_U+r_B\cdot B\cdot\tau_C\\&\equiv E\left[\tilde{r}_S\right]\cdot S_L+r_B\cdot B\end{aligned} \tag{12.1}$$

From Eq. (12.2), we have: $V_L\equiv S_L+B=V_U+B\cdot\tau_C$. Substitute $V_U=S_L+B-B\cdot\tau_C$ into Eq. (12.1'), we obtain:

$$E\left[\tilde{r}_{WACC}\right]\cdot(S_L+B-B\cdot\tau_C)+r_B\cdot B\cdot\tau_C=E\left[\tilde{r}_S\right]\cdot S_L+r_B\cdot B$$

or

$$E\left[\tilde{r}_S\right]=E\left[\tilde{r}_{WACC}\right]+(B/S_L)(1-\tau_C)\left(E\left[\tilde{r}_{WACC}\right]-r_B\right) \tag{12.3}$$

Comparing Eq. (12.3) with Eq. (8.3) in Chap. 8, we know that with corporate income taxes, the expected rate of return on equity of a levered firm will be less than that of an unlevered firm.

In practice, there may be both corporate income taxes and individual income taxes.[1] Suppose that there are corporate income tax rate: τ_C, individual income tax rate for equityholders: τ_S, and individual income tax rate for debtholders: τ_B. Thus, the after-tax annual expected cashflow paid to equityholders is: $(1-\tau_C)\cdot$

[1] Miller and Merton (1977) Debt and taxes. *Journal of Finance* 32: 261–275.

$\left(E\left[\tilde{X}\right] - r_B \cdot B\right) \cdot (1 - \tau_S)$, and the after-tax annual cashflow paid to debtholders is: $(1 - \tau_B) \cdot r_B \cdot B$. The sum of the two payments for the two capital providers is:

$$E\left[\tilde{X}\right] \cdot (1 - \tau_C) \cdot (1 - \tau_S) + r_B \cdot B \cdot (1 - \tau_B) \cdot \left[1 - \frac{(1 - \tau_C)(1 - \tau_S)}{1 - \tau_B}\right] \quad (12.4)$$

where $E\left[\tilde{X}\right] \cdot (1 - \tau_C) \cdot (1 - \tau_S)$ is the annual after-tax expected cashflow paid to the equityholders of the unlevered firm. Thus, the market value of the unlevered firm is calculated as:

$$V_U = E\left[\tilde{X}\right] \cdot (1 - \tau_C) \cdot (1 - \tau_S)/E\left[\tilde{r}_S\right] \quad (12.5)$$

Since the after-tax interest rate of the risk-free debt is: $r_B(1 - \tau_B)$, we can use $r_B(1 - \tau_B)$ as the discount rate to discount the annual cash flow: $r_B \cdot B \cdot (1 - \tau_B) \cdot \left[1 - \frac{(1-\tau_C)(1-\tau_S)}{1-\tau_B}\right]$, i.e.,

$$r_B \cdot B \cdot (1 - \tau_B) \cdot \left[1 - \frac{(1 - \tau_C)(1 - \tau_S)}{1 - \tau_B}\right] / (r_B(1 - \tau_B)) = B \cdot \left[1 - \frac{(1 - \tau_C)(1 - \tau_S)}{1 - \tau_B}\right] \quad (12.6)$$

From Eq.'s (12.4)–(12.6), the market value of the levered firm under both corporate and individual income taxes is calculated as:

$$V_L = V_U + B \cdot \left[1 - \frac{(1 - \tau_C)(1 - \tau_S)}{1 - \tau_B}\right] \quad (12.7)$$

In Eq. (12.7), if $(1 - \tau_C) \cdot (1 - \tau_S) = 1 - \tau_B$, then $V_L = V_U$, i.e., the Modigliani–Miller first proposition (i.e., the capital structure irrelevancy) holds. If $\tau_S = \tau_B$, then $V_L = V_U + B \cdot \tau_C$, i.e., only corporate income tax matters.

Shirking and Perquisites or On-the-Job Consumption

Low debt means low pressure for the management team of the firm to pay in cash. This can create two transaction costs: (a) shirking behavior which is not easy to observe by outsiders; and (2) on-the-job-consumption: e.g., luxury office, expensive cars, etc. If the managerial stock ownership is very low, these two transaction costs could be very high (since every dollar lost has little impact on the management team), and the firm will have lower market value.

The above two transaction costs may not consider the competition in labor market for managers and free choice of resource providers. Suppose the market value of the firm decreases because of managers' shirking and on the job consumption, resource providers (e.g., labors, stockholders and debtholders) could leave the firm and move to some other places. Managers are also face competition in the labor market. The total benefit a manager receives from the firm is equal to the summation of the benefit of shirking and of on-the-job-consumption and of salary and bonus. This total benefit could still be a constant if shirking and on-the-job-consumption exist. Demsetz and Lehn's (1985) empirical study finds that in the

511 US companies, no significant relationship between annual accounting rates of return and managerial stock ownership.[2] Morcket al. (1988) find that when managerial stock ownership increases, Tobin's Q (which is the ratio of market value of assets to replacement cost of capital) will first increase and then decrease. They argue that this inverted U shape phenomenon may come from: (1) when managerial stock ownership increases, it will align the interest of outside stockholders with that of inside management team, i.e., less shirking; (2) when managerial stock ownership increases more, it will become more difficult to replace the incompetent management team by take-over (i.e., entrenchment effect).[3]

Bureaucracy

In governments, bureaucrats may try to expand the budget for their own benefit. Unlike governments, all resource providers in a company have free choice to stay or move to another company. Managers in a large firm will have higher salary and higher social status than those in a small firm. Thus, managers in a low debt firm may have incentive to expand the size of the firm. The free cash flow hypothesis claims that managers act as agents to use free cash flow to invest in projects with negative net present value (NPV), which can increase the firm size but decrease the firm's market value. Hence, managers may be reluctant to debt financing or pay out dividends, as these moves reduce free cash flow in their hands.

Some argue that when a firm has more free cash flows than it needs to invest, there will be more shirking and overinvestments. Solutions for these problems are: let the firm have more debt and/or less free cash flows.[4] However, suppose the management team works harder to produce more free cash flows and the firm will distribute these cash flows to stockholders as cash dividends. Then, why will the management team work harder? This is similar to the case of a regulated public utility firm: If the firm produces more efficiently to earn more excess profits, then the regulatory agency will lower the regulated prices. The result is lower efficiency and lower work moral in regulated firms.

In some cases, overinvestments may be exaggerated. For example, in semiconductor industry, chip manufacturing companies may build new plants to increase their capacity even in economic recession. This is because market share is an important factor for competition if the economy starts to recover. This kind of overinvestment hence can be regarded as the company's buying a real option.

---

[2] Demsetz and Lehn (1985) The structure of corporate ownership: causes and consequences. *Journal of Political Economy* 93: 155–1177.

[3] Morck, Randall, Andrei Shleifer and Robert Vishny (1988) Management ownership and market valuation: an empirical analysis. *Journal of Financial Economics* 20: 293–315.

[4] Jensen (1986) Agency costs of free cash flow, corporate finance, and takeovers. *American Economic Review* 76: 323-339.

12.2 Transaction Costs with High Debt

Higher debt may lead to financial distress even bankruptcy, underinvestment or overinvestment.

Financial Distress or Bankruptcy

The Robin Hood story in Chap. 2 has no transaction costs in cooperation and no bankruptcy costs, i.e., after each robbery, gangsters liquidate and split the spoils according to ex ante contract. In modern economy, however, there will be transaction costs if the firm liquidates or goes bankrupt. Bankruptcy costs (or financial distress costs) can be direct or indirect. Direct financial distress costs are the costs paid to lawyers and accountants if the firm liquidates. Higher debt means higher probability of bankruptcy and hence, the firm has higher chance to pay these direct costs which can reduce the market value of the firm. Indirect financial distress costs are the transaction costs when the firm is in financial distress, valuable employees may leave the company, suppliers may want cash payments (hence, higher accounts payable turnover ratio), customers may not buy the products (especially, durable goods). These indirect costs can increase the firm's operation costs and costs of new investment projects. Also, if a big company goes bankrupt, lots of people may be unemployed which governments and politicians want to avoid (too big to fail?).

In some civil law countries, when a company cannot pay its debt, it will go bankrupt and liquidate directly. But in some common law countries, when a firm is in financial distress, the management team may seek for order of reorganization from courts. During the reorganization process, if the court agrees, the incumbent management team can still keep their jobs, and more importantly, the stockholders in fact are using the debtholders' money to invest and operate. That is, if the firm finally goes bankrupt, the debtholders lose more; and if the firm succeeds, the stockholders gain. Senior claimants (debtholders) want liquidation and junior claimants (stockholders) want reorganization. The legal proceeding may take a long period of time and the company (in fact, the debtholders) will pay more to lawyers. Thus, senior claimants (debtholders) may agree with junior claimants' (stockholders') demand for reorganization. Interestingly, judges of courts may not have the expertise of management but can judge whether a company can be saved by reorganizing.[5] Furthermore, when liquidating, the courts may distribute the firm's wealth to employees or outsiders. Because of these costs, debtholders in the beginning will ask for higher interest rates on the debt.

Underinvestment

The underinvestment problem is an agency problem between stockholders and debtholders: a levered company may forego valuable investment opportunities

[5] Weiss and Wruck (1998). Information problems, conflicts of interest, and the asset stripping: Chapter 11's failure in the case of Eastern Airlines. *Journal of Financial Economics* 48: 55-97.

because debtholders will obtain a portion of the benefits of the project and leave insufficient returns to the stockholders. For example, suppose that the market value of the firm's is only $100 and after two months the firm need to pay $200 to its debtholders. There is a positive NPV project: invest $150 to earn $210 immediately, i.e., the NPV is $60. But in this case, the stockholders will not invest additional $50 to this project even if this is a positive NPV project. The reason is very simple: after the stockholders invest additional $50, in the end they can only get back $10 (= 210 – 200).[6] It is possible, though, that the stockholders and debtholders can reach an agreement on how to split $210 if the transaction cost of their negotiation is small.

High debt can also lead to the so-called debt overhang, which is related to firm's debt capacity: When a firm gradually increases the level of its debt, at some point, the firm can no longer borrow more from creditors. It is possible that the firm's debt is so large that all earnings generated go directly to paying off existing debt instead of going into new investments or projects. This leads to firm's underinvestment and declining in growth opportunities.

Overinvestment

Suppose that in the above example, the NPV project needs $100 to invest and the firm's market value is also $100. The project has a 0.2 chance to produce $300 and a 0.8 chance to produce $0. The equityholders of the firm will be happy to invest in this project because they are actually using the debtholders' wealth to invest. If the project succeeds, the equityholders obtain $100 and the debtholders obtain $200. If the project fails, both the equityholders and the debtholders obtain nothing. This example shows that managers may not act in the best interests of the debtholders and invest potentially in negative net present value projects.

12.3 Pecking Order Theory and Trade-Off Theory

Practitioners have long noticed pecking order in corporate's financing policy. Companies usually will first use internal fund to finance a new project, and then debt, and equity will be the last resort. The reason why first using internal fund is that using internal fund incurs almost zero transaction costs, and there will be no issuance costs, and the existing equityholders will receive all benefits of the project. Borrowing more debt may signal the company's management team is confident that the company will have more and enough cash flows in the future. However, if the firm chooses to issue new shares to finance, in addition to the issuance costs, outsiders will infer the project must be a negative present value project, and the firm plans to use new stockholders' wealth to subsidize old stockholders.

[6] Myers (1977). Determinants of corporate borrowing. *Journal of Financial Economics* 5: 147-175.

Myers and Majluf (1984) argue that managers know better about true condition of the firm than outside investors.[7] This asymmetric information problem can lead to pecking order of firm's financing. When the firm issues new equity to finance, investors will interpret this signal as: managers believe that their firm is overvalued. Therefore, issuing new equity will decrease the stock price of the firm. However, in growth firms, issuing new equity may represent: (1) the firm is making a long-term plan to finance its profitable projects; and/or (2) the firm is selling new equity to strategical partners, e.g., suppliers, and invites them to the board of directors.

Companies usually are financed by debt and equity. The trade-off theory of capital structure emphasizes the benefits and costs of debt- and equity-financing. As discussed in the previous section, taxes, financial distress, and transaction costs incurred due to agency (asymmetric information) problems can all affect a firm's capital structure. Cost and benefit analysis of debt financing may lead to the so-called target debt ratio or optimal capital structure. This is questionable. For example, a firm which has a lot of cash on hand and does not need debt financing may still borrow money from banks. This may be because the firm wants to build a good connection/relationship with the banks in case that in the future the firm may need outside funding. Miller (1984) argues that because taxes are sure and large, and bankruptcy is rare, if the trade-off theory were true, then firms ought to have much higher debt levels than we observe in reality.[8] But financial distress costs of firms (including salary and future career) could be very high for managers. When these costs affect the living standard of managers, the management team will be reluctant to accept high debt.

Graham and Harvey's (2001) survey of the US firms finds that the management team will first consider financial flexibility, and then credit rating.[9] About 44% of the firms have target debt ratio; corporate income tax but not individual income tax will be considered when using debt financing; issuing new equity when share price increases; using internal fund to finance is the first choice; free cash flow hypothesis and over- and under-investment because of high debt do not hold; debt-equity ratios of the firms in the same industry are not different (i.e., may be a herding behavior); firms will not use debt as a signal and do not change the debt-equity ratio according to customers, employees, or suppliers' responses. Among the firms in different countries, Germany's and UK's have lower debt; Japan's has higher external funding; and the US' use more internal fund to finance.

Summary and Conclusions

- When there are transaction costs, low debt means less financial distress costs but higher corporate income taxes.

[7] Myers (1984) Corporate financing and investment decisions when firms have information that investors do not have. *Journal of Financial Economics* 13: 187–221.

[8] Miller (1977) Debt and taxes. *Journal of Finance* 32: 261–275.

[9] Graham and Harvey (2001) The theory and practice of corporate finance: evidence from the field. *Journal of Financial Economics* 60: 187-243.

- Because of competition in managerial labor market, managers' shirking behavior and on-the-job consumption may not be as serious as bureaucrats in governments.
- In practice, pecking order is popular in corporate's financing policy. Firms will first use internal fund to finance, and then debt, and equity will be the last resort. This may be due to the transaction costs of issuing new equity.

Problems

1. Explain why firms in the same industry usually have similar capital structure.
2. In both government and business, they usually intend to expand their sizes. Why?
3. What are the assumptions of the pecking order theory and the trade-off theory?
4. List the possible conflicts between shareholders and managers. Some shareholders complain that the high-ranking officials get too much compensations. Is this complaint reasonable?
5. Explain why a firm has a lot of cash in hand but still issues corporate bonds to borrow from the markets.

References

Demsetz, H., & Lehn, K. (1985). The structure of corporate ownership: Causes and consequences. *Journal of Political Economy, 93*, 155–1177.

Graham, J. R., & Harvey, C. R. (2001). The theory and practice of corporate finance: Evidence from the field. *Journal of Financial Economics, 60*, 187–243.

Jensen, M. C. (1986). Agency costs of Free cash flow (FCF), corporate finance, and takeovers. *American Economic Review, 76*, 323–339.

Miller, M. X. E., & Merton, R. (1977). Debt and taxes. *Journal of Finance, 32*, 261–275.

Morck, R., Shleifer, A., & Vishny, R. W. (1988). Management ownership and market valuation: An empirical analysis. *Journal of Financial Economics, 20*, 293–315.

Myers, S. C. (1977). Determinants of corporate borrowing. *Journal of Financial Economics, 5*, 147–175.

Myers, S. C., & Majluf, N. S. (1984). Corporate financing and investment decisions when firms have information that investors do not have. *Journal of Financial Economics, 13*, 187–221.

Weiss, L. A., & Wruck, K. H. (1998). Information problems, conflicts of interest, and the asset stripping: Chapter 11's failure in the case of Eastern Airlines. *Journal of Financial Economics* 48: 55–97

Payout Policy 13

Investment is for consumption. After resource providers finance (provide) resources to a firm and producing and selling, the firm needs to split and distribute the big pie generated to all the resource providers. Payout policies are usually proposed by the management team to the board of directors and then to the annual shareholders meeting. In the case of cash dividends, after the announcement of cash dividends (the declaration date), there will be ex-dividend date (buyers of stock on or after this date will not receive dividends), record date (shareholders recorded by the company by this date will receive dividends), and payable date (the date shareholders receive cash dividends). In this chapter, Sect. 13.1 shows that in a complete and perfect market, payout policies do not affect the market value of the firm. Cash dividends or share repurchases can benefit equityholders at expense of debtholders. Section 13.2 discusses how market imperfections, e.g., taxes, asymmetric information and signaling costs, influence firms' decisions on payout policy.

13.1 Payout Policy with Zero Transaction Costs: Financial Diversification Irrelevancy

When a firm earns free cash flows, the question is whether different ways to pay resource providers will affect the market value of the firm and each resource provider's wealth. A simple answer is: With no transaction costs, i.e., with a perfect capital market, different ways (but according to the ex-ante contract) to pay resource providers is irrelevant to both the market value of the firm and each resource provider's wealth. For example, in the Robin Hood story of Chap. 2, after each "operation" (robbery), the big pie generated is split and paid to: the cook (debtholder), and Robin Hood, the archer and the lookout (equityholders) according to their ex-ante contract (i.e., the cook: \$2,000; Robin Hood: 20%; the archer:50%; and the lookout: 30%). Whether the payments paid to the resource

K.-P. Chang, *Corporate Finance: A Systematic Approach*, Springer Texts in Business and Economics, https://doi.org/10.1007/978-981-19-9119-6_13

providers are in gold and/or in silver is irrelevant because with no transaction costs, a resource provider can always without losing any value exchange gold for silver, or vice versa. In this example, the payout policy is irrelevant to both the market value of the firm and all resource providers (i.e., an example of financial diversification irrelevancy).

Suppose that in the above example, the three "equityholders" (Robin Hood, the archer and the lookout) want some cash dividends before liquidating the gang (the firm) according to their ex-ante contract. Then the total market value of the firm will still be the same, but the 'paying cash dividends first' policy which changes the ex-ante contract will benefit the three equityholders at expense of the debtholder (i.e., the cook). The reason is as follows. As shown in Eq. (9.2) in Chap. 9, at $t = 0$, every uncertain asset (firm) has a corresponding put-call parity:

$$c + \frac{K}{1+r} = S_0 + p, \tag{13.1}$$

or

$$S_0 = c + \left(\frac{K}{1+r} - p\right) \tag{13.2}$$

where S_0 is the market value of the firm, c is the market value of the equity, $\left(\frac{K}{1+r} - p\right)$ is the market value of the risky debt, p is the insurance (put option) that insures the debtholder can obtain K at $t = T$, and r is the simple risk-free interest rate for the period between $t = 0$ and $t = T$. The put-call parity, i.e., Eq. (13.2), shows the ex-ante contract of the distribution of the firm's wealth for the equityholders and debtholders.

Suppose that at $t = 0$, the firm decides and announces to pay cash dividends: c_d at $t = T$, where the payment of cash dividends c_d contains no information. Then the firm's market value S_0 will still remain the same and Eq. (13.2) becomes[1]:

$$S_0 = \left(c' + \frac{c_d}{1+r}\right) + \left(\frac{K}{1+r} - p'\right) \tag{13.3}$$

where c' is the market value of the equity, $\frac{c_d}{1+r}$ is the market value of the cash dividends, and $\left(\frac{K}{1+r} - p'\right)$ is the market value of the risky debt. Note that this new put-call parity (i.e., Eq. (13.3)) is the distribution of the firm's wealth for the

[1] Equation (13.3) can be derived as follows. Consider two portfolios at $t = 0$:

Portfolio A: one European call option c'. with strike price $(K + c_d)$, and cash $\frac{K+c_d}{1+r}$ deposited in a bank;

Portfolio B: one European put option p' with strike price $(K + c_d)$, and one unit of the underlying asset S_0.

On the expiration date $t = T$, both portfolios give exactly the same payoff: $Max[S_T, K + c_d]$. Thus, the costs of the two portfolios at $t = 0$ must be the same, i.e., $c' + \frac{K+c_d}{1+r} = S_0 + p'$.

equityholders and debtholders **after** the announcement of cash dividends changes the ex-ante contract.

Deduct Eq. (13.3) from Eq. (13.2), we have:

$$c - c' = \frac{c_d}{1 + r} - (p' - p) > 0 \tag{13.4}$$

where $p' - p > 0$. The reasons why $c - c' > 0$ and $p' - p > 0$ can be found from Table 13.1:

(i) For debt: at $t = T$, the value of $Min[K, S_T]$ is greater than that of $Min[K, S_T - c_d]$, which implies paying cash dividends will decrease the market value of debt at $t = 0$, i.e., $\frac{K}{1+r} - p > \frac{K}{1+r} - p'$ or $p' - p > 0$. Also, because at $t = T$, the market value of $Max[0, K - (S_T - c_d)]$ is greater than that of $Max[0, K - S_T]$, we have: $p' > p$ at $t = 0$, i.e., paying cash dividends will increase the risk level of debt.

(ii) For equity: at $t = T$, the value of $Max[0, S_T - K]$ is greater than that of $Max[0, S_T - K - c_d]$, which implies: $c - c' > 0$ at $t = 0$. Also, the value of $[Max[0, S_T - K - c_d] + c_d]$ is greater than that of $Max[0, S_T - K]$, which implies that paying cash dividends will increase the market value of equity at $t = 0$, i.e., $c' + \frac{c_d}{1+r} > c$, or $\frac{c_d}{1+r} > c - c'$. Therefore, we have: $\frac{c_d}{1+r} > c - c' > 0$. Note that in Eq. (13.2), if $r = 0$, the put-call parity still holds, i.e., $S_0 = c + K - p$. Thus, Eq. (13.4) becomes:

$$c - c' = c_d - (p' - p) > 0 \tag{13.5}$$

where $p' - p > 0$, and $c_d > c - c' > 0$ implies that even with a zero risk-free interest rate, the stock price falls less than the amount of the dividend. This result rejects the claim that "in a perfect capital market, when a cash dividend is paid, the share price drops by the amount of the dividend when the stock begins to trade ex-dividend." These two inequalities: $c_d > c - c' > 0$ (for equity) and $K - p > K - p'$ (for debt) indicate that cash dividends can change the ex-ante contract to benefit

Table. 13.1 The market values of equity and debt with and without cash dividends

	$t = 0$		$t = T$	
	Original	With cash dividends	Original	With cash dividends
Equity	c	$c' + \frac{c_d}{1+r}$	$Max[0, S_T - K]$	$Max[0, S_T - K - c_d] + c_d$
Debt	$\frac{K}{1+r} - p$	$\frac{K}{1+r} - p'$	$Min[K, S_T]$	$Min[K, S_T - c_d]$
The firm	S_0	S_0	S_T	S_T
Put option/insurance	p	p'	$Max[0, K - S_T]$	$Max[0, K - (S_T - c_d)]$

equityholders at expense of debtholder. This might explain why in practice, firms issue dividends despite their tax disadvantage, i.e., the so-called dividend puzzle.[2] Also, because cash dividends can hurt debtholders' wealth, debtholders may ask for higher interest rate to compensate their loss. Firms' constant cash dividends policy (i.e., dividend smoothing) may help alleviate this problem.[3]

Suppose that the market value of the firm is $S_0 = \$100$, the market value of the equity $c = \$62$, and the market value of the debt $\frac{K}{1+r} - p = \$38$ where $r = 0$.

(i) Paying cash dividends $c_d = \$2$. Then from Eq. (13.5), $\$2 - (p' - p) = \$62 - c' > 0,$

where $c = \$62$. Because $c_d = \$2 > 0$ results in $p' - p > 0$, we have: $\$60 < c' < \$62$. The share of equity of the firm's value changes from $c/\$100$ to $c'/(\$100 - \$2)$.

(ii) Use share repurchase to pay the equityholders \$2. This result is the same as paying cash dividends $c_d = \$2$. After paying \$2, the share of equity of the firm's value changes from $c/\$100$ to $c'/(\$100 - \$2)$.

(iii) Homemade dividends \$2. The equityholders can sell (2/62) of their equity (\$62) to a new investor to obtain \$2. This will not change the market value of the firm (\$100) and the share of equity of the firm's value (62/100).

(iv) Issuing new equity to pay \$2 to the existing equityholders. This will not change the market value of the firm (\$100) and the market value of the equity (\$62). The existing equityholder's share of equity will drop to 60/62. The new shareholder's share of equity will be 2/62.

(v) Suppose that the firm (a) is totally equity-financed or (b) has riskless debt and cash dividends or share repurchase do not make the debt risky, i.e., p does not exist. Then cash dividends or share repurchase will not affect the market value of the firm and the equityholders' wealth.

Proposition 13.1 (Payout Policy Irrelevancy)

In a complete market with no transaction costs (i.e., perfect market), the market value of the firm is independent of the firm's payout policy.

(i) Cash dividends or share purchase can increase equityholders' wealth at expense of debtholders.

(ii) If the firm (a) is totally equity-financed or (b) has riskless debt and cash dividends do not make the debt risky, then cash dividends or share purchase will not affect the equityholders' wealth.

---

[2] Black, Fischer (1976) The dividend puzzle. *Journal of Portfolio Management* 2: 5–8.

[3] Lintner, John (1956) Distribution of incomes of corporations among dividends, retained earnings and taxes. *American Economic Review* 46: 97–113. Miller, Merton and Franco Modigliani (1961) Dividend policy, growth, and the valuation of shares. *Journal of Business* 34: 411–433.

(iii) Homemade dividends by selling part of equity to outside investors do not affect the market value of equity.
(iv) Issuing new equity to pay cash dividends to the existing equityholders does not affect the market value of equity.

13.2 Payout Policy with Transaction Costs

In an imperfect market, i.e., with transaction costs, different payout policies can affect both the market value of the firm and the distributions between equityholders and debtholders.

Taxes
Equityholders need to pay taxes on the dividends they receive. They need to pay capital gains taxes when they sell their shares. This means capital gains have tax deferral benefits. Higher income people may prefer stocks with low cash dividends and high capital gains. Lower income people may prefer stocks with high cash dividends and low capital gains. This is called the clientele effect.

Payback Period Strategy
The old saying: *"A bird in the hand is worth two in the bush"* can be changed into: *"A bird in the hand is the same as a bird in the cage as long as you own and have the cage in your hand"*. The bird in the hand theory is a dividend relevance theory, which states that investors prefer dividends to capital gains from their stock investment because investors prefer current certain returns (dividends) to uncertain future gains (capital appreciation). This theory also argues that with lower dividends, firms will have more retained earnings (internal fund) which can lead to higher growth and higher stock prices.

The preference for dividends over capital gains may imply that investors are using the payback period method to invest in an environment with high inflation and/or political risk. For example, in highly unprotected environments, dividends can be used as a replacement of legal protection to enhance the firm's reputation of good treatment to investors.[4] However, this also means that for low dividend firms in low protection environments, minority investors, because the firms may tunnel money to major shareholders and/or firms' high-level insiders, will offer low prices to buy the stocks. Thus, if there is no difference between dividend tax rate and capital gain tax rate, high or low dividends should make no difference.

[4] La Porta, Rafael, Florencio Lopez-de-Silanes, Andrei Shleifer and Robert Vishny (2000) Agency problems and dividend policies around the world. *Journal of Finance*, 55: 1–33.

Signaling Theory

The signaling theory regarding payout policies was developed by Lintner (1956). Lintner finds the so-called sticky dividends phenomenon, i.e., companies' share prices usually adjust in response to changes in dividend payments, and hence, they tend to smooth dividends over time, not making considerable increases in dividend levels that cannot be maintained in the near future. An increase in dividends can signal that managers expect good future prospects (Miller & Rock, 1985).[5] However, with high signaling costs, there may be a separating equilibrium, i.e., high-quality companies can use high dividend payments to signal their good qualities, but low-quality firms cannot imitate because they cannot keep sustainable levels of dividend payments, and cuts on payouts could cause a decline in the shares price.

Comparing with constant dividend payouts, share repurchases are more volatile and may have substantial changes related to corporate earnings and business cycles. After firms announce an open market share repurchase, the actual amount spend may take several years and usually is much less than the planned amount. This indicates that share repurchases give firms more financial flexibility. If the management team doesn't like a major shareholder (e.g., she threatens to take over the firm), the firm may use the so-called greenmail to buy out the shareholder, i.e., pay a price higher than the current stock price. Also, a firm's announcement of share repurchase may signal that its corporate insiders believe the stocks are undervalued and want to boost share price. Regulatory agency may regard it as a manipulation of stock price.

Cash dividends can reduce free cash flows and help reduce the agency costs when there is an information asymmetry between managers and outside investors. Stock dividend and stock split may signal the management team's confidence in the firm's future cash inflows. That is, managers believe the firm can still pay the same cash dividends per share even with more shares of the stock. More profitable firms can accumulate more internal fund for future investment opportunities, and hence, is less levered. Young firms will retain earnings to finance good investment opportunities. Mature firms which have higher profits and few attractive investment opportunities will distribute free cash flow to shareholders to reduce agency costs.[6]

Summary and Conclusions

- In a complete market with no transaction costs (i.e., a perfect market), the market value of the firm is independent of the firm's payout policy.
- Cash dividends or share purchase can increase equityholders' wealth at expense of debtholders.

---

[5] Miller, Merton and Kevin Rock (1985) Dividend policy under asymmetric information. *Journal of Finance* 40: 1031–1051.

[6] Fama, Eugene and Kenneth French (2002) Testing tradeoff and pecking order predictions about dividends and debt. *Review of Financial Studies* 15: 1–33.

- If the firm (a) is totally equity-financed or (b) has riskless debt and cash dividends do not make the debt risky, then cash dividends or share purchase will not affect the equityholders' wealth.
- Homemade dividends by selling part of equity to outside investors do not affect the market value of equity.
- Issuing new equity to pay cash dividends to the existing equityholders does not affect the market value of equity.
- If the tax rate on dividends is higher than the tax rate on capital gains, high (low) income investors may choose low (high) dividend stocks. This is the clientele effect.
- Increase cash dividends may signal the firm will have higher profits in the future. Firms usually give constant cash dividends. Because of financial flexibility, managers may prefer share repurchases than cash dividends.

Problems

1. Comment on the following statement.
   When a firm announces cash dividends, it is equivalent to the case that the firm changes part of its equity into a senior debt, and the original debt becomes junior. Thus, cash dividends can benefit equityholders at the expense of debtholders.
2. Some people argue that cash dividend can reduce free cash flow so that it will not only lessen the management team's shirking problem but also may reduce the chance to invest in positive NPV projects. Are these arguments correct?
3. What are the assumptions of the bird-in-the-hand hypothesis?
4. When a firm announces share repurchases, does it mean that the firm's stock price is over- or undervalued?
5. Explain why firms usually provide constant cash dividends.

References

Black, F. (1976). The dividend puzzle. *Journal of Portfolio Management, 2*, 5–8.

Lintner, J. (1956) Distribution of incomes of corporations among dividends, retained earnings and taxes. *American Economic Review, 46*, 97–113; Miller, M., & Modigliani, F. (1961) Dividend policy, growth, and the valuation of shares. *Journal of Business, 34*, 411–433.

Miller, M., & Rock, K. (1985) Dividend policy under asymmetric information. *Journal of Finance, 40*, 1031–1051.

14 Mergers and Acquisitions, and Corporate Governance

Mergers and acquisitions are competitions for firms' controlling right and interest. Different takeover strategies and defensive tactics can affect the interests of the target firm's senior management and shareholders. They are basically about the conflicts between shareholders and the management team. There is a wide variation of regulations and practices in corporate governance structures in the world because differences in civil law or common law; paternalism or less paternalism tradition; bank-based or market-based financial system, etc. Section 14.1 of this chapter discusses ways to merge and take-over. Section 14.2 explains various defensive tactics for takeovers. Section 14.3 discusses the role of the board of directors. Section 14.4 introduces different corporate governance systems.

14.1 Ways to Merge and Take-Over

Merger

A takeover is defined as: an acquiring company assumes control of or acquire a target company. Takeovers can be done through mergers and acquisitions. A merger is the combination of two firms, which subsequently form a new legal entity under the banner of one corporate name. If two firms combine into an entirely new firm, it is a consolidation. Merger can be horizontal merger, vertical merger or conglomerate merger.

(i) Horizontal merger is the merger of two firms which produce similar or related products. This may help the new firm to achieve economies of scale, i.e., produce outputs with lower unit/average cost. It may also create monopoly power in the industry.
(ii) Vertical merger means that an acquiring firm acquires a target firm which supplies or sells products to the acquiring firm. Vertical integration can eliminate the hold-up problem between the supplier and the supplier's downstream

K.-P. Chang, *Corporate Finance: A Systematic Approach*, Springer Texts in Business and Economics, https://doi.org/10.1007/978-981-19-9119-6_14

firm. Hence, it may reduce operating costs of these two firms. But again, vertical merger or vertical integration may create monopoly power and regulatory agencies may forbid it. Vertically integrate a downstream firm could also mean the firm becomes a competitor to its customers.

(iii) Conglomerate merger happens when an acquiring firm acquires a target firm which is in a different industry. Conglomerate was popular in the US in the 1960s, and is still common in other parts of the world. It is argued that conglomerate can diversify risk for investors. But this reason is dubious since investors can diversify the risk by themselves (may be at a lower cost). Some conglomerates are family-owned, and each descendant controls and manages one firm. Conglomerate may have the benefit of economies of scope, i.e., different production lines/factories are managed by the same management team. Real option could be another reason for conglomerate, e.g., a semiconductor firm acquires an electric vehicle firm or a biotech firm to have the option (choice) to expand to other new profitable business.

Tender Offer

A tender offer is a public, open offer by an acquirer to buy shares of a target firm. The offer is made directly to all stockholders of the target firm where the directors of the firm may or may not endorse the tender offer proposal. Cash or securities may be offered to the target firm's shareholders. An acquirer who owns and controls more than 50% of the target firm's outstanding shares (i.e., has a controlling interest) can direct the course of a firm and make strategic and operational decisions.

Proxy Contest

Proxy votes are votes by one individual or institution as the authorized representative of another. A proxy contest is an unfriendly contest initiated by dissident shareholders who oppose the current corporate policy and attempt to persuade shareholders to use their proxy votes to install new management. Shareholders may appoint a person (i.e., the shareholder's proxy) to attend shareholder meetings and vote on their behalf. Once the new board of directors is formed and in control, management will be replaced. In some countries, proxy contests are illegal. In other countries, the contests are legal but expensive and difficult to win. However, the threat of a proxy contest may persuade management to change corporate policy. This is like the contest market theory which states that even in a monopoly or oligopoly, incumbents will act competitively when there is a lack of barriers, such as government regulation and high entry costs, doing everything they can to prevent new entrants from one day putting them out of business.

Going Private

Going private means the purchase of all outstanding shares of a public firm by private equity buyout or management buyout. After the buyout the firm's shares are withdrawn from being traded in the open market, i.e., shares are delisted in the stock exchange. A private equity buyout means a private equity firm purchases a controlling share in the target firm. Private equity buyout is usually financed with large amounts of debt, i.e., the leveraged buyout (LBO). The assets and cashflows of the acquired company are used to pay for those debts. A management buyout means a company is taken private by its own management team. The LBO is also used to finance the management buyout. Tax benefit is one reason of using the LBO. When a firm is owned and managed by the same persons, less agency costs and more efficient production can lead to more profits.

14.2 Defensive Tactics

In response to hostile takeover techniques, target firms usually devise various defensive tactics. Target firms' defensive tactics on the one hand can encourage competition among bidders and benefit the target firm's shareholders. On the other hand, the management team of a target firm may use the firm's wealth to defend, and it becomes more difficult to replace inefficient management.

Green Mail

Stock repurchase (also known as self-tender offer) is a purchase by the target of its own-issued shares from its shareholders. For a corporate raider (greenmailer) who has bought enough shares in a target firm, the firm may use a greenmail payment (i.e., repurchasing the corporate raider's shares at a substantial premium) to stop the hostile takeover. This practice though is a solution to disputes between shareholders may be seemed as an extortion, i.e., it hurts both minority shareholders and debtholders. Greenmail may also be accompanied by a standstill agreement, which is an undertaking by the acquirer not to acquire any more shares of the target firm within certain period of time.

Poison pill

A poison pill is a shareholder rights plan used to dissuade any outside takeover attempt by giving shareholders the right to buy more shares at a discount if one shareholder buys a certain percentage (say, 15%) or more of the company's shares. This plan can be issued by the board of directors as a choice (an option) attached to existing shares, and only be revoked at the discretion of the board. Using poison pill tactic can considerably dilute the acquirer's shareholding in the target and thus can deter a takeover. Examples of poison pill are: flip-in (i.e., a target firm gives its shareholders, except for the acquirer, to purchase additional shares at a discount); flip-out (i.e., a target firm enables its stockholders to purchase the acquirer's shares after the merger at a discounted rate).

Staggered board

Staggered board is a board in which only a certain number of directors, usually one third, is reelected annually. Although staggered boards are useful in preventing hostile takeovers, they are also considered to be disadvantageous to shareholders.

Golden parachutes

In a golden parachute, a firm provides additional compensations to its top management in the case of termination of its employment following a successful hostile acquisition. includes a large payout to a senior executive's contract to make the takeover more expensive for the acquiring company. It mainly protects senior management but harms the target firm's shareholders.

14.3 Role of the Board

The board of directors oversees important decisions which might impact stakeholders' interests. Usually, the board should be able to make decisions on hiring or firing senior executives, monitor business activities, and determine corporate strategy, compensation and risk management. When there is a lack of trust, corporate governance will not be an easy task.

(i) Because of high transaction costs, the board's monitoring to ensure compliance with laws and ethics relies heavily on accounting reports and suggestions from accountants and lawyers (especially, when the board directors do not have these specialties). A firm may buy the directors' and officers' liability insurance to cover the cost of compensation claims made against the company's directors and key managers (officers) for alleged wrongful acts.

(ii) Lack of domain knowledge about the industry and the firm's products makes it difficult for the board to devise company's strategies and long-term goals. Also, when the company's management team makes good and continuous profits, the board usually will not reject the team's more aggressive proposals such as merge and acquire another firm or develop a new product in a new field. These projects may end up losing money. Some directors may be the investors who make technological investment or financial investment in the firm. Technological investment (for a long-term goal) and financial investment (for a short-term goal) can create conflicts within the board.

(iii) In addition to the risk management of accounting fraud, corporate information security (CIS), and product liability, the board needs to monitor how the firm uses derivatives to hedge risks, e.g., hedge the exchange rate risk. Management may also use the firm's money to invest in derivatives to gamble when the firm is in trouble.

(iv) Even with outside (independent) directors, there is no guarantee that the board is able to be unbiased to stakeholders. Afterall, outside independent directors are invited by the CEO or the chairperson of the board (i.e., to some extent, they are "captured"). It is argued that strong, outside directors recommended by major shareholders might help alleviate these problems. However, in practice, these strong directors may sometimes be too risk-averse to accept new corporate policies and strategies. More regulations and bylaws can not only help corporate governance but also increase the firm's operating costs. Interestingly, we have regulations, rules and laws for corporate governance, but we do not have those for "family governance".

Compensation policy for top management is a big issue in corporate governance. Usually, a combination of salary and stock options, restricted stocks and cash bonus is used. The ratios of these payments require serious consideration. For example, when a new CEO is hired, to reduce the uncertainty for the CEO higher salary and lower bonus connected to performance may be first used because the CEO is not sure how long this cooperation can last. After a few years with good performance, the compensation package for the CEO may change to less annual salary but more discretionary bonuses related to company performance.[1] Bonuses related to performance can create other problems too. For example, push for higher earnings per share (EPS) can lead to delay important investment which can hurt the prospect of the company. Also, management's owning the company's stock can reduce managers' perquisite consumption. But it may also increase management's entrenchment effect, i.e., it will be harder to fire managers. Finally, it may be meaninglessly to argue that the pay to the top management is too high because after all, every resource provider has a free choice to join or not to join the company.

14.4 Corporate Governance in Practice

Wide variation of regulations and practices in corporate governance structures in the world may be due to: civil law or common law; paternalism or less paternalism tradition; bank-based or market-based financial system; etc. It is often argued that bank-based financial system may provide less protection for investors than market-based financial system. But one principle remains the same: As long as the interests and money are not in your own pocket, even you hire an agent to take care of them, these interests and money may disappear. That is, there won't be a perfect corporate governance structure which can always protect and help increase all resource providers' wealth.

Cross Shareholding

Interfirm cross-shareholding means one publicly-traded company holds a significant number of shares of another publicly-traded company. In Asia and some parts of Europe, because of strong emphasis on social relationships and networking in culture and weak restriction of cross shareholding in corporate law, cross shareholding among firms is quite popular. Some studies find that companies can create business alliance through cross shareholding, which may help

[1] Discretionary bonuses are often paid as an annual reward to employees following a successful year. Employees feel rewarded and valued by the company. Non-discretionary bonuses are paid on an agreed schedule, when employees hit a defined target. Employees feel extra motivation to reach the goals the board has set.

firms share resources, reduce operation costs, improve financial performance and corporate governance, enhancing information advantages, corporate cooperation, and financial capacity.[2] An extreme case could be the Japanese keiretsu system, in which the members' companies own small portions of the shares in each other's companies, and individual managers have considerable autonomy in their own companies but coordinate their activities through the president council and a common main bank. Keiretsu helps insulate each company from stock market fluctuations and takeover attempts, thus enabling long-term planning in projects. A disbenefit of keiretsu's very long-term relationship is lack of flexibility, i.e., firms (and their employees) cannot easily change partners to cooperate with.

Pyramidal Ownership Structure

Pyramids are family business groups, in which an individual or a family controls a firm, which in turn controls another firm, which could itself control another firm, etc. Pyramidal structure allows a family to achieve control of a firm using only a small cash flow stake. For example, a family which directly owns 51% of a firm which in turn owns 51% of a different firm gains control of the latter firm with an ultimate cash flow stake of only 26.01%. Significant separation of ownership and control in a pyramid structure can also benefit the controlling family to expropriate minority shareholders. Transfer pricing is a way to do it. For example, the top firm can sell its product at a much higher price to the bottom firm in the pyramid so that it moves the bottom firm's profits to the top firm where the controlling family has a higher cash flow right. Of course, in a weak investor protection environment, minority shareholders will expect expropriations and will pay less for the shares of firms that are low in the pyramid. That is, the controlling family in a pyramid sells the bottom firm's shares to minority shareholders at a lower price in exchange for expropriations later on.[3]

Summary and Conclusions

- Mergers and acquisitions represent changes of controlling interest (right) in firms. An efficient acquirer may take over an inefficient firm. Similarly, a firm may spin off inefficient divisions.
- As discussed in Chap. 2, the size of the firm is determined by Coase's five different transaction costs (i.e., the costs of discovering, informing, bargaining, contracting, and monitoring). If the monitoring cost is less than the sum of the other four costs, merger and acquisition will increase the market value of the firm. However, in

[2] China's state-owned firms may help expand environmental social governance (ESG) by cross-shareholding of non-state-owned firms.

[3] Another way for families to achieve control over firms even without majority shares is to issue dual class shares. Dual-class stock is often designated Class A and Class B, where Class B is generally the one with more potent voting status. Both classes are common stock.

merger and acquisition, top management and shareholders of the target firm may not have the same interest.

- Various takeovers strategies include: tender offer, proxy contest, and going private. Colourful defensive tactics for takeovers are: greenmail, poison pill, staggered board, and golden parachute.
- Wide variation of regulations and practices in corporate governance structures in the world may be due to: civil law or common law; paternalism or less paternalism tradition; bank-based or market-based financial system, etc.
- The role of the board of directors includes hiring or firing senior executives, monitor business activities, and determine corporate strategy, compensation and risk management. When lack of trust, the transaction costs of corporate governance can be very high.
- For controlling rights over firms, there are: cross shareholdings, pyramidal organizational structure, dual class shares. They all have their own benefits and costs when implementing.

Problems

1. After mergers and acquisitions, firms on average do not perform well. Explain why?
2. Mergers and acquisitions usually do not benefit the acquiring firm's equityholders. Why will mergers and acquisitions still exist?
3. What are the benefits and costs of a regulated monopoly and an unregulated monopoly?
4. Some researchers suggest more rules and regulations, more frequent revelations of firms' financial status, and independent directors. What are the benefits and costs of these suggestions?
5. The entrenchment effect, tunnelling, and perquisite consumptions may happen to both major shareholders and management. Are these transaction costs reasonable?

International Corporate Finance 15

Multinational corporations (MNC) are prevalent in the world. Financing and investment criteria in MNC are not much different from domestic firms. But there exists advantages and disadvantages of managing multinational companies. Section 15.1 of this chapter discusses benefits and costs (and risks) of multinational companies. Section 15.2 discusses the purchasing power parity and the interest rate parity which are related to the exchange rate risk and the interest rate risk.

15.1 Advantages and Disadvantages of Multinational Corporations

A multinational corporation (MNC) can be defined as a company that has business operations in at least one country other than its home country. As mentioned in Chap. 2, Schumpeterian entrepreneurs are those who can innovate to devise new product, new producing method and new organization structure, and find new markets and new resources. Schumpeter terms capitalists as the persons who do not innovate but only provide capitals and take risks, and entrepreneurs as the persons who innovate and do not take any risk. Innovations can bring in excess profits which lead to entrepreneurs' power and authority in an organization. A MNC can at a lower transaction cost access new markets and sales opportunities by coordinating different local resources (i.e., lower labor costs and more advanced technology), spread research and development costs and advertising expenditures over global sales, pool global purchasing power over suppliers, have higher reputation and bargaining power when dealing with domestic and foreign governments/politicians, and diversify operation risks in different countries. MNC can also help local economy by paying taxes, hiring more local people, and providing the same quality product at a lower price (e.g., some publishing companies charge lower prices for textbooks sold in developing countries).

K.-P. Chang, *Corporate Finance: A Systematic Approach*, Springer Texts in Business and Economics, https://doi.org/10.1007/978-981-19-9119-6_15

In addition to exchange rate risk and interest rate risk, the disadvantages of MNC are: (i) domestic jobs move overseas and unlike other resources, labors are not easy to move to foreign countries; (ii) MNC may become monopolies to increase prices for consumers, stifle competition and impede innovation; (iii) MNC may hurt the environment and deplete local and natural resources; and (iv) languages and cultural differences within MNC. More subtle issues such as languages and cultural differences may create problems and transaction costs in MNC. Domestic as well as foreign politicians may in the name of national security become more hostile to MNC. The political risks of censure, sanction, and even frozen foreign assets are more prevalent in recent years. After all, there is no world government that can enforce rules and laws.

15.2 Purchasing Power Parity and Interest Rate Parity

Exchange rate and interest rate are closely related. When one country's interest increases, foreign capital may come in to earn more interests. But when the foreign capitalist wants to take the money out and exchanges into her own country's currency, she earns more interests but may suffer loss on exchange. Governments have the power to influence their domestic interest rate and exchange rate but not so much power to affect domestic inflation rate. In general, higher inflation rate means too much money in the market and lower purchasing power.

Purchasing Power Parity

Suppose that there are two countries: domestic and foreign. At $t = 0$, the domestic price level is: $P_h(0)$, the foreign price level is: $P_f(0)$. Between $t = 0$ and $t = 1$, the domestic inflation rate is: $\pi_h(0) \equiv \frac{[P_h(1) - P_h(0)]}{P_h(0)}$, and the foreign inflation rate is $\pi_f(0) \equiv \frac{[P_f(1) - P_f(0)]}{P_f(0)}$. At $t = 0$, one unit of foreign currency can exchange for $s(0)$ units of domestic currency. Then,

$$P_h(0) = s(0) \cdot P_f(0),\ P_h(1) = s(1) \cdot P_f(1)$$

and,

$$\frac{P_h(1)}{P_h(0)} = \frac{s(1)}{s(0)} \cdot \frac{P_f(1)}{P_f(0)} \tag{15.1}$$

or,

$$\frac{1 + \pi_h(0)}{1 + \pi_f(0)} = \frac{s(1)}{s(0)} \tag{15.2}$$

Deduct 1 from both sides of Eq. (15.2),

$$\frac{\pi_h(0) - \pi_f(0)}{1 + \pi_f(0)} = \frac{s(1) - s(0)}{s(0)}. \tag{15.3}$$

If $\pi_f(t)$ is quite small, then

$$\pi_h(0) - \pi_f(0) \approx \frac{s(1) - s(0)}{s(0)}. \tag{15.4}$$

For example, in Eq. (15.4), suppose that at $t = 0$, the original exchange rate is: $s(0) = 1$, i.e., one unit of foreign currency can exchange for one unit of domestic currency. If between $t = 0$ and $t = 1$, the domestic inflation rate is: $\pi_h(0) = 10\%$ and the foreign inflation rate is: $\pi_f(0) = 4\%$, then at $t = 1$, one unit of foreign currency can exchange for $s(1) = 1.06$ units of domestic currency. That is, higher inflation rate in a country leads to its currency depreciation.

Interest Rate Parity

In the foreign exchange market, there are spot-exchange rate and forward-exchange rate. At $t = 0$, the spot exchange rate is the current market price for exchanging one currency for another, e.g., $s(0) = 1$ means that one unit of foreign currency can exchange for one units of domestic currency. Also, at $t = 0$, two parties can set up a forward-exchange rate, $F(0)$, which is an exchange rate at which a party agrees to exchange one currency for another at $t = 1$ when it enters into a forward contract with another party.

Suppose that at $t = 0$, one unit of foreign currency can exchange for $s(0)$ units of domestic currency. $F(0)$ is the forward exchange rate which means that at $t = 1$, one unit of foreign currency can exchange for $F(0)$ units of domestic currency. $i_h(0)$ is the domestic interest rate, and $i_f(0)$ is the foreign interest rate between $t = 0$ and $t = 1$. In equilibrium, the following two strategies should give the same value: (a) at $t = 0$, deposit one unit of domestic currency with interest rate $i_h(0)$ in a domestic bank, and at $t = 1$, use the exchange rate $1/F(0)$ to exchange $(1 + i_h(0))$ units of domestic currency for $(1 + i_h(0))/F(0)$ units of foreign currency; (b) at $t = 0$, exchange one unit of domestic currency for $1/s(0)$ units of foreign currency and deposit it in a foreign bank with interest rate $i_f(0)$, and at $t = 1$, obtain $\left(1 + i_f(0)\right)/s(0)$ units of foreign currency. That is,

$$(1 + i_h(0))/F(0) = \left(1 + i_f(0)\right)/s(0). \tag{15.5}$$

Deduct $\left[s(0) \bullet i_f(0)\right]$ from both sides of Eq. (15.5),

$$\frac{F(0) - s(0)}{s(0)} = \frac{i_h(0) - i_f(0)}{1 + i_f(0)}. \tag{15.6}$$

If $i_f(t)$ is quite small, then

$$\frac{F(0) - s(0)}{s(0)} \approx i_h(0) - i_f(0). \tag{15.7}$$

For example, in Eq. (15.7), suppose that at $t = 0$, the exchange rate is: $s(0) = 1$, i.e., one unit of foreign currency can exchange for one unit of domestic currency.

If between $t = 0$ and $t = 1$, the domestic interest rate is: $i_h(0) = 10\%$ and the foreign interest rate is: $i_f(0) = 4\%$, then at $t = 1$, one unit of foreign currency can exchange for $F(0) = 1.06$ units of domestic currency. That is, higher interest rate in a country leads to its currency depreciation in terms of the forward exchange rate.

Summary and Conclusions

- Multinational corporations (MNC) can at a lower transaction cost access new markets and sales opportunities by coordinating different local resources (i.e., lower labor costs and more advanced technology), spread research and development costs and advertising expenditures over global sales, pool global purchasing power over suppliers, have higher reputation and bargaining power when dealing with domestic and foreign governments/politicians, and diversify operation risks in different countries. MNC can also help local economy by paying taxes, hiring more local people, and providing the same quality product at a lower price.
- The disadvantages of MNC are: (i) domestic jobs move overseas and unlike other resources, labors are not easy to move to foreign countries; (ii) MNC may become monopolies to increase prices for consumers, stifle competition and impede innovation; (iii) MNC may hurt the environment and deplete local and natural resources; and (iv) languages and cultural differences within MNC.
- Language barriers and cultural differences may hinder MNC. Domestic as well as foreign politicians may in the name of national security become more hostile to MNC. The political risks of censure, sanction, and even frozen foreign assets are more prevalent in recent years.
- Exchange rate risk and interest rate risk also affect MNC. Purchasing power parity argues that higher inflation rate in a country leads to its currency depreciation. Interest rate parity shows that higher interest rate in a country leads to its currency depreciation in terms of the forward exchange rate.

Problems

1. Is it true that higher inflation rate in a country leads to its currency depreciation.
2. Multinational corporations are claimed to be stateless. What kind of protections can these firms have?
3. Some argues that overseas investments will decrease domestic investments. Is this claim reasonable?
4. What additional factors does a multinational corporation need to consider when making investment decision?
5. What are the benefits and costs of a multinational company?

Author Index

K.-P. Chang, *Corporate Finance: A Systematic Approach*, Springer Texts in Business and Economics, https://doi.org/10.1007/978-981-19-9119-6

Subject Index

K.-P. Chang, *Corporate Finance: A Systematic Approach*, Springer Texts in Business and Economics, https://doi.org/10.1007/978-981-19-9119-6

The manufacturer's authorised representative in the EU is Springer Nature Customer Service Centre GmbH, Europaplatz 3, 69115 Heidelberg, Germany. If you have any concerns regarding our products, please contact ProductSafety@springernature.com

Printed and bound by CPI Group (UK) Ltd, Croydon, CR0 4YY
30/09/2026
02225246-0007